EXPLORING MAINE

on Country Roads and Byways

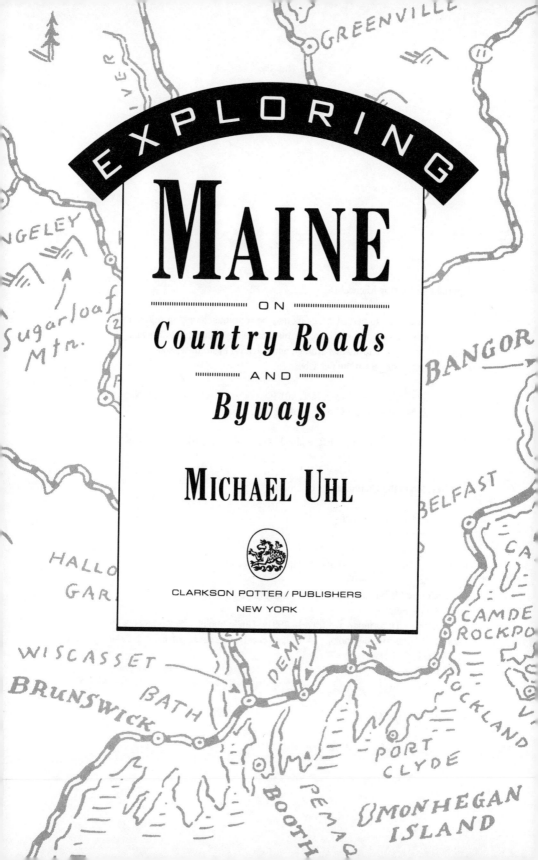

EXPLORING

MAINE

ON

Country Roads

AND

Byways

MICHAEL UHL

CLARKSON POTTER / PUBLISHERS

NEW YORK

Copyright © 1991 by Michael Uhl

Published by Clarkson N. Potter, Inc., 201 East 50th Street, New York, New York 10022. Member of the Crown Publishing Group.

CLARKSON POTTER, POTTER, and colophon are trademarks of Clarkson N. Potter, Inc.

Manufactured in the United States of America

Book design by Jane Treuhaft
Maps by Eric Hanson

LIBRARY OF CONGRESS CATALOGING-IN-PUBLICATION DATA
Uhl, Michael.
    Exploring Maine on country roads and byways / by Michael Uhl.
    Includes index.
    1. Maine—Description and travel—1991—Guide-books. 2. Automobile travel—Maine—Guide-books. 3. Uhl, Michael—Journeys—Maine. I. Title.
F17.3.U34   1991
917.4104'43—dc20   90-47217
                                                                       CIP

ISBN 0-517-57455-1

10   9   8   7   6   5   4   3   2

FOR GERALD FOSTER
1910–1989

▪

*Friend, neighbor—and the last farmer
in Bristol, Maine*

CONTENTS

▪

Take you a ride in the car-car . . .
WOODY GUTHRIE

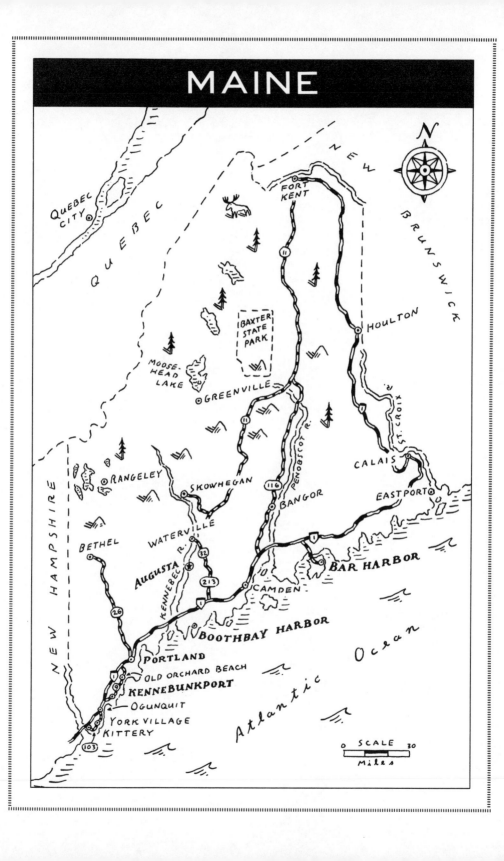

INTRODUCTION

⅟⅟⅟⅟⅟⅟⅟⅟⅟⅟ ■ ⅟⅟⅟⅟⅟⅟⅟⅟⅟⅟

THE MAINE IMAGE

Think of Maine as a territorial cul-de-sac, a sizable chunk of the northeastern United States existing somewhat apart geographically from the rest of the country. The northern half of Maine bulges into Canada, which surrounds the state on three sides, the national boundary having been established, by design or accident, in rough correspondence to the outline of a parabola suggested by two rivers, the St. John and the St. Croix. "This is the forest primeval," wrote Longfellow at the beginning of his poem *Evangeline,* awed by the antiquity of these northern woods even as late as the mid-nineteenth century. Of that original Acadian forest, much has fallen since the poet's day, but vast stretches remain undeveloped and wooded still, often regenerated as second growth. Such wilderness lands as the eastern United States may yet boast of in any volume are to be found in this sector of Maine bordering Quebec Province to the west and New Brunswick to the north and east.

The bulk of Maine's population resides below this northern bulge, mostly along the coast and in the linings of three great river valleys that occupy central and western portions of the state. Western Maine rises out of the mountains and slopes gradually to the sea, draining rain and snowfall through many channels, forming great rivers and lakes among the sometimes rolling, sometimes jagged elevations that are characteristic of the state's interior landscape. Coastal Maine embodies a nice spatial paradox: from southern tip to farthest point "Down East," the Maine coast measures a scant 225 miles as the birds fly; but that modest distance swells to continental proportions, some 3,500 miles of sea frontage, if you trace your measurement along the banks and indentations of every bay and harbor that winds up the coast. This watery seam, dotted with islands, hems the fabled rocky coast of Maine, where scores of peninsulas, large and small, reach into the Atlantic Ocean like so many mini-Maines—each a replication of the state's essential cul-de-sac motif, approachable by land from one direction only.

Maine's bottom half is itself only tenuously connected to the rest of the country. Road access to Maine from along New Hampshire's wide western border is for the most part of a neighborly sort, a network of secondary roads not meant for great commerce. Maine's exclusive link to the country's interstate highway system is via the New Hampshire corridor to the south, a narrow strip of geography separating Maine from Massachusetts and providing otherwise landlocked New Hampshire with its only access to commercial sea lanes at Portsmouth Harbor. Here at the Kittery Bridge, which spans the swift Piscatagua, is Maine's front door.

Maine's geographic isolation, the density of its timberlands and rockiness of its soil, its elongated, serpentine coastline and rugged winter climate have combined to shape the state's population and economic development in certain ways that are distinct from the prevailing currents of the American mainstream. For decades during this century, Maine was one of the very poorest of all the states—if not in fact the poorest—at least when income was the measure. Low incomes, however, merely masked a more significant distinction. When much of the country became fully integrated into the cash economy and the so-called mass culture following World War II, Maine remained tenaciously rooted to its barter system and to its tradition of self-sufficiency as a means of compensating for low wages and scarce employment.

Mainers traditionally generated cash income from lumbering, agriculture, and fishing—seasonal vocations organized for the most part around small businesses and individual producers. Mills and other centralized industries always existed in pockets along the coast and in river towns throughout the state; boatbuilding, shoe manufacture, poultry production, canning, and quarrying each may have experienced its boom epoch, but such enterprises rarely absorbed the bulk of any area's labor potential. Many people, primarily in the towns, found steady employment in a variety of shops, services, trades, and professions—albeit for wages at the very bottom of the national scale. To be sure, Mainers had accompanied the rest of the country's assimilation of major technological advances as each in turn appeared in this century. Motor vehicles and gasoline engines were put to work immediately on farms and in fishing boats; telephones, radios, televisions—and recently VCRs—quickly became necessities, though other domestic luxuries, such as indoor plumbing and central heating—indeed, even electrification—were slower to come in more remote areas. By the 1950s, while the country at large was rapidly being homogenized into a consumer society, the majority of the people here continued to live largely as they had for generations, eking out an existence in this or that activity, minimally dependent on cash to resolve their needs.

Large portions of the state's population still raised and put up fair quantities of their own food (or bartered for it with their labor). Many added to the larder by hunting and fishing, and gathered their fuel from the woodlots. When such tasks as harvesting or haymaking required extra hands, neighbor helped neighbor in exchange for similar considerations, or for fellowship over a hearty supper of baked beans, apple cider, and such other staples as a body could afford to share. You might say Mainers were traditionally underemployed but never underworked. Except for the foolhardy and the truly unfortunate, they paid their taxes and held on to their land and traditions, counting themselves well off in the bargain.

And then, of course, there was the summer trade. Thoreau probably wasn't the first traveler who came to savor the Maine wilderness as a getaway experience. But he is certainly the best known of his generation from the mid-1800s who were conscious of the shrinking frontier to the west, and who sought in the Maine wilderness a spiritual balm for the creeping materialism of their own age. "The wilderness is simple, almost to barrenness," Thoreau observed approvingly in *The Maine Woods*. He further noted the reason why the Maine wilderness had remained pristine at the very time when the more distant and sparsely inhabited western lands were being rapidly settled. Except for those limited numbers who came to hunt meat and gather pelts, the Maine interior, in Thoreau's day, had only one commercial attraction: the towering white pine, much in demand by our citizens, then as now, to frame and sheath their houses. After the pine was removed, the bulk of the forest was left standing until a later, second wave of loggers found in the spruce a suitable substitute. And even when one toiled mightily to clear the remaining trees and brush, the land as often as not was unsuitable for farming on any scale, unlike that of the Ohio Valley, or the great central prairie where hordes of natives and foreign immigrants were flocking by Thoreau's day.

The coastal and mountain regions of Maine tell a different tale. These lands were settled from the early days of European discovery, and resettled time and again during the seventy bloody years of the French and Indian Wars—from the late 1600s to the mid-1700s—when the English were constantly being driven from the buffer lands between French Acadia and British Massachusetts. Only four villages (Kittery, York, Wells, and Appledore on the Isle of Shoals) near Maine's southern tip took root and held on without interruption during these years. Thus the settlement of Maine must be seen as an occurrence that largely followed rather than preceded the War of Independence. But in the footsteps of those first waves of permanent settlers soon trailed a class of visitors who were known somewhat tongue-in-cheek as "rusticators." These were the summer folk who fled their own sticky, humid regions to the south in exchange for a dose of Maine's fresh air and serenity. Here they could still commune with a nature that had yet to be dismantled and with a sea that remained untamed. And they could sleep through August nights that required the use of a blanket, rather than a cry of deliverance from the oppressive heat they had left behind.

Thoreau came to the Maine woods for the first time in 1846. And while he was more of a true naturalist than a rusticator, he also intuitively perceived his role as an advance man when, referring to his climb of Mount Katahdin, he remarked in his journal that "it will be a long time before the tide of fashionable travel sets [this] way." His prediction proved correct, but it wasn't as long as he had perhaps imagined, and his insight also seemed to imply that if he was drawn thither, others would surely follow, fashionable or otherwise. And, of course, they have, and continue to do so in ever-increasing numbers with each passing year.

Over the years, Maine's Yankee natives formed an easy alliance with the rusticators—whether they were genuine outdoorsmen, like Thoreau, or summer visitors of a more delicate and domestic constitution. The natives gladly shared their delightful summertime with the outsiders, from whom they would receive a welcome patronage in the form of odd jobs, or employment as off-season caretakers of summer properties, and whom they would serve as guides to good fishing and well-stocked hunting grounds. Each group would have its complaints or prejudices about the other, but in general, the exchange was satisfactory to both parties. This was especially so because the tourist season was short in relation to the length of the year, and the best season, the fall, was largely reserved for the natives along with a limited number of serious hunters from away. As for the long winter—well, that was part of the terms you accepted to live the kind of independent life that Maine offered, one that kept you at a reasonable distance from your neighbor's chimney.

It was 1980 when I first came to summer in Maine. The world I have sketchily described above was then still faintly extant in the place where I settled, though living its final chapters. By the mid-1980s the drift of change—systemic change, I believe—was already in the air. Suddenly, Maine was no longer at or near number fifty among the states in economic indices; she had climbed to the top of the lower third—a great leap in a short space of time. The impetus came from several sectors—increased tourism and speculation in real estate primary among them. Maine was being discovered by a whole new generation of pioneers and rusticators, and she was beginning to show signs of development along lines that had transformed rural zones elsewhere throughout the country since World War II into exurban communities where consumer values outweighed traditional patterns of self-sufficiency.

Those who came to Maine in this latest migratory wave not only sought cheap land, but were attracted just as often by the simpler, unhurried style of life that had thrived here, and which they wished to emulate. So compelling was this attraction that for many it canceled out the fear of a climate they had once viewed as inhospitable for full-time residence. Sadly, on the heels of this migration has followed a rootless speculation in the land, speeding the steady and rapid erosion of the traditional values that sustained the vision of simplicity that all concerned—natives and outsiders alike—found at once so unique and appealing.

In my own town, one registers the transition to which I refer, not so much in population increase, subdivision of land, or new construction—though these have occurred more or less dramatically—but in the gradual replacement of the old ethos with the new as the local elders pass from the scene. These are the folk whose lives have spanned—all in this century for the most part—two very different social and economic orders. And for the first time, owing to the pressures of development, the old order to which they are the last remaining witnesses is not being passed on to their descendants. Faced with the enormous pressures of development, a new generation of Mainers will have to resolve how much of the old values can yet be salvaged if anything is to remain of the past beyond the commercially exploitable Maine image.

SOME NOTES

This book is a guide to pastoral, seafaring, small-town, and forested Maine by way of the state's seemingly endless network of secondary roads: a work conceived as an informal orientation for the confirmed touring motorist who wishes to explore the state in whole or in part, from top to bottom. The guide is organized into fifteen chapters that embrace Maine's three principal geographic divisions: *coast, rural interior,* and *wilderness area.* Wherever possible, the most heavily traveled arterial roads—such as Route 1—as well as the state's single interstate highway (the combined Maine Turnpike/Route 95) are avoided. Of course, these more direct alternatives are always there if you want them. The coastal routes followed hew as closely to nature's outline of the shore as the presence of suitable road surface will allow. The interior sections are traveled over secondary roads that lie within or near the valleys of three mighty river systems: the Androscoggin, the Kennebec, and the Penobscot. And finally, the narrative accompanies you along the settled periphery of the state's wilderness area, penetrating its zones of solitude wherever the roads are passable, and where points of interest justify the traveler's consideration.

Because this book is meant to be a road guide in which the regions between the destinations are considered as important as the destinations themselves, it is written in the form of an old-fashioned travelogue, rather than as a compendium of facts and listings. I have tried to look at Maine through fresh eyes, applying with some consistency two guiding rules: to travel extensively throughout the state and repeatedly over the same ground, so that my portrait bears some resemblance to Maine's rich contemporary reality; and to write about only those things I have actually seen or done during the course of my travels. For your convenience, however, a selected listing of those facilities referred to in the text follows each chapter, often supplemented by recommendations that came to me by word of mouth. When available, the name and telephone number of a good local source of information—usually the Chamber of Commerce—for a given township or county is also included. A single area code (207) is used throughout Maine.

For a categorical listing of lodgings and attractions in Maine, I recommend that you take advantage of the voluminous promotional material made available through the Maine Publicity Bureau (97 Winthrop Street, Hallowell, ME 04347; 207-289-2423), mailed to you free of charge. What this material lacks in critical perspective, it makes up for with its all-inclusive coverage. Also keep in mind that Maine is camping country; campsites are widely available throughout the state, especially during the warmer months. A complete directory of private and public camp grounds may also be requested of the Maine Publicity Bureau.

As for restaurants, when it comes to eating out in Maine, my advice is to keep it simple. One does not come to Maine expecting culinary excellence. Generally to be avoided (unless otherwise indicated) are the seasonal restaurants—eateries that are open from Memorial Day to Labor Day, and that charge high prices for food often prepared by nonprofessionals. I have eaten many a mediocre meal in such places, and paid the equivalent of a half-day's wages in the bargain. My personal *modus operandi* while touring in Maine is to carry a well-stocked cooler of my favorite snacks, and to eat at roadside stands, diners, and small local restaurants where, by and large, straightforward, tasty meals are served without pretense and at reasonable prices. I have taken pains to incorporate as many of these establishments as possible within this guide. And then, of course, there are the seaside lobster shanties and fishermen's co-ops open in the summertime. In this category, the greatest emphasis has been given to those places where you may dine on fresh boiled lobster or soft-shelled clams—the typical, no-frills, inexpensive fare.

Nature walks, old housing stock (of which Maine has the greatest volume among all fifty states), junk collectors, literary and historical reference points, small-town museums and collections, ferries, fine art and folk art, and such folklore and contemporary viewpoints as I could glean from scores of interesting individuals I encountered in the course of my many wanderings—these are what form the substance of the text and string together the vast network of roads over which I have traveled. Ultimately, I hope you will find in these itineraries a simple orientation to a mode of touring that not only guides you off the beaten track, but opens up endless possibilities for individual discovery as well. The point is not to imitate or duplicate the journey I have taken, but to see the road as a destination in its own right—to allow the currents of spontaneity and serendipity to carry you along at your own pace, consciously embracing the opportunity to view the living tableaux of simpler times and the incomparable scenic beauty that are still to be found in practically every corner of Maine.

Happy trails!

NOTE ■ A recommended map is the *Maine Atlas and Gazetteer,* published by Delorme Publishing Company, P.O. Box 298Q, Freeport, ME 04032.

SOUTHERN MAINE

N

NEW HAMPSHIRE

ANDROSCOGGIN RIVER

BETHEL

26

26

NORWAY

5

LONG LAKE

AUBURN

LEWISTON

122

100

FRYEBURG

BRIDGTON

NAPLES

132

KENNEBEC RIVER

AUGUSTA

114

SEBAGO LAKE

FREEPORT

BRUNSWICK

BATH

302

26

PORTLAND

77

SACO
BIDDEFORD

OLD ORCHARD BEACH

1

9

KENNEBUNKPORT

Atlantic Ocean

1

OGUNQUIT

YORK VILLAGE

103

KITTERY

SCALE

0   15
miles

Off-Season on the Southern Coast

KITTERY TO PORTLAND

In the idiom of traditional tourism, Maine's southern coast is a Down East version of Spain's Costa Brava: dense with seasonal spas and summer havens, yet uniquely scenic and, for the most part, remarkably unspoiled. During July and August, the population of the region swells threefold. Diverse social castes return with migratory regularity to their favorite seashore hideaways. For Yankee bluebloods, the retreat of choice is tony Kennebunkport; blue-collar Quebecois have deep roots in Old Orchard Beach, a gritty honkytonk resort; the style-conscious, the art-minded, and the literati flock to long-established colonies around York and Ogunquit. And when you add the day-trippers and vacationers to the year-round residents and summer folk, the scene along this whole stretch of south coastal Maine between Kittery and Portland stays pretty lively from July Fourth till Labor Day.

The summer crowd in southern Maine is a beach crowd, attracted by the state's only extensive stretch of sandy seashore. If you want to swim comfortably in the ocean off Maine shores, this is where you come. Once you get much above Portland, the ocean waters seem to be chilled by invisible ice cubes. Swimming days are few in Maine anyway, even in the warmer south; and the summer tourist season, if occasionally intense, is short. By early September, the pace of life downshifts abruptly. As the crowds of vacationers diminish, the natural beauty of Maine's south coast seems to rush into the visual and sensual spaces vacated by the fading human camouflage. There is a wholesale closing, coastal-wide, of businesses that cater primarily to seasonal guests; a lot of restaurants, good and bad, seafood shacks down by the water, most inns and village museums, certain gift shops and galleries are all bedded down for the long off-season. What remains to engage the cognoscenti of off-season travel is the region's scenic appeal, the perennial buzz and scutter of town life as it occupies Mainers during the "other" ten months of the year, and in general, ideal conditions for a day of unharried rambling along the shore, or a laid-back getaway weekend.

Nature itself never shuts down during the off-season. A virtually unbroken succession of public pathways, village squares, town landings, coves and peninsulas, beaches and nature sanctuaries provide one excuse after another to stop for a breather and a bit of scenic leg-stretching as you motor up the coast. The larger towns are marketplaces for daily necessaries as well as fine handicrafts and other specialty goods, and many shops are open year-round. Several small museums that enshrine fragments of the local heritage also remain open throughout the year. The whole south coastal region is rich in history and colonial architecture. An almost palpable sense of the past is apparent in the abundance of seasoned colonial and early-nineteenth-century houses and public buildings that one passes from one end of our itinerary to the other. And not just the structures, but their roomy, agrarian-age settings have likewise escaped great leaps in development or modernization. This well-preserved scale of the bucolic past frozen in the Maine landscape is the essence of the state's seductive, fantasy-laden appeal for residents and vacationers alike.

In the summertime, the population congestion makes getting around on the region's wonderful back roads a bit hectic. The tour I describe here took place during the height of the low season, but one might encounter the same uncrowded conditions anytime from mid-October until well into June. The landscape and the weather change radically, of course. Both late fall and late spring—the latter marred a bit by insects—promise the mildest weather, not to mention spectacular displays of nature's growth cycle at its two extremes. The drive from Kittery to Portland on the turnpikes takes roughly an hour under normal circumstances. The alternate route laid out here, assuming frequent and leisurely stops, can *easily* soak up eight hours or more. It really depends on what stays your course, and how fast you want to get to Portland. The account that follows is based largely on a tour my wife and I fashioned for ourselves as a day-long drive up the coast; material from prior solitary "research" visits has been interwoven, however, and so the time sequence should not be taken literally.

KITTERY, KITTERY POINT VIA ROUTE 103

O ur visit began on a morning late in February. The sky above Kittery was, paradoxically, bright and dull. With spring approaching, the sun was already scribing its arc visibly higher each day; but the bruised clouds along the horizon served notice that in Maine winter was far from over, and a storm might yet develop before the day was done. The dark, warm days of the mid-January thaw were now long past, and the air was brittle but bearable; March and April are generally less hospitable to outdoor activities in Maine than February, what with the frigid winds of the former and the bothersome mud of the latter.

At 8 A.M., we were sitting in Alice's—part luncheonette, part tavern —along Kittery's very short main drag, eating an unexpectedly tasty breakfast. Behind us, following Route 1 across the old Memorial Bridge at a place where the Piscataqua River narrows, lay the attractive city of Portsmouth, New Hampshire. The skeleton of this old Yankee port has been preserved: the odd-shaped, oversized brick buildings that overhang the old wharf, the stone-paved, perambulating streets and alleys. But today these relics of the town's longevity have for the most part been resheathed in the service of fashion. The streets are softly lighted, and the buildings house many fine shops and restaurants, making a very pleasant atmosphere for strolling, pub-hopping, and browsing.

But we had turned our backs to Portsmouth, and from within this unadorned eatery that guards one entrance to the Portsmouth Naval Shipyard, we lingered over coffee and maps, soaking up a different kind of atmosphere, that of a workingman's hangout outside the factory gate. Signs proclaiming rooms for rent along this string of small, clapboard buildings

marked the street as the transient, low-rent district in the village. And
while numerous plaques and monuments in the vicinity also attest to Kittery's honored place in American colonial history, the town today is no
showcase for tourists. The major attraction Kittery has, for many Mainers
and visitors alike, is the mile-long strip lining both sides of old Route 1 with
scores of specialty stores and self-proclaimed discount outlets, just north of
the village. It is said that these stores regularly attract shoppers from as far
away as Boston, even beyond.

The first leg of our drive took us east along Route 103 in the direction of
Kittery Point. Just minutes beyond utilitarian Kittery, the setting softens
into the picture of a colonial river town, as the quiet road winds among the
venerable houses, spotted at decent intervals between the rolling heights
and still waters of the harborside. Just past the little bridge, the road curves
sharply, and the spire of a plain white meetinghouse comes into view on the
left. This is the site of the first church built in Maine. The current building,
the First Congregational Church, dates from 1730 and opens on days of
scheduled worship. It is said to contain some original woodwork, including
a delicately paneled pulpit, and two rough-hewn box pews. Across the road,
along the opposite sweep of the curve, are a historic Georgian mansion and
an old burial ground on a promontory overlooking the harbor.

While not, strictly speaking, open to the public, this is a much-visited
scene, considered an emblematic tableau depicting without fanfare how the
Maine settlement actually appeared during mid-colonial times. We turned
the car into the empty church parking lot and crossed over to walk among
the old slate grave markers that peek, half-buried and cockeyed like shark's
teeth, through the ground, and whose inscriptions, where visible, are worn
thin by weather and time and are for the most part illegible. On a granite
stone of a slightly later period, a brass plate bears an original inscription by
Robert Browning to honor the husband of a local poet, Celia Thaxter. The
Thaxters lived offshore on the nearby Isle of Shoals, and Celia was a muse
much courted by early-nineteenth-century literary circles, visited by such
worthies among her contemporaries as Hawthorne, Whittier, and Lowell.

While it is tended with apparent care, no attempt has been made to
landscape the tiny graveyard, which dips and rises over the natural contours of this knoll above the riverbank, and where the bushes and brambles
are such that nature provides for common vegetation along this shoreline.
The harbor beyond was once the private cove of the shipowning Pep-
perrells—and still carries their name. William Pepperrell, Sr., amassed a

fortune in fishing, and his son Sir William—a rare knight among colonial natives, who secured his baronetcy by leading a successful assault against the fortress at Louisbourg in French Canada—added to the family wealth as an ocean trader. The mansion contiguous to the burial ground was built for Sir William's widow in 1760. Lady Pepperrell—a Tory during the War of Independence—lorded it over her Republican neighbors, though much of the family property and riches were reportedly confiscated during the revolution. The house, currently the offices of a professional association, may have appeared ostentatious in its day, yet it now seems a stunning, relatively simple structure, its exterior graced somewhat sparingly by details of a revived classical architecture, and set among well-proportioned, if modest, formal grounds.

We continued up Route 103 East, on the lookout for several other examples of colonial architecture, and found the drive so exhilarating that when we reached the cluster of buildings around the Kittery Point post office, not a mile down the road, we turned around and retraced our course twice more over the same ground. The season and time of day worked to our advantage; there were so few cars on the road that we inconvenienced no one as we crept slowly along, not wanting to miss a single element in what amounts to Maine's oldest, most unspoiled neighborhood. Back at the post office we parked in the lot next to the Frisbee General Store, established in 1828, and—according to its sign—still in the hands of the original family. Beyond Captain Simeon's Gallery and Seafood Restaurant, where the original Frisbee store was located, is the Kittery Point town wharf, highly recommended for its wide and magnificent view of the mouth of Portsmouth Harbor.

The wharf is a working one for local fishermen. Lobster gear was piled high on the dockside in parking spaces reserved for town residents on this winter day, when few visitors could be expected. At water level, a lobster boat was already tied up to a floating pier and unloading the morning's first haul. The view beyond, as if by design, seemed a compilation of the elements we associate with a quintessential New England harbor: two lighthouses stand on the most distant points of land; huge Victorian houses dot the hillside on the opposite shore. Close by is the blockhouse of Fort McCleary (1812), original site of the Pepperrell family stronghold, the more recent structure dating from the early 1800s and named for an officer who fell at Bunker Hill.

Just east of the general store stands the original Pepperrell house (1682), a large, gambrel-roofed affair that now has an unappealing, over-renovated look. Several houses beyond, however, is a delightful, many-cornered Cape, painted red, which was the childhood home (1662) of Marjorie Bray, Sir William's mother. But the real gem is still farther up the road, a long, low red house (dated 1738 but believed to be even older) with three chimneys, "magic cottage" windows, and tiny doorways, which seems wedded to the land like an old hedgerow. Surely its early inhabitant, the carpenter Peletiah Fernald, who provided finish work for Lady Pepperrell's mansion, was more Hobbit than man. There are many other worthy structures and cove-side vistas along this meandering road (once an Indian trail, or, as its topographical winding attests, a "natural" trail).

From Kittery Point to York Harbor, Route 103 rides over a landscape that is primarily barrens and marshlands, best appreciated in the fall, when the natural light endows the straw-colored grasses with the visual power of Flemish paintings from the Middle Ages. Wildlife sightings, on the other hand, are possible almost anytime, and with virtual certainty during migratory and nesting months. As you drive on, note how each bend in the way seems to speed you forward in history as well as space. By the time the bridge across York Harbor is reached, you have driven in a few miles through three centuries of American architecture, from ancient Capes to classic Maine farmsteads, from homy fisherman's cottages of this century's early decades to tasteful, timber-framed imitations of the past that are being built today; and no two houses are the same. There is not a hint of the suburbanization that now dominates the outskirts of so many of Maine's oldest towns.

Seldom along this route will you actually catch a glimpse of the sea, though occasionally the tail end of a tidal flat or estuary will approach or cross beneath the road. To view the ocean, you must choose a secondary road that leads from Route 103 to the edge of some point or cape. The first such digression we chose for the day was along the Chauncey Creek Road to Seapoint Beach, indicated by roadside signs just beyond Kittery Point.

While I am told that rising property values have all but driven out the traditional fishing families hereabouts, there are no obvious signs of rapid development. The land seems no more crowded today than it might have been 300 years ago, and some of the old farms and faded houses along the way elicit an involuntary nostalgia for the past, no matter how cold an eye the observer may turn on this remarkably wild landscape of woodlots, meadows, and marshlands. The land rises near the road's end, and the surf can be seen pounding an invisible shore for several seconds before the so-called beach—a tiny cove of stony black sand—comes into view. A small parking area is littered with unfriendly signs that announce "Parking for Kittery Residents Only." So we kept to our car and digested the beautiful seascape, our disappointment at being confined to quarters solaced by the drive back along this road that communicates so much of the reality from which the myth of Maine is drawn.

THE YORKS VIA ROUTE 1A

When Route 103 suddenly approaches a wide expanse of water, and a fleet of fishing boats can be seen bobbing at their moorings even in the wintertime, you have arrived at York Harbor. Just beyond the bridge, Route 103 terminates at a junction with Route 1A, and here you turn left to enter York Village. In the early 1600s, these lands were occupied by Native Americans in a village known as Agamenticus, first discovered by English explorers and fishermen in their early quest for New World trade. Exposure to smallpox and other diseases to which the Europeans were by then relatively immunized soon decimated the Indian population, and in 1639 their former lands were conveyed by royal charter to Sir Ferdinando Gorges, an English adventurer officially proclaimed the Father of Maine. Gorges's plans for his plantations were ambitious. The settlement he sponsored became the first charted English city in the New World, named Gorgeana in his honor. But the colony did not prosper, and was subsequently purchased by the Massachusetts Bay Colony in 1652 for a pittance from Gorges's heirs, restructured municipally as a town, and given the name of York.

York Village has preserved something of its heritage and colonial look in a unique local museum comprising six historic buildings. York apparently owes the preservation of these, as well as its other numerous and privately owned architectural relics, to the hardships that accompanied "Mr. Jefferson's War" with the English in 1812. Maine dominated U.S. shipping in the early days of the Republic, and by ordering U.S. harbors closed to foreign ships, the president sparked a depression that plagued the Maine coast for years and hampered its development. When York became a fashionable literary watering hole at the turn of the century, several celebrated writers, including Mark Twain, were so charmed by the accidental legacy of under-development that, to preserve the visual integrity of their beloved village for posterity, they purchased the structures that formed the core of the original and very pastoral village common, including the old "gaol," a public roadhouse, a one-room school, and a genteel dwelling.

Before our arrival, I had called ahead to the York Historical Society, which manages the buildings and their exhibits, to see if an off-season tour might be arranged. Happily, the staff was accommodating. After all, it is one thing to drive by and admire the exteriors of old houses, and quite another to gain admittance, somewhat akin to a step back in time, especially when the structures in question are crammed with period artifacts and furnishings. You can almost slip into the skins and personae of your pred-ecessors and act out—at least in fantasy—the intimate minutiae of their lives. This was certainly the feeling I had as I stepped across the threshold and into the "Old Gaol" (c. 1720), one of the first public buildings in the country to be used as a museum and repository for local history.

This former "King's prison" is a large, gambrel-roofed structure of wood and stone that occupies a knoll above an old burying ground. From a modern perspective, its interior seems oddly arranged with the inmates' cells on the periphery opening directly into the gaoler's residential quarters at the core. The cells are roomy enough, most having fireplaces and some sparse addition of furnishings, today embellished somewhat against the grain of authenticity. (One, called "the cobbler's cell," contains a work-bench, leather scraps, and tools of the trade.) Gang-saw blades, once used to saw planks and boards by hand, are embedded as bars in window casings set in walls at least two feet thick. The gaoler's quarters are hardly more commodious, and everywhere the woodwork and plaster are worn into sensually irregular surfaces from centuries of human usage. A "museum of colonial relics" occupies several less-ancient rooms at the rear of the jail, where we might easily have spent half a day meditating on the many intriguing displays of prison records, assorted written and pictorial docu-ments, tools, household items, and personal objects that so perfectly re-flect the times.

We next toured the Emerson-Wilcox House (c. 1740) on the same square, an equally entrancing experience of time travel, albeit into a world of domestic prosperity that contrasts sharply with the stark simplicity of the gaoler's life. Then we drove down Lindsay Road a mile or so to the Historical Society headquarters in the old George Marshall general store, a small yellow building that sits on high ground above the York River. The Historical Society has an excellent genealogical library, open to the public during normal business hours year-round, Tuesdays through Thursdays. On the grounds below the old store, we looked around the John Hancock Warehouse (c. 1800), a business that the first signer of the Declaration of Independence owned but apparently never visited, coming into its possession to "bail out" the previous owner, a friend in debt. The warehouse, now filled with exhibits of Maine's agrarian and seafaring past, once served the community as a store for various dry goods, such as molasses from the West Indies trade, delivered in bulk from Boston on a coastal barge called a "gundalow," a replica of which occupies a slip at the wharf behind the building.

In our brief spin through York Village, we'd already passed a fair number of roadside inns, all nice enough. But as we stood on this spot behind Hancock's wharf, soaking up the softness of the surrounding riverscape, it was clear that here was the ideal setting for a getaway night or weekend in York, assuming there was a nearby inn that could live up to the scenery. As it turned out, we discovered Hutchins House a few hundred yards up the road, but it was closed to guests for the season. Hutchins House juts out like a bold prow above the York River, offering an even more complete picture of the dreamy little river valley than from the wharf. We interrupted innkeeper Linda Hutchins in the midst of her Jane Fonda exercises. Rising to the intrusion, she showed us around the spacious and comfortable house where she and her husband have raised six children, and now let out three rooms a night, with breakfast, from Memorial Day through October.

A special feature at Hutchins House is the outdoor terrace that faces a bend in the river spanned by Sewell's Bridge—the oldest pile-driven bridge in the country—and on the opposite shore, another of the Historical Society's period museums, Perkins House. York Village has wisely retained a public walking path along the river that passes conveniently close to Hutchins House and leads to, among other picturesque points, Harbor

Beach, a half-mile downstream. The best restaurant in the area, according
to Linda Hutchins, is the Cape Neddick Inn, where you can expect to pay
New York City prices but dine well, she allows. Also "reliable on a day-
to-day basis," she says, is the Dockside Restaurant on Harris Island, not
far from the bridge in York Harbor. Among rival inns, her own favorite is
the Canterbury House in York Harbor; this was not the first time I heard
this hostelry referred to with praise. Canterbury House is open year-
round, and is reputed to serve an exquisite breakfast.

We fueled up with fresh coffee and doughnuts at a pizza shop right in the
middle of York Village, then poked around for a few minutes in the Emporium next door, which houses a bike shop up front, and a gallery of
Maine crafts and products in the rear. The quality of the items was
mixed, from excellent to awful, but to each set of eyes lurks a potential
find. We were satisfied with a couple of old hardcover books purchased
for spare change. Our treasures in tow, we left town on Route 1A,
heading for York Beach just up the road. When a wide view of the ocean
suddenly filled the windshield as we crested a curving hill, it was as if we
had entered into a completely different movie. The suave gentility of
make-believe colonial life and gourmet comforts just behind us gave way
here to a simpler, more democratic beach town. Crowded cheek by jowl
on every available plot of ground up and down the shore, summer cottages with façades of many windows stand like a congregation of wide-
eyed worshipers transfixed before the awe-inspiring sea. Long Sands is
the first and larger of the two public beaches at York, backed by houses
that are relatively new, the oldest perhaps dating from the 1940s. Farther up the road, opposite Short Sands beach, the homes have a more
Victorian appearance, like workers' housing on the outskirts of a mill
town, and many a rough gem stands among them. Most of the beach
shops and food stands are old, lopsided wooden buildings, boarded up,
and with the low-overhead look of game booths on a carnival midway
from an earlier time. Between these two strands at York Beach is Cape
Neddick, known locally as the Nubble, a proboscis-shaped peninsula perpendicular to the shoreline, and therefore exposed to the wilds of the
ocean on all three sides.

A cabinetmaker friend living in Portsmouth has since mentioned that he
spent many childhood summers camping on York Beach, in his grandpar-

ents' trailer. His comments confirmed pretty much the impression we got just from driving through. "It's a blue-collar beach," he told me, "traditionally French. You don't find a lot of doctors and lawyers like in Ogunquit, but the old middle class who had the house by the ocean. It's always been pretty congested. If they had a yard, they sold it off, and another house went up. But there was a family feeling about the place. Every Fourth of July until the late sixties, there would be a big torchlight procession out to Cape Neddick, where we'd gather driftwood and have a big bonfire." The bonfire and close-knittedness were now in the past, but Scott felt that the beach was still offbeat in a way that suited him personally: honky-tonk commercial, and not transformed as yet into condo-land. Besides the good beaches—possibly the best in Maine—there's an animal and amusement attraction geared to kids right in the village center, called the Wild Kingdom and strictly seasonal. The lit-up vacancy signs on a few motels along the strip showed that York Beach hosts at least a trickle of overnight visitors year-round.

Despite the town's off-season pallor, we weren't in a great hurry to move on. There's a certain hypnotic magic about a winter beach. And besides, we were on a drive, not a guided tour. We could take our pleasures as we found them, often with the aid of our map, where we first spied the four- or five-mile road that loops around the Nubble.

Just past the Sea Turn Motel on Route 1A, we entered onto that peninsular road, which is indicated by a hatrack of road signs. The drive winds close to the water, among larger, more costly houses than those on the mainland. The vegetation is sparse and gnarled in that peculiar way of plants that adapt to the perpetual pruning of high winds and salt air. We passed several inns as we drove, not the ramshackle variety typical of the beachfront, but more upscale, each sporting its own version of the carved colonial sign with gold-leaf lettering that has become the entrepreneurial rage on the coast of Maine. From a small parking area at land's end, opposite Nubble Light, the views of the mainland and the sea are equally wide-angle. Nubble Light, one of the last manned lighthouses in the country, occupies an island just offshore, and was erected in 1879 to protect mariners from the "savage rock" scattered everywhere beneath these local waters. A basket suspended from a cable over a thoroughfare of pounding surf once was used to transport the keeper's kids to and from the school bus, as well as supplies from the mainland.

AGAMENTICUS VIA ROUTES 1A AND 1, AND THE MOUNTAIN ROAD ■ OGUNQUIT VIA SHORE ROAD

Just beyond York Beach, the road forks, and I propose that you find a way of traveling both stretches. To the west, via the village of Cape Neddick, is Mount Agamenticus, a hill really, but with its elevation at nearly 700 feet, a prominent and long-standing navigational feature on this otherwise flat coastal plain. The summit is accessible by car, and on a clear day you can stand above a landscape blanketed by treetops and a prominent pond, taking in a view that reaches the sea and includes some amazingly close-up details of Portsmouth harbor. To reach Mount Agamenticus, follow Route 1A to Route 1 and turn right. Opposite Flo's Steamed Hot Dogs, turn left onto Mountain Road and drive for approximately three miles until the road ahead abruptly turns to dirt. Here you continue sharply to the right, remaining on the asphalt till you arrive on top of the hill. The summit is cluttered with towers belonging to, among others, a local radio station, the forest service, and the FBI, and a large wooden building that was once a ski lodge. It is not an attractive ensemble, but the vista is superb, and the hiking (or snowmobiling) is good around the two neighboring hills of slightly lower elevation, prosaically named Second and Third. Flo's hot dogs, by the way, served with a home-made spicy relish, are a wildly popular specialty of the region. And Flo is a Maine character writ large in local lore. One Ogunquit resident I met called Flo "the orneriest woman you'll ever meet, especially when you hit her with a large order." A recent spat in the courts put Flo in the local head-lines; seems Cape Neddick's hot-dog maven was out to block a competitor who was marketing his own brand of relish under the oddly deprecating name of "Almost Flo's."

Our route, continuing up the coast, follows Shore Road from 1A. This is a scenic bypass that avoids Route 1, and slithers and rolls some four miles along the shore to Ogunquit, a village sometimes referred to as the Carmel of New England. This I have taken to mean artsy but not highbrow, and still picturesque, not deformed by overdevelopment. And so it is. Ogunquit has a spectacular beach, a few special corners, and—from the looks of the houses and estates you pass along Shore Road—a well-heeled citizenry.

I liked this road a lot. One reason is that the contours of its surface are so irregular that you can't make good time even if you want to. You have to go along for the ride, a rare combination of the peaks, twists, and dips of a roller coaster with the gentle cadence of a carousel. A strip of residential land tapers along at varying widths between the road and the shoreline, the homes half-hidden at the ends of long driveways and on grounds for the most part thickly wooded. The murky green of the North Atlantic, topped by a patch of Maine's no-two-alike skies, occasionally strobes through the trees into sight. But you get no ocean view per se. The sea is a tease along this slow, prosperous shoreline drive, until you reach Perkins Cove, a harborside hamlet and gallery district astride the pilings of a large wharf that overlooks Ogunquit's most picturesque inlet and only safe anchorage.

You'll know you're approaching Perkins Cove when the houses along Shore Road thicken into a village and you've passed a stunning, pagoda-style house that sits above you on a hillside. At a fork in the road, you would bear left to enter the village proper, but I suggest you bear right and go first to Perkins Cove. You can drive onto the wharf and circle a little lane where fishermen once resided. Their shacks were long ago commandeered by a mob of *fin de siècle* artists who were thrilled to rough it for a month or two in a fish shack overlooking the Atlantic on the coast of Maine. The colorful colony endured for several generations, but what with the inevitable improvements to the shanties and the scene's capacity to draw crowds, whether true collectors or the merely curious, Perkins Cove had no way to go but commercial. The atelier has now given way to the gallery and to a host of shops and boutiques selling crafts or finished goods. The shops are mostly seasonal, but a lady walking her dog, and one or two other folk circulating about, made me realize that some home fires are still burning on Perkins Cove.

If you need a better reason for coming to Perkins Cove in the winter than to gratify an affinity for life in slow motion, there is a famous old restaurant, the Whistling Oyster, open year-round, and a draw-footbridge that adds unique dimension to the cove's general attractiveness. But the best reason is so you can walk along a rocky path eighty feet above the ocean, called the Marginal Way. The mile-long promontory, complete with benches, runs along the edge of Bald Head Cliff between the village and the cove. Armed with a bag lunch and a good book, you will find plenty of elbow room despite the popularity of the path, and no better spot along this coast to pause and contemplate how the granite meets the sea.

In the village of Ogunquit there are more galleries, more restaurants,

more shops to be found. A block from Route 1, a footbridge crosses an
in-town river, providing quick local access to one end of Ogunquit's justly
celebrated beach, a crescent-shaped strand three miles long. Years back,
the town bought the beach to prevent private development, and even in
February the public presence on the sands attests to the sagacity of this
decision. We saw small pockets of people everywhere, running their dogs,
walking meditatively, even picnicking on this day that unexpectedly had
brightened up. The view westward looks back on the long cliff that is the
terrain signature of this coastal town, where the rambling wooden buildings
of the old resorts still crowd the shoreline. At peak season, Ogunquit has
the facilities—some hundred different resorts, motels, B-and-Bs, cottages,
and guest houses—to lodge a fair number of vacationers. Parking is at a
premium. There are several public lots charging reasonable fees, and most
folk, visitors and residents alike, leave their cars in favor of the four trolleys
that circulate among the principal sights during the summer months only.
These include several respected cultural entities, a summer-stock theater,
and the Walt Kuhn museum, which is the old art colony's most lasting relic,
though it too serves the public only in the vacation months.

Today we park where we want, and that is directly alongside Einstein's
restaurant and café, the Ogunquit oasis that makes a perfect pit stop during
the sleepy season on Maine's south coast. The fact that it's open at all this
time of year is Einstein's most indisputable attraction, followed by the
reliable deli food, the layout—part diner, part bistro—its status as a local
landmark, and the restaurant's convenient location at the junction of Shore
Road and Route 1. Steve Einstein, formerly of Long Island, New York,
bought the building a few years back, gutted what was then a Chinese-style
restaurant, dragged up the old counter, stools, and booths from the basement, and, after consulting with a number of old-timers, restored the look
of the eatery that had served the village for fifty years. He did, however,
change the menu: pastrami, corned beef, potato pancakes, chopped liver—
good Jewish-style eats, plus the usual blue-plate specials.

For an out-of-stater, Einstein has done all right for himself both in business and in local politics. As chairman of the town's five-person committee
of selectmen, he's achieved a rare degree of acceptance for an "outsider"
in clan-conscious Maine. But as he is quick to point out, the "outsiders" in
Ogunquit now outnumber the natives. Of the 1,600 year-rounders, sixty
percent are sixty-five or older, people who have come here to retire or
slow down," he says. Ogunquit has always been a summer community, and

the pressures of development are its perennial problem. But all of Maine these days is confronted by the same issue: How much change do we want, and at what pace? To complicate matters, as Steve Einstein astutely observes, "everybody who comes wants to close the door on somebody else."

WELLS, KENNEBUNKPORT VIA ROUTES 1 AND 9

Until now, we had avoided Route 1, the principal caravan route up and down the coast and mostly an unharmonious commercial strip that demonstrates the wisdom and necessity of zoning in some form, a solution Mainers traditionally have opposed as an intrusion of an individual's right to make of his property what he will. It is precisely this random willfulness that makes our next destination, Wells, a place you want to drive through as quickly as possible. And that is perhaps the way local residents want it. Strung out for several miles along Route 1 are the transient lodgings, restaurants, outlets, and gift shops packed among the car agencies, banks, fast-food joints, and the usual miscellany of services you'll find on commercial strips practically anywhere in the country. Most of the town's rocky beaches, moreover, are in private hands, with public access a cause for many lawsuits in recent years.

To get any sense of the Wells that was first settled in 1640, you must detour frequently from Route 1. Turn eastward onto any cross street to reach the outer drive along Moody and Wells beaches, a straight run between rows of summer cottages; one line of houses faces the ocean, the other is backed by lovely brackish wetlands. A modern hotel called the Forbes Lakeview Inn, complete with swimming pool, is open year-round on Wells Beach. So Wells too has its getaway possibilities, though the atmosphere at Forbes Lakeview is more corporate-like, a venue you might select for an offbeat business meeting. Marshlands similar to those along the beach are the resource in Wells most accessible to the touring public. The Laudholm Trust (on Laudholm Road, off Route 1) oversees a 1,600-acre estuarial reserve comprising five different habitats: uplands and open fields, woodlands, marsh, estuary, and beach. Laudholm's mission is mostly research, but a number of trails are open to the public, and tours are accompanied by nature experts. The big public event at Laudholm, much of which was once the provincial estate of a Boston railroad man, is the annual Nature Craft Festival mounted among the fields and within a monumental antique barn on the second weekend in September.

We left Wells via Route 9, en route to Kennebunkport. Route 9 is also the back way into the twin mill towns of Biddeford-Saco. For a self-guided nature walk at any time of the year, turn into the Rachel Carson Refuge, just a few hundred yards up the road after turning off Route 1. You can park your car and, without further instruction, follow the gravel pathway till you reach a view of the sea a mile away. The path, which is accessible to wheelchairs, crosses a lightly wooded grove and accompanies a narrow tidal river surrounded by earthy, golden marshlands (visible except when covered during winter by ice or snow). "The trail is not the best for wildlife observation," we were cautioned by the resident ecologist, who is on duty during business hours and can provide you with brochures and a trail map that describes the varied habitats at a dozen stations along the way.

Route 9 has a good blacktop surface, and initially passes through a largely undeveloped area, densely wooded with evergreens. The scene is thematic in Maine, the familiar ecology of a saltwater woods repeated on a lesser or greater scale up and down the coast. Some places you can drive for the better part of an hour over a bumpy, sand-splattered roadway, closed in on both sides by the endless ranks and files of the pungent conifers, and those alone. The patch of barrens on this stretch of Route 9 is brief, but has strangely imprinted on my memory a weighty image, vaguely allegorical, as if Nature, with the sparse formality of a pine or spruce barren, were demonstrating the kinship between wildness and order. What you can always bank on, however, is the scent of balmy resin that saturates the air, invigorating the lungs and awakening the senses. At the boundary of this deep and medicinal forest, the scene accelerates into a hybrid suburb, where the houses have an off-the-shelf look about them, but their spacing is generous in the rural mode. The land is suddenly unwooded. Old farmsteads—rural pre-suburbias?—appear like a succession of windows flung open onto faint vistas of the agrarian past. And at least one estuary that creeps to the edge of the road offers a telescopic view to the sea.

Our map indicated several beaches along the local shoreline. To visit them, we picked a road at random that led to a small, sandy cove and onto a road that paralleled the ocean, running the length of a fair-sized summer-home community. The bright sun bleached the foreground, limiting visibility as we drove southwest down the beach. Squinting at a sign on a guest house, I deadpanned, "Suicidal Inn." The power of suggestion enhanced by the glare led my wife, Carol, to imagine she had also seen those exact words; and she clucked at the morbid humor, though she mistook its author. The "inn" was a simple, shingled beach house, and the name it actually goes by is "Sundial." A bit farther up Route 9, at a crossroads called the "four corners," we again turned toward the water and looped the gold coast of the Kennebunk beaches, returning to the main road just before the bridge that leads into the village of Kennebunkport. This is no doubt an attractive village when animated in season by many visitors, but off-season it has the look of an abandoned stage set. To Carol, it looked like Provincetown on Cape Cod, "full of T-shirt and fudge factories." But if Kennebunkport's commercial core is hollow out of season, and the signs along its famous Dock Square just so much colorful copy hanging over closed shops, the environs beyond this mothballed mall are anything but stagy.

For a quick study of grand living at its finest, turn right just beyond Dock Square onto Ocean Avenue. A white wooden marker on a pedestal of stone indicates the road, also called Shore Drive. The houses along the drive are quietly opulent, as is the watery view across the harbor that takes in the beachscape on the opposite shore. A narrow promenade called Parson's Way not only allows some public access to this privileged shoreline, but the several benches, as we discovered, make fine human perches for watching the long-necked cormorants as they dive for food or assume cultic poses while sunning themselves on a distant jetty. The immediacy of the ocean on this drive is a source of steady exhilaration.

As we rounded the cape, Walker Point, the summer home of the George Bush family, came fully into sight. The house is well removed from the road, and certainly was among the largest of all the impressive "cottages" we passed. True to his word, as the presence of boats off the point attests, President Bush has not used security considerations as an excuse to bar local lobstermen from these traditional fishing grounds, though the fellas are now hollering that the constant Coast Guard presence is playing havoc with their gear. Complementing the studied naturalism of Walker Point was another scene, slightly more surreal. Several clusters of pedestrians were stationed at various intervals on the edge of the road, standing quietly and gazing at the President's compound. What was odd was that they were all women who looked remarkably like Barbara Bush, white-haired, round,

and sportily dressed. One cannot help but wonder what was on their minds.
Were the President at home, they would not have been allowed to take up
their vigils quite so near his compound. Police checkpoints and car searches
apparently make the Shore Drive a less pleasant excursion when the
Bushes are on the scene.

KENNEBUNK VIA ROUTES 9A/35 AND 1 ■ CAPE PORPOISE VIA ROUTE 1, BACK ROADS, AND ROUTE 9

At the junction of the Shore Drive with Route 9, you have the
option of continuing up the coast (east) to Cape Porpoise, or
making a side trip (west) to nearby Kennebunk. Should you
elect the side trip, return through Kennebunkport, recross
the bridge, and, following signs for routes 9A/35, in ten minutes you will
come to a village that would make the perfect base in this area for an
off-season getaway weekend. Kennebunk, set between two small rivers, is
a regional center, active all year. While a number of inns and motels offer
year-round lodgings, the place I would choose is the Kennebunk Inn. Not
only does the inn have the rare look of a genuine roadhouse, complete with
an excellent restaurant and backroom tavern, but there are other advan-
tages to being lodged right on Main Street in the center of town. For one,
you will always find the company of other wayfarers at the Kennebunk Inn,
even in February. ("Forget about trying to get a room when Bush is at
Walker Point," the bartender told me. "He travels with an entourage of
three hundred.") Another intown attraction is the charming, diminutive
Brick Store Museum, combining a historic shipmaster's home (c. 1803),
furnished in the period, with several galleries for rotating or permanent
exhibits that focus on subjects ranging from social and maritime history to
local crafts and fine art.

To return to the coast, travel a mile or so on Route 1 north of Kennebunk
and turn right onto the road, otherwise unmarked, opposite the Arundal
Inn. When the road branches, bear right and you will cross a wooden-sided
bridge into an especially picturesque farm scene that vanishes all too soon.
Continue on this road, and you will rejoin Route 9 at Cape Porpoise, en
route to Biddeford. A fishing village and summer community, Cape Por-

poise offers the off-season visitor a view of its active harbor, and a unique craft shop called Womanswork that has become nationally known for selling durable work gloves and tool aprons scaled to women's sizes, rather than to men's as is usual with similar items found in hardware stores and lumber yards. Farther up Route 9, we took a brief detour down to Goose Rocks Beach, and saw an elegant stand of young white birch in a landscape that shimmered in the light like an Oriental watercolor brought to life. Fortunes Rocks Beach and Biddeford Pool—two summer colonies at the mouth of the Saco River, just beyond Goose Rocks—are both exposed to the howling winds and the crashing seas and present classic studies of winter desolation along this strip of rock-strewn coast.

BIDDEFORD-SACO VIA ROUTES 9 AND 1

Five miles farther up Route 9, with the river occasionally in view, is Biddeford, one of several centers in Maine that retain their predominantly French-American cultural identity. Every June the townsfolk reaffirm their heritage with a lively street festival called "La Kermesse." Across the river—separated by the former millworks of Factory Island—is Saco. It is said that the French workers lived in Biddeford, and the mill owners, mostly of English origin, inhabited Saco. To this day, the appearances of the two towns still suggest a similar social division. Saco is a postcard New England village, while Biddeford is rugged and plain. There are many offices and storefronts in the red brick buildings along Biddeford's principal commercial streets, but little sign of gentrification. The stores, as often as not bearing names that are clearly French, are those that provide no-frills goods and day-to-day services. But we find a bit of plumage in one very essential shop.

On Main Street, attracted by a window display of well-crafted pastries, we wandered into a bakery called Our Daily Bread and loitered at the counter for a good half hour, drinking coffee, sampling the sweets, and chatting with the young owners, Don and Lise Martell. Both are Biddeford natives, and Don recently left a well-paid chef's job to realize his ambition of becoming a small-town baker. Lise is friendly and quiet, while Don regales his customers with a running, good-humored monologue, blarney *à la français.* Even the slogan on Don's business card is a bit of a goof—"Fine Baked Goods Since 1988"—but as your tastebuds will tell you, the substance of his claim is no jest.

Several factories still operate in Biddeford, but no longer on Factory Island—where the voluminous floor space in the old brick manufactories is gradually being given over to shops, offices, and apartments. The mills here have been idle since the 1950s, but when York Manufacturing—a great wooden millworks—occupied this site in 1825, it was the country's largest textile producer, specializing in common shirting—calicos, checks, and ginghams. On the Saco side of the river, the grand white mansions of the former mill owners and executives are likewise preserved on Main and North streets. Though Saco is now a bedroom community for nearby Portland, the nineteenth-century brand of refined paternalism that once bound the two towns and cultures has long been severed.

"We're only fifteen minutes from the Maine Mall" (the state's largest shopping center), bemoaned anthropologist Tad Baker, director of the York Institute, Saco's miniature museum, built in 1866 and one of Maine's oldest. Baker provided some insight on local history and current issues as we toured this appealing repository of preindustrial artifacts, decorative and fine arts, furnishings and tools, as well as some specimens of natural history, all of which added up to a rich collage of town life in Maine during the federal period. Like other desirable colonial-era locales in southern Maine, Saco faces "explosive growth," Baker said, characterizing as "hamburger alley" the creeping commercial expansion taking place on Route 1 just north of the town. And while Tad Baker is more bemused than bitter as he speaks, his comments reflect the concerns one hears everywhere in the state these days from those who fear that the Maine coast is losing its traditional character in a brushfire of real-estate speculation. A bit later we sat in the Golden Rooster, a lunch counter on Saco's "downtown" strip, and listened to an old Frenchman who registered the receding past in his own unique way. He makes his living fishing for eels in the Saco River, and he described how the creatures are hooked on a bob of worms the size of a softball. He can still make $100 a day for a trashcan full of eels, but it takes him a lot longer to fill the can than it used to.

At Tad Baker's suggestion, we explored some of the countryside west of Biddeford, just a short spin on South Street and then along Hollis Road, following the Saco River upstream. If land is becoming dear and scarce around the coastal towns and villages, inland Maine is still a reservoir of open spaces, with many more working farms than one might expect. Or at least, if family farming is no longer a full-time vocation for these rural residents, everyone with a fair patch of land seems to be using some portion of it to squeeze a bit more cash from the local economies, whatever their other occupations. A sign at the Cole Farm Dairy proclaimed maple syrup for sale, so we drove up to the farmhouse and I rang the bell. An ancient lady, near ninety for certain, but still more wiry than frail, opened the door. She said that the farm's milking operation now belonged to a large dairy corporation, but that her nephew ran a sap camp out back, and sold maple syrup to locals and passing motorists. When she asked the purpose of my inquiry, I told her I was writing a book, and she offered this advice: "Take your Bible along. It helped Abe Lincoln. He never would have been able to write anything without that Bible."

OLD ORCHARD BEACH, CAMP ELLIS VIA ROUTE 9 ∎ PROUTS NECK, CAPE ELIZABETH, PORTLAND VIA ROUTES 1, 207, AND 77

The last obligatory stop on our coastal itinerary was to be nearby Old Orchard Beach, so we picked up Route 9 again, this time driving down the opposite bank of the Saco River. Tidy as a sociologist's model community in Anywhere, USA, the layout of the houses we passed for some time reminded me of seamless suburban images from early television sitcoms like "Ozzie and Harriet" or "Life with Father." But gradually this domestic anonymity gives way to the more familiar ancestral settings of the Maine coast, where the colors of the land and the growing things reappear in snatches, like earth and grass breaking through an asphalt road that becomes more and more worn the longer you follow it. At a point where Route 9 seems to end—but actually jogs radically to the left—we continued straight on, intrigued by an ambiguous sign announcing our arrival at "Camp Ellis." Unexpectedly, we had entered an active fishing village. The local hangout, Langevin's, was surrounded by pickup trucks, so we stopped to see what had drawn such a winter crowd. Inside, the fisherfolk sat playing cards, their pastime on days like this when an ill wind whips up the surf and keeps the fleet in port despite what has developed into an almost cloudless sky.

Camp Ellis occupies a small sandy point, noted for its 2,000-foot-long beach to the leeward of the river mouth. The village itself has that unfinished, informal beach-town look, the narrow lanes and alleys etched at random, warrenlike, over the dunes, and tightly bordered by cottages— mostly seasonal, judging from their mothballed, lifeless appearance. A perimeter road, running one way, winds close to the water, perilously in places where the shoulder has been washed away by a succession of winter squalls. As we drove near the tip of the point, we spotted a small neon sign on a large wooden building, the word OPEN lighted in red. By chance, we'd come upon the Wormwood Restaurant, a chowder house and family-style restaurant open year-round, a rare luxury along this dismantled off-season coast, and one all the more welcome in such an evocative seaside setting. Spacious, yet underlit, the place had a clubby warmth about it, pleasantly anachronistic; the menu was varied and reasonable. But Camp Ellis, too, is feeling the pinch of success, as we learned when the bartender pointed through the window to a plain, shingled bungalow across the street. "They've been offered $350,000 for it," he said, referring to the owners. "Everybody's selling out." "Why?" I asked, with feigned reportorial naiveté. "There are no B-and-Bs in Saco," was his somewhat enigmatic reply, suggesting no doubt that there would soon be many B-and-Bs in Camp Ellis. At the end of the road outside the Wormwood, a wide rock pier extends a good quarter-mile beyond the land, and one imagines it could be walked in good weather, though always with caution; not uncommonly in the summer, when the coast is saturated with vacationers, the sea rises up and plucks a wide-eyed landlubber into a watery grave.

The next stretch of Route 9, between Camp Ellis and Old Orchard Beach, has a very rural, uncluttered appearance. Off the road is a state beach called Ferry Park, along which summer retreats belonging to various religious communities are discreetly arranged beneath the pines, some with roadside signs that invite visitors at fixed hours. What with this bucolic introduction, you would hardly anticipate the proximity of Maine's most disreputable playground, tacky and brassy to many whose eyes don't decipher—and delight in—the kitsch among all the visual chaos. Certainly, no one could accuse Old Orchard Beach of being pretty, especially in the dead of winter. Hardly a soul is stirring along the main ocean drive that tunnels for miles past cut-rate motels and other architectural bric-a-brac, modified only occasionally by a new wave of overdesigned condos—genuine eyesores, there being nothing worse than the attempt to cover shabbiness with pretension.

Old Orchard's strength is that the town has never pretended to be Bar Harbor, any more than the dance-hall scenes in the paintings of Toulouse-Lautrec can be mistaken for debutante cotillions. The hoi polloi prefer a carnival atmosphere, those singular old-time ingredients that make a day in a seaside resort like Old Orchard a kind of irresistible nostalgia trip during the summer months, as you jostle shoulder-to-shoulder with the noisy crowds, shuttling between the sand and the boardwalk attractions, filling your nostrils with the strong smell of fried dough and humanity. Tragically —a word justified by the grief of a true fan—Maine's Triple A minor-league baseball team, formerly of Old Orchard, now has packed off to warmer quarters, turning the local stadium into a permanent venue for rock concerts. But the condos, according to the owner of Langevin's Market back in Camp Ellis, are not selling as expected, so Old Orchard is likely to retain its rough-edged, funky appeal for some time to come.

Surprisingly, despite the nearness of Portland, the remaining drive from Old Orchard can be remarkably long and countrylike, if, after driving inland to bypass the vast Scarborough marsh, you return to coastal roads rather than zipping quickly into South Portland on Route 1. Just before Route 9 hinges west to ascend the Scarborough River, we drove out to Pine Point, onto a wharf with a fisherman's co-op, where you can buy lobster and steamed clams in season, served in cardboard containers with plenty of napkins and melted butter, and eat on the deck with its fine view across what is Maine's largest estuarial marsh, some 2,700 protected acres in all. The opposite shore is near enough, but to reach it and continue up the coast, you must circumvent the marsh, by no means an unpleasant task since the wetlands and the twisted beds of two rivers, first the Scarborough and then the Nonesuch, remain your constant companions for miles. A field guide to salt-marsh environments and wildlife would be a good reference to carry with you on any excursion up Maine's south coast, for help in identifying the wetland flora and fauna.

Were it summer, we certainly would have dropped in on the seasonal Audubon nature center on Route 9, where canoes may be rented, the best mode of transportation for getting a truly close-up view of the marshlands. As it was, we drove on until Route 9 joined Route 1, then doubled back to the shore on Route 207, which leads all the way to Prouts Neck, an exclusive community that shuns casual visitors, as their many "Do not . . ." signs rudely convey. But, while you will find no place to stop and walk, you cannot be prevented from driving the public roads and imbibing the beauty of the sea prospects or the sweeping view back over Saco Bay, clear to Biddeford Pool. Marring the shoreline at the depth of that deep cove are a half-dozen concrete monstrosities that look like giant telephone relay buildings or shore defense emplacements, circa World War II. These turn out to be the aforementioned condos, providing further painful visual evidence of their undesirability along such a priceless ecological and—let's face it— aesthetic resource as the Maine coast. Prouts Neck is Winslow Homer country. The artist, whose work first popularized this stretch of shore, lived here at the turn of the century, and he might still be moved today by the unsullied beauty of the local surroundings and the undisturbed intimacy of the sea.

The final leg of our journey followed Route 77, accessed from Route 207 just above Prouts Neck. Though there appeared to be many corners to explore off the road, we were rapidly losing daylight, and so, by necessity, these had to be shelved for future explorations. We did manage to fit in a quick visit to Two Lights overlook, a very appealing ocean-view picnic facility distinguished by two lighthouses set among attractive modern and vintage Victorian homes. For the rest, we were pleased to end the day as we had begun it, keeping to a leisurely pace and enjoying both the drive and the unexpectedly open landscape around Cape Elizabeth. On a previous excursion we had spent a day at the Inn by the Sea, a grandly appointed, somewhat pricy hotel just minutes outside Portland. Enhancing the attractiveness of the inn is the raised wooden pathway through a small wildlife sanctuary that connects the hotel grounds to the sandy beach at Crescent State Park. On this occasion, however, we passed the inn by and crossed the bridge linking Route 77 to the city of Portland, and we could not have anticipated a more satisfying finale: the orange orb of the sun was melting into the western horizon at the far end of the harbor, diffusing the moment of dusk with that mottled, fading half-light that heralds the night.

INFORMATION ■ *Portsmouth Chamber of Commerce* (603-436-1118), P.O. Box 239, Portsmouth, 500 Market St., Portsmouth, NH 03801. Distributes the free pamphlet "Historic Kittery." ■ *York Chamber of Commerce* (363-4422)*, P.O. Box 417, York 03909 ■ *Ogunquit Chamber of Commerce* (646-2939), Box 2289, Ogunquit 03907 ■ *Kennebunk/Kennebunkport Chamber of Commerce* (967-0857), 105 Main St., Kennebunk 04043 ■ *Biddeford/Saco Chamber of Commerce* (282-1567), 170 Main St., Biddeford 04005 ■ *Old Orchard Beach Chamber of Commerce* (934-2091), P.O. Box 600, First St., Old Orchard Beach 04064.

KITTERY/THE YORKS

LODGINGS ■ *Whaleback Inn* (439-9570), Kittery Point 03905. Near the scenic wharf. Open Memorial Day to Columbus Day. ■ *Hutchins House* (363-3058), 173 Orgunug Rd., York 03909. Overlooking the York River. Open Memorial Day through October. ■ *The Canterbury House* (363-3503), P.O. Box 881C, York Harbor 03909. Near the beach. Open year-round. ■ *Dockside* (363-2868), Harris Island, P.O. Box 205, York Harbor 03909. Cottages, rooms, and restaurant on the wharf. Seasonal. ■ *Edwards Harborside Inn* (363-3037), Stage Neck Rd., York Harbor 03911. Overlooks the ocean at harbor entrance. Open year-round.

CAMPING ■ *Flagg's Tent 'n' Trailer Park* (363-5050), Webber Rd., P.O. Box 232, York Beach 03910. ■ *Libby's Oceanside Campgrounds* (363-4171), Rt. 1A, P.O. Box 67, York Harbor 03911.

RESTAURANTS ■ *Chauncey Creek Lobster Pound* (439-1030), Chauncey Creek Rd., Kittery Point. Lobster and clams, including raw bar. Seasonal. ■ *Cape Neddick Inn* (363-2899) Rt. 1, Cape Neddick 03902. Open year-round. ■ *Dockside Dining Room* (363-4800), Harris Island, York Harbor. Open May through Columbus Day, except Mondays. ■ *The Goldenrod* (363-2621), York Beach. Family-style restaurant and soda fountain operating since 1896. Open Memorial Day to Labor Day.

*Unless indicated otherwise, telephone numbers here and throughout this book are in area code 207.

OUTLETS ■ The following outlet malls are located on Route 1, immediately north of Kittery; all are open year-round: ■ *The Kittery Trading Post* (439-2700): an L.L. Bean without the mail-order business. ■ *Maine Outlet Mall:* Samuel Robert (men's clothing); Eurosport (sportswear); Scandinavian Design (furniture); Oneida (flatwear); Talbots (women's clothing); Timberland (shoes and boots); Mikasa (china and glassware); Ripoffs (men's wear). ■ *Tidewater Outlet Mall:* Lenox (china); North Country Leather (luggage); Boston Trader (men's and women's sportswear). ■ *Kittery Outlet Center:* Van Heusen (dress shirts); Totes (raingear); Royal Doulton Shoppe (china); Towle (silverplate); Mighty-Mac (raingear); Le Sportsac (luggage); Waterford (crystal). ■ *Kittery Mall:* Dansk (kitchenware). ■ *Maine Gate Outlets:* Corning (cookware); Leather Loft (accessories); Georges Braid (painted ice buckets). ■ *Kittery Factory Stores:* Bass, Dexter, Dunham, Eastland (shoes); Hathaway (shirts); Black & Decker (tools); American Tourister (luggage).

OGUNQUIT

LODGINGS ■ *Perkins Cove Inn* (646-2232), Woodbury Lane (off Shore Road), Ogunquit 03907. Overlooks Perkins Cove. Open May through Columbus Day; two-night minimum. ■ *Beachcrest Inn* (646-2156), P.O. Box 673, 16 Beach St., Ogunquit 03907. Turn-of-the-century summer hotel overlooking the sea, open year-round.

RESTAURANTS ■ *Whistling Oyster* (646-9521), Perkins Cove. Ogunquit institution, open year-round. ■ *Einstein's Deli Restaurant* (646-5262), 2 Shore Rd. Reliable for eats, bar, and nightlife. Open year-round. ■ *Lobster Shack* (646-2941), Perkins Cove. Reasonably priced lobster and trimmings. Open May through mid-October.

THE KENNEBUNKS

LODGINGS ■ *The Kennebunk Inn* (985-3351), 45 Main St., Kennebunk 04043. Dining room and bar. Open year-round. ■ *The Kennebunkport Inn* (967-2621), Dock Square, Kennebunkport 04046. Open year-round, with shoulder-season packages in late spring and early fall that include meals. ■ *The Ocean View* (967-2750), 72 Beach Ave., Kennebunk Beach 04043. A B-and-B with a unique beach setting. Seasonal.

RESTAURANTS ■ *The Kennebunk Inn* and *The Kennebunkport Inn*, mentioned above, have their own dining rooms, which are said to be reliable. ■ *Bartley's Dockside Dining by the Bridge* (967-4798), by the bridge in Kennebunkport. Inexpensive seafood entrees and good chowders. Open year-round. ■ *Tilly's Shanty* (967-5015), Pier Rd., Cape Porpoise. Take-out fried seafood and boiled lobster, with outdoor deck on the water. Seasonal.

2

PORTLAND: ALMOST A CITY

A DESTINATION

Beware of Portland, Maine; many travelers come here with the intent of "just passing through," and never return home. Invisible Sirens seem to charge the sights and sounds of this old port with a seductive pull too powerful for many visitors to withstand. Portland, the closest thing in Maine to a genuine city, has won recognition in recent years for its "quality of life," and young professionals in particular are finding a boom employment market here as well. And yet, by any comparative measure, Portland is hardly a city at all. Rather it is a sprawling, nineteenth-century town by the sea, transformed into a new-age haven: three parts provincial—quiet, relatively crime-free, and unpolluted; one part urbane, with just enough cultural attractions to take the edge off its backwater past. A single day in Portland is sufficient to get a feel for the town, but a two- or three-day stopover would be ideal to allow a fuller sampling of the many engaging sights and attractions.

In appearance, Portland belongs primarily to the period of American industrial development that spanned the years between the Civil War and the turn of the century. During those years and before, Portland was a bustling and prosperous harbor, a depot for Maine's Third World–style economy, which exported raw materials—mostly lumber—and received finished goods in return. Individually, many of Portland's merchants and traders were enriched by this exchange, as the city's surplus of fabulous mansions dating from this time still attest. But Portland never entered the Age of Steel, that boom epoch when other port towns of the Northeast and Midwest were transformed into producers of goods and forests of skyscrapers by the engines of twentieth-century industry and mass production.

When, throughout New England, the factories in mill towns lapsed into idleness, and the warehouses lining old harbors came to store only the echoes of their own emptiness, the massive buildings were allowed to fall into ruin. If a wave of development happened to follow on the heels of such a decline, as often occurred elsewhere during the years of American industrial expansion, the mills and warehouses were plowed under and replaced by modern plants and buildings. If no such development occurred, they were allowed to decay until they either collapsed or were revitalized and put to some new use.

Such was the case in Portland. The old five-, six-, and seven-story wholesale and warehouse structures that survived the boom years of the harbor were reclaimed in the 1960s by artists and artisans at a time when most of Portland's citizenry viewed the seedy waterfront alleys and decrepit wharves as a civic eyesore. Port activity—except for the local fishing industry—had shifted to the opposite bank of the Fore River, into South Portland, where the oceangoing tankers emptied their cargoes of oil—the only tonnage to speak of now entering the port—into ugly rows of storage tanks for distribution throughout the state. Surrounding the "old port," the city's other commercial streets and residential neighborhoods held their own, despite the inevitable flight of residents and businesses to the suburbs and shopping malls; and so Portland slept the slumber of recession that set in during much of this century.

The entrepreneurial impetus that reversed this trend came not from the cautious imaginations of the town's fathers and merchants, but from the pioneering zeal of a marginal group of counterculturalists and artists who valued the old lofts and storefronts for the space and cheap rent, and in whose eyes the abandoned or underutilized buildings had taken on the romantic characteristics of monumental ruins. Inevitably, as demand for space in what quickly became a chic zone displaced many original pioneers to the city's remaining low-rent districts, the back streets of the waterfront have become homogeneously elegant, filled with fine shops and restaurants.

This is not the first time during its more than three hundred years of intermittent existence that Portland has risen from the doldrums of ruination. Three previous—and greatly more devastating—periods of decline saw Portland virtually wiped from the map. The city was known as Falmouth until the 1780s, having been first settled in the early 1600s. Disaster number one occurred in 1690, when French and Indian raiders burned the settlement to the ground and massacred most of its inhabitants, after which Falmouth reverted to wilderness for almost thirty years. By the 1720s, a new generation of colonists had returned to what was then popularly called "The Neck," and began to resettle and rebuild the town. By the eve of the American Revolution, Falmouth had grown enviably prosperous from mast-cutting and the lumber trade. The inhabitants had also grown increasingly seditious toward their English masters, and the outcome of one rebellion was the leveling of the city for the second time at the hands of an invading enemy. As the story goes, a certain Captain Mowatt of the British Navy, who had been arrested and harassed in Falmouth in April 1775, returned that same October with a fleet of warships and subjected the town to a cruel bombardment, demolishing 414 of its 500 buildings and houses.

The dispossessed residents thought it wise to delay rebuilding until the cessation of hostilities, but over the next seventy-five years the city—now called Portland—once more recovered and witnessed impressive growth. Then, just after the close of the Civil War, on July 4, 1866, tragedy struck again. A firecracker carelessly discharged among the wood shavings of a wharfside shipyard ignited a fire that "ate through the heart of the city. Homes, banks, stores, newspaper offices, warehouses, churches, schools and landmarks that went back to the foundation of the city were destroyed . . . and ten thousand people were made homeless." Portland became a city of tents, but this time the recovery was almost immediate, as the construction dates—late 1860s and early 1870s—of the core of Portland's Old Port Exchange buildings bear witness. Following this last major disaster, the city of Portland adopted for its motto—as well it might—the Latin word *Resurgam:* "I shall rise again."

My own recent visit to Portland was a delightful experience. For all the years I've been summering—and lately living—in Maine, I'd never taken the opportunity to explore the city in depth. After several preliminary day trips, I resolved to stay overnight in a B-and-B, and to create a Portland itinerary that fellow travelers with two or three days on their hands could easily simulate. Portland is divided into three sections. The West End occupies Bramhall Hill, slopes down to the old downtown at sea level, then rises once again to the East End, above Munjoy Hill. Running the length of the city along an ancient ridgeline is Congress Street, Portland's principal thoroughfare. The city fronts Casco Bay and is surrounded on three sides by water; seeing it from its fourth side, along Highway 295, one is left with the illusion of Portland as a citadel, self-contained, high upon a ridge and virtually detached from the mainland.

Portland is ideal for long, pleasant walks—and not overly taxing, since the elevations are modest and the climbs seldom abrupt. On one initial visit, however, I dutifully drove out to the Eastern Promenade, a somewhat bleak promontory with a commanding view over Casco Bay and its closest offshore islands. Beyond the promenade—and the 1807 observatory tower (open seasonally)—Portland's East End neighborhoods are of little interest to the touring visitor. A building buff might find a drive through the east side worthwhile, and a visit to Levinsky's, a large and hip clothing store on Congress east of Franklin, is a sensible digression. The Old Port Exchange, occupying the center ground, is elegant and highly commercial, inclining, especially on sunny weekends, toward a kind of theme-park intensity that overwhelms one with crowds and choices. Not that this revitalized center is a place to avoid; a lot of charm shines through the glitter. But I preferred the West End and chose a B-and-B there for my base; and besides, Portland is such a small town that my room was barely a twenty-minute walk to the farthest point on the downtown waterfront.

From the Inn on Carlton, the West End home of a young bookbinder with two sons, I was also only minutes from Longfellow Square on the quiet end of Congress Street where the art museum and two excellent cafés provided all the stimulus I needed for one morning's excursion.

But I'm getting ahead of my tale. I had actually gotten into Portland on the previous morning, parked my car on Free Street in a public lot (five dollars a day) and immediately headed for Raffle's Café Bookstore to plot out the day's adventure. Raffle's owners, Mary and Tim Follow, migrated from New Haven a few years back, and decided to open their business on upper Congress Street, preferring this untampered urban setting over the more studied quaintness of the Old Port. The rack of out-of-town newspapers just outside the entrance is your first hint of having stumbled upon a den of quiet sophistication. Inside, café tables with barrel-back chairs and a small counter share the ground floor with several shelves of top-quality hardcover editions, while the brick walls on the morning in question showcased the exciting, sensual paper sculptures of an artist friend of the Follows. On this occasion I happily munched on a real cheese Danish, about as rare a find in Maine as the sun in April. And while I had previously lunched here very happily on a platter of salad with a flavorful humus flecked green with fresh parsley, it is obviously the genuine café atmosphere of the place, as much as the reliable, healthy food, that hooks the clientele.

It was Tim Follow who suggested to me that Portland's greatest asset was its varied architecture, and therefore a long walking tour was the most satisfying activity the city had to offer its visitors. Portland, he said, was also endowed with many rare and old book shops and he suggested that I drop by Pat Murphy's out-of-print bookstore on High Street while I was heading toward Greater Portland Landmarks, as the local historic preservation group is known, to pick up brochures for self-guided walking tours. Murphy's shop is indeed a treat, crammed with thousands of old titles priced between three and five dollars. Pat Murphy himself is an affable local poet and raconteur who claims, without any hint of melancholy, to "enjoy life now that fame and fortune have passed me by." He makes ends meet by trading his more valuable finds with dealers, and proudly displayed several bound volumes that had just come into his possession which contained the original issues of *The Strand* magazine—the periodical in which Conan Doyle first published his tales of Holmes and Watson. Murphy also shared some of Portland's offbeat literary lore, noting that the author Erskine Caldwell ran a bookstore here on Congress Street during the late 1920s.

The landmark organization's office is itself located on a landmark street. State Street and its surrounding blocks were developed after the American Revolution, when local merchants "looked to the western edges of the town for suitable locations on which to build their homes." Today, some two dozen extraordinary dwellings from the Federal and Greek Revival periods—1800 to 1860—lie within the rectangle created by Congress, High, York, and State streets. None, however, can rival for sheer mass and fancy the Ruggles Sylvester Morse House—the so-called Victoria Mansion—that occupies an uncrowded corner plot at Danforth and Park streets. The mansion, built in the grand Italianate style by a hotel magnate, is open to the public only during the summer months and for a brief period around Christmas.

At Greater Portland Landmarks I picked up four walking guides—entitled "Congress Street," "State Street," "Old Port Exchange," and "Western Promenade"—and then wandered down Spring Street in search of a restaurant called Alberta's to eat lunch and to examine my brochures. It was then I spotted the Inn at Park Spring, the name derived from the intersection of those two streets. Rather than an owner-operated B-and-B, the accommodation actually is a tiny, well-appointed hotel with a resident manager on hand day and night to greet guests and facilitate their requests. The seven rooms here are lovely, just under $100 a night (less in the off-season), and the rates include a light continental breakfast plus the unusual amenity of a common parlor where a decanter of brandy and a selection of traditional teas are available to guests throughout the day without charge. Across the street from the inn, going toward the waterfront, is the Park Street Row, a line of town houses built on speculation in the 1830s that held the western line against the consuming flames of the 1866 disaster.

Alberta's Restaurant on nearby Pleasant Street, just above the intersection of Danforth and Center streets, is the perfect starting point for a walk around Portland's historic West End, located as it is at the foot of the incline that rises toward the Western Promenade. There's a slightly in-crowd preciousness in the air at Alberta's, but the food is true to its reputation. Over a draft of Bass ale, and a sumptuous chef's omelette filled with fresh corn, cheese, and avocado, accompanied by a side dish of steamed rice and wheat berries (less than $10 with tip), I spread out my papers, and gave full appreciation to the wonderfully illustrated brochures provided by Greater Portland Landmarks. The line drawings of the old houses have the texture and grace of old prints, and I was particularly awed by the unexpected grandeur of the mansions depicted in the guide to the Western Promenade, which I would soon explore.

At the beginning of Danforth Street, just above wide Commercial Street, which runs along the docks, is a line of red brick warehouses that provide space for an appealing variety of workshops and galleries. There is still a feeling of the outpost about these buildings, since the development of the Old Port has yet to extend much beyond Temple Street, several blocks to the east. In the first building, the old J. B. Brown Molasses Warehouse at number 20, I walked unannounced into a wholesale print and custom frame shop housed in a large loft, where much of the space is given over to framemaking, and the walls are filled from top to bottom with framed pictures, in the manner of a French salon. In a far corner sat the proprietor, Ronald Rubin, behind a desk centered on a mid-sized Oriental rug and bordered by several chairs.

I was gestured into one of the chairs, served a cup of freshly ground coffee, and entertained for the next forty-five minutes by Mr. Rubin, who shared with me the name of his favorite Portland restaurant (Hugo's), disclosed the locations of several desirable off-the-road hideaways scattered throughout western Maine that he hoped I might investigate for possible inclusion in this guide, discoursed on the problems inherent in a former New Yorker's adjustment to the temperament of Mainers, and instructed me on the ins and outs of the print business, producing a sheaf of sixteenth-century engravings by Albrecht Dürer for my pleasure and admiration. While not in the retail trade per se, Ron Rubin confesses to enjoying occasional visits from drop-ins who demonstrate an interest in his art. The remainder of this vast converted building houses fifty-two other tenants, all owner-operated businesses that include woodworkers, papermakers, fashion designers, and a host of other artisans, each a potential encounter—like my impromptu chat with Ron Rubin—for someone trekking about Portland in the manner described here.

On the street once more, I began to ascend Danforth, passing another line of red brick warehouses (numbers 34–36) given over to artists, craftspersons, and retailers, and across the street, the Tree Café, Portland's hottest night spot for many years, though recently under threat of foreclosure. A young woman in Ron Rubin's print shop had volunteered that the Tree draws a fair-sized, youngish crowd most nights of the week and often features live reggae. Rumor has it the Tree will survive, or rise again at the same location in a different form. The afternoon was already well advanced, and so I found myself climbing into the face of a setting sun; an earlier hour is therefore recommended for those following this route, or one may reverse the course, entering directly onto the Western Promenade via Bramhall Street, off Congress. I chose this route because I found it the most dramatic approach, evolving gradually into a fine scenic and architectural finale.

For the first half-dozen blocks, the street scene is transitional, the structures an eclectic mix of styles and periods, and in various states of repair, though by no means devoid of visual appeal. Side streets and alleys open narrow vistas to the harbor below, but neither the forward march of state philanthropy nor the forces of private development have yet to reclaim this priceless stretch of stagnant waterfrontage. Sidewalks of red brick evoke a decidedly Victorian feeling, confirmed by the age and design of the imposing mansions that begin to appear above Emery Street, though one of Portland's oldest Federal homes—Vaughan House (1799)—is also tucked in their midst. Toward the top of the hill, Western Cemetery comes into view, and the road curves rightward, a pedestrian path being worn at curbside into the lawns of the few privileged homes that command this spot where no sidewalks have been installed.

Shortly beyond this point the actual promenade begins. The wind has played havoc with the tombstones and monuments in the burial ground (where Longfellow's parents are interred); not a single marker seems to stand plumb, but all incline like seasick landsmen on a rocking ship. The narrow strip of ground where the promenade is laid out occupies a steep promontory, 175 feet at its highest elevation, and looks over a disappointing landscape in the foreground, the dregs of an industrial waterway. Along the western horizon, some sixty miles distant, the peaks of New Hampshire's Presidential Range, Mount Washington among them, can be seen, the clearer the day, the sharper their outlines. Along the many side streets behind this bulb of land, Greater Portland Landmarks has designated thirty-seven buildings of historic and architectural interest, accounting for one of the most stunning concentrations of late-nineteenth-century residences in the nation.

It was during this walk that I first came upon the Inn on Carlton, and decided to spend the night there. Innkeeper Susan Holland purchased what was already a functioning B-and-B in this graceful Victorian town house a little over a year ago. Formerly a college instructor, she now pursues the Zen-like craft of custom bookbinding. She will be only too happy to show off her well-bound volumes and small basement workshop, where the hardy aromas of leather and paste, the hand-powered-cutting machines and sewing racks, reflect the fundamental simplicity and subtlety of this ancient handicraft. The seven high-ceilinged guest rooms at the Inn on Carlton, like the public spaces, are designed for home comfort with country style furnishings and antiques, and depending on the season range in price from $35 for a small single to $80 for the largest third-floor room with private bath.

Ms. Holland keeps a supply of menus in her front parlor, often donated at her request by guests who wish to share a successful dining experience. When I told her I was interested in an ethnic meal, she suggested the

Afghan Restaurant on Congress, not far from Raffle's, and I dined superbly there that evening. (The Afghan Restaurant has since moved to Exchange Street in the Old Port area; see listings for exact address.) The neighborhood restaurant that Susan recommends most frequently is the West Side, around the corner on Pine Street. Also nearby, at 155 Brackett, is the Good Day Market, a food co-op open to the public, where soups and sandwiches are served at lunchtime, and a full deli restaurant is soon to be opened above the shop.

The next morning I was out early to explore Congress Street, a super strip for a morning constitutional, regardless of where you spend the night in Portland. The street's most singular feature is its length, broken up by three diminutive squares. From Monument Square to Longfellow Square, with Congress Square in between, you will run the gamut of several distinct social and institutional environments, beginning with City Hall opposite Exchange Street, and ending with the serenely seated statue of Longfellow where State and Pine join with the principal thoroughfare. In between are the many unadorned storefronts that substantiate the claim that this remains the city's traditional shopping street. The overall effect recalls an image of similar commercial streets I retain from the 1950s. Here on Congress Street, one's relationship to the marketplace seems more voluntary than in the refurbished Old Port Exchange, where the spirit of aggressive consumerism fairly displaces all other stimuli, even invading the private spaces of the imagination that seek a wider spectrum of experience from city streets than the one-dimensional obsession with buying and selling. "Street life," "commercial archaeology," label it how you will; there's a dose of it on Congress Street (even an umbrella-shaded hot-dog stand).

One senses that this nagging alienation from the pushiness of the theme-ridden establishments beyond the periphery of Congress Street is shared, albeit unconsciously—and no doubt most strongly in the quiet morning hours—by the clientele who lounge comfortably over breakfast in the Good Egg, a veritable Noah's Ark of humanity embracing every social type from yuppie professionals and city bureaucrats to blue-collar workers and bohemians. Among the counter staff and waiters here are several youths whose nonconformity is expressed in purple hair and subdued punk regalia. And, as one might almost guess, most of the staff are struggling artists of one stripe or another, among them several students of the Portland School of

Art, housed nearby in a former library, a most appealing structure of mixed inspiration, somewhat obscured by the seediness of its surroundings.

With art and artists, Maine has been blessed. Some first-rate modern painters have spent their productive days illuminating on canvas their respective visions of Maine's unblemished land and seascapes. Many examples of this creative output—including works of Hopper, Wyeth, Homer, and Zorach—have been assembled into the State of Maine Collection by the Portland Museum of Art, a tidy complex of buildings, old and new, on High Street opposite Congress Square. The bulk of the collection hangs under natural lighting on bright white walls in an I. M. Pei–designed wing that opened in 1983. I find it an attractive structure, one that the museum's publicity folk label "postmodern," in this instance referring to a mix and match of architectural motifs from various ages and cultures. The building is also of a perfect size to allow for viewing most of the museum's collection in a single visit. Cornerstones of the Maine Collection are the seventeen Winslow Homer works that shuttle between the private quarters of a wealthy Maine family, the Paysons (former owners of the New York Mets and of Van Gogh's *Irises*), and the museum, which exhibits the paintings during the spring and summer only.

My stop at the museum included a brief tour of the McLellan-Sweat House, where the institution's earliest collection had been housed, and which, on occasion, is open to the public. The old mansion (c. 1800) is a striking example of Federal architecture, but completely unfurnished, and with a rickety center stairway that my companion and I had to climb one person at a time. When scheduled, tours of McLellan-Sweat House focus on the stages involved in the restoration of old houses to their original interiors and decor. On display, as it were, are certain interior architectural details, patches of plaster walls or segments of wainscoting and molding, each of which has been stripped of successive layers of paint or paper and numbered in the manner of a relic from an archaeological dig. The effect not only reveals the restorers' skills, and the choices made by various generations of residents when redecorating the mansion, but each station has the immediate appeal of an abstract design in its own right.

After leaving the museum, I headed down Congress toward another of Portland's historical attractions, the Wadsworth-Longfellow House, adjacent to the Maine Historical Society. The sign of the Hotel Everett, at the corner of Oak and Congress, caught my eye for the umpteenth time, and this time I decided to investigate. The fifty-five-room Everett, Portland's oldest hotel, turns out to be a find of sorts for visitors easily accommodated by simple surroundings, and especially for those on a tight budget. The rooms are pleasant, clean, and inexpensive, as little as $26 for a single without bath, and no more than $32 for a double with bath. According to the desk clerk, guests often include many young travelers from abroad.

Three blocks farther east, I found myself standing in front of the home where America's most successful poet spent his boyhood. Built in 1785 by Longfellow's maternal grandfather, Peleg Wadsworth—a general in the American Revolution—the house is the oldest one remaining on the Portland peninsula. It contains furnishings that belonged to both the Wadsworth and Longfellow families, including the desk where the poet wrote "My Lost Youth," his nostalgic ode to Portland. Both the house and its quiet backyard garden, a popular lunch spot for local office workers, are open only during the summer months. The Historical Society is open year-round, and visitors may make use of its extensive library facilities or simply view the collection of marine oil paintings that express a whole period of Maine's maritime development.

From a strictly architectural point of view, one of the most cohesive streetscapes in Portland can be found among the blocks of the Old Port Exchange. At its core, bounded roughly by Middle, Exchange, Fore, and Temple streets, is the area of greatest interest. It is quite striking to realize that so many of the buildings to be seen here—solid, squat, four- and five-story red brick structures with highly decorative façades—bear construction dates of 1866 and 1867, revealing that the ashes and rubble of the Great Fire had barely cooled before Portland rebuilt itself with renewed vigor and style. Fore Street is a personal favorite because—owing to an inexplicable twist of fortune—several of its buildings of the Colonial period escaped the condemnation of the flames, leaving behind a faint image of that time when exotic foreign sailors were no less commonplace along the New England waterfront than were Quaker sea captains. Look for the Samuel Butts House and Store (1792) at number 332, the Portland peninsula's second-oldest surviving building. Exchange Street, on the other hand, seems to be the fulcrum of the district's new-age commercial development, but the entire zone is fairly saturated with fine specialty shops, arts-and-crafts galleries, restaurants, taverns, and clubs. Off a tiny, graceful square at Milk and Market streets, the massive Armory now houses the Regency

Hotel, which has many features to commend it, particularly to those who wish to lodge in a full-service hotel, albeit it at the ground zero of Portland's touristic center.

The massive granite and brick buildings that line Portland's mile-long waterfront also escaped the 1866 fire. Before 1850, the water's edge had come up to Fore Street, but tons of landfill were hauled in to create the hundred-foot-wide Commercial Street that currently hems the score of working wharves projecting into the bay. I had come down to the waterfront with the special intention of boarding a mailboat of the Casco Bay Lines and touring for two and a half hours the water roads among those Calendar Islands that fall within the Greater Portland city limits. The archipelago received its poetic name from the legendary explorer Captain John Smith, who fancied this bay an American Aegean with as many islands and exposed reefs as there are days in the yearly calendar. The islands are indeed many, but their true number does not approach Captain Smith's metaphoric census. The larger islands nearest the shore serve both as bedroom communities and summer colonies within the Portland orbit.

The ferry line operates from the docks off Franklin Street, and as I walked in that direction I was distracted by the rough appearance of Custom House wharf—somewhat exceptional on a waterfront that has increasingly been adapted to retail trade, floating restaurants, and a spate of condominium construction. At the far end of the wharf, a hundred lobster traps were piled in neat stacks, and I asked a fisherman whose boat was secured to the dock if an active fishing fleet still functioned out of the Portland harbor. He said it did, but that he was from Rockland, en route to New Bedford, Massachusetts. He'd been scalloping all winter, as was evidenced by the heavy dragging rig attached to the stern of his boat, but that to avoid the Maine summer prohibition against dragging within three miles of the shore, he was headed to Massachusetts, "where they have no laws," he said, to try his luck in those anarchistic waters.

I was intrigued by the Hole, a restaurant and fisherman's hangout right there in the middle of the wharf. The early-April sky was mixed cloudy, and while the air was mild, a gusty wind was blowing intermittently, and I imagined the ride around the harbor would be a chilly one. So I ducked into the Hole for a take-out coffee. Something appealing about the place made me decide to sit at the counter and drink my coffee there. The waitress, who caught me eying the turkey platter my neighbor was eating, suggested that I order the dish for myself. At first I begged off. It was only eleven-thirty, and I wasn't quite ready for lunch. "I'll come in when I get back from the islands," I said. "If you do, you won't get any," she warned. "The boys from Bath Iron Works come in at noon, and by two there's nothing left." I mention this because the dish in question was one of those glorified cafeteria meals—piles of fresh turkey, mashed potatoes, stuffing, and canned green beans, smothered in white, starchy gravy. It was too irresistible to pass up, and for $3 it was about the best bargain, pound for pound, that I'd found so far in the whole state of Maine.

With my load of ballast well settled, I loped off to tour the bay, but soon learned that I'd missed my mailboat and that the next one would not depart for over an hour. A ferry at dockside was, however, just leaving for Peaks Island. I decided to modify my plan on the spot, opting for an island walk over a long boat ride. The crossing took only fifteen minutes to what is Portland's most populous island suburb, and its nearest, not counting several smaller mounds closer in, where the defunct forts of the harbor's defenses may still be seen. As we approached the island, I was surprised at the density of the hardwood trees, still leafless, that covered it, having assumed that all Maine islands were blanketed predominantly with evergreens. But these stands were the sign of long-standing domesticity, shade and ornamental growth cultivated by generations of inhabitants.

As the boat docked at the town landing and several dozen passengers strode over the gangway—presumably en route to their homes—I took in the island's back-cove view and what could be considered the town's center, modest frame houses, a few stores, notably a dockside restaurant with a terrace facing back toward Portland. A wide asphalt avenue rose from water's edge and disappeared up a hill toward the center of the island. Other roads seemed to follow the shore, and I chose one of these, executing a series of right turns as necessary in order to stay within view of the water. There was little sign of human presence, despite the number of clearly occupied houses and the fine weather. But the sky was filled with birds and their cheery noises. Songbirds chirped melodic, uplifting choruses as sweet as madrigals as they flitted among the bare branches of trees and brambles in open celebration of their mating days. From the vicinity of backyard garbage bins, crows, fearing my approach, rose defiantly and cawed warnings to their sultry fellows. Mourning doves grieved like lonely foghorns from the peaks of barn roofs, while seafowl and water birds pursued their own inscrutable objectives, the sea gulls forever soaring and screeching, the cravat-necked loons, swimming and bobbing, suppressing their full-blown laughter as they chortled under their breath at some endless source of secret amusement.

Beside the cove where the loons swam, there stood one of those great wooden public buildings with which Maine is richly endowed. Painted canary yellow and embraced all around by a green deck, it goes by the name of the Maine Fifth Regiment Memorial Hall. By chance, the building was open, undergoing repairs by a crew of carpenters who were indifferent to my taking an informal tour of the main meeting room. One glance at the military portraits on the walls and the several display cases of battlefield paraphernalia made it clear that the Fifth Regiment fought during the Civil War, and this was the reunion hall of the unit's veterans and their descendants. A grisly illustrated map—drawn from memory by a Maine private—documents the horrible conditions in the Confederate prisoner-of-war camp at Andersonville, and should not be missed, assuming one can gain access to the building.

Had I not miscalculated the return of the ferry, I would have been able to make the five-mile circuit of Peaks Island—roughly an hour and a half's walk. As it was, I stayed relatively near the landing, next walking off to the island's northeast side, past the market and a small cabin restaurant, to a short, rocky strand called Centennial Beach, which looked out on Little and Great Diamond islands. Returning by the same route, I noticed the sign of the Moonshell Inn in a distinct putty-gray building near the firehouse, the only year-round B-and-B on Peaks Island. Day-trippers, however, tend to congregate at Jones' Landing, a pub and restaurant adjacent to the ferry dock, and Portlanders themselves often make the crossing after work just to sit on the restaurant's outdoor deck and watch the sun set over Casco Bay.

Before departing Portland, I made one final stop on the West Side, en route to collect my car. The name of the Pomegranate B-and-B had been given to me by a woman in the landmark office, and I did not want to leave town without paying a brief visit there. The house, on Neal Street, is owned by Alan and Isabel Smiles, recently of Greenwich, Connecticut, where Mrs. Smiles was in the antiques and interior design business. With a remarkable eye for color and effect, and exquisite taste in materials, she has combined an unusual assortment of furnishings and objects d'art with the skills of several gifted decorators and painters to create a formidable interior for her home and six guest rooms. The style is thoroughly unique, and defies categorizing, but the visual impact is exhilarating and dramatic. The rooms rent for $95 a night, and in a radical departure from conventional B-and-B protocol, each is equipped with a phone and a television.

A final excursion I would recommend for anyone stopping in Portland is a drive out to Fort Williams Park, in the direction of Cape Elizabeth. A friend who serves as night editor at the *Portland Press Herald* likened the setting there—the steep promontories that rise high above the water—to Golden Gate Park in San Francisco. The great difference, of course, is that the water in question is the rugged Atlantic of the Maine coast. Further, Fort Williams Park is home to Portland Head Light, one of the nation's oldest lighthouse stations, commissioned by President Washington himself in the late 1700s. Paths along the heights allow for broad prospects on the sea, which can be seen swirling, foaming, and exploding against the rock outcroppings of several nearby islands.

A PORTLAND POSTSCRIPT

Portland, it should be noted, is a gateway to Yarmouth, Nova Scotia, via the *Scotia Prince,* a combined car ferry and cruise ship that makes daily crossings from early May to late October. During the summer, the ship functions primarily as a ferry, especially popular with tourists bound for Nova Scotia who want to save the more than 800 miles of driving there and back. Overnight mini-cruises (for as little as $118 per person, with cabin, breakfast, and buffet; less for children) attract the majority of the ship's passengers during the spring and fall. In style, the mini-cruise appeals primarily to a social group that would find an overnight stay in Atlantic City much to their taste. Casino gambling on a small scale, complete with an upbeat, if modest, cabaret show, operates through the night and the following day, but the majority of the passengers seem perfectly satisfied to spend the crossing—back and forth—in the constant grip and companionship of the many "one-armed bandits" that whir and clang endlessly throughout the voyage.

I boarded the *Scotia Prince* in Portland with my wife and then-nine-year-old son on a Saturday night in May with not the slightest interest in gambling, but simply for the novelty of making the overnight crossing. What I wanted to test was whether the gaming atmosphere would be so intrusive as to render a more relaxing cruise experience impossible. I had reasoned in advance that, as long as we had a comfortable cabin and the availability of a few gambling-free environments and activities, my wife and I, at least, could tune out the gaming as we saw fit and enjoy the cruise as a twenty-four-hour shipboard holiday. We hoped that our son, Simon, would find a friend or two to share the adventure kid-style. And that was basically what happened.

It was past 9:00 P.M. before the ship left the dock. Following a creditable dinner in the main restaurant, we left Simon asleep in his berth and made a quick tour of the various clubs and salons before retiring ourselves. It was clear that most of the passengers had come to party and gamble. The most animated among them were the slot-machine players and the capacity audience who gave active encouragement to two disco dancers and a pair of singers as they trooped gamely through their routines. The more serious gamblers slumped around the gaming tables, accepting losses and winnings alike with the same air of dour indifference. On deck, the night was foggy, and only the ship's wash could be seen as we plowed gently over the water.

Our cabin, equipped with four wide berths, two lower and two upper, plus a small bathroom complete with shower, was quite comfortable. But still, only the young and the innocent can hope for uninterrupted sleep in a strange bed; the rest of us adapt as best we can, especially on the rolling seas. The following morning, by 9:00 A.M. ship's time, we had landed in Yarmouth. The stopover allows just enough time to leave the ship for a stretch and a quick walking tour of this unextraordinary Canadian coastal town. Yarmouth dates from the mid-1700s but retains little in the way of a colonial appearance. The place, particularly on a quiet Sunday morning, seemed very much a backwater of the twentieth century. Enough gift shops were open, however, to absorb the several hundred passengers who disembarked and quickly faded from the main street into the various emporia. We walked among the back streets, though Simon finally wore us down with his badgering and dragged us into a store packed to the rafters with hideous *tchotchkas*.

The ship left Yarmouth by 11:00 A.M., due to arrive in Portland by eight in the evening. And as it turned out, the return was quite pleasant. There was a movie to distract the afternoon hours, but mostly Carol and I slept or read—or walked the deck—while Simon and a new-found friend roamed at will, endlessly rode the elevators, and begged quarters for the slots and video games every time they ran into us. For lunch we were more or less self-sufficient, as we had carried on board our own wine and a small cooler filled with fruit, cheeses, and the like (frowned upon, I believe—but we were discreet). The late-afternoon buffet, as part of the package, drew every passenger on board, and so a line formed that actually snaked up a stairway between decks. But we waited till the end, ate our fill, and spent the remaining two hours as we had the earlier part of the day. Leave it to U.S. Customs to attach a slight blemish to what was an otherwise refreshing excursion. In Canada there were no such formalities, but back home we all had to stand in line for an hour while agents tracked down a few extra cartons of cigarettes and liters of booze for the required duty.

INFORMATION ■ *Portland Chamber of Commerce* (772-2811), 142 Free St., Portland 04101. The Maine Publicity Bureau maintains an information center in the same building (same phone number). ■ *Greater Portland Landmarks* (772-5561), 165 State St., Portland 04101.

LODGINGS ■ *Inn on Carlton* (775-1910), 46 Carlton St., Portland 04102. ■ *Pomegranate Inn* (772-1006 or 800-356-0408), 49 Neal St., Portland 04102. ■ *Inn at Park Spring* (774-1059), 135 Spring St., Portland 04101. ■ *Portland Regency Inn* (774-4200), 20 Milk St., Portland 04101. ■ *Sonesta of Portland* (775-5411 or 800-343-7170), 157 High St., Portland 04101.

RESTAURANTS ■ (Many people I talked with in Portland shared the names of restaurants that were either their personal favorites or were at least establishments where they felt the food was generally reliable. For the most part, the following list reflects that informal survey.) ■ *Maria's* (772-9232), 337 Cumberland Ave. Traditional Italian. ■ *Village Café* (772-5320), 112 Newbury St. Continental. ■ *Rafael's* (773-4500), 36 Market St. Northern Italian. ■ *Bruno's Italian Restaurant* (773-3530), 35 India St. Pizza. ■ *Christopher's* (772-6877), 688 Forest Ave. Greek cuisine. ■ *Hugo's Portland Bistro* (774-8538), 88 Middle St. Irish food. ■ *Baker's Table* (775-0303), 434 Fore St. Continental, some vegetarian dishes. ■ *The Seaman's Club* (772-7311), 375 Fore St. Seafood. ■ *Alberta's* (774-5408), 21 Pleasant St. Nouvelle cuisine. ■ *Boone's Restaurant* (774-5725),

6 Custom House Wharf (next to the Hole). Seafood. ▪ *West Side* (773-8223), 58 Pine St. Continental. ▪ *Good Egg Café* (773-0801) 705 Congress St. Breakfast, open till noon only. ▪ *Raffle's Café Bookstore* (761-3930) 555 Congress St. Café. ▪ *The Afghan Restaurant* (773-3431), recently moved to Old Port area; now on Exchange St. ▪ *Woodford's Café,* Spring at Park. Offbeat neighborhood hangout for gays and straights.

NOVA SCOTIA CRUISE/FERRY ▪ *Prince of Fundy Cruise Limited,* P.O. Box 4216, Station A, Portland, Maine 04101; telephone 800-341-7540.

3

SOUTHWESTERN MAINE AT FAIR TIME

E ach year, during the first week of October, Maine's oldest and largest agricultural fair takes place in Fryeburg, a small town bordering New Hampshire at the head of the Saco River. A first-time visit to the Fryeburg Fair provided the perfect excuse for a two-day swing through the state's southwestern interior, departing from Portland via Route 302 and returning over Route 136 to the coastal town of Freeport, home of the famous outfitter for the outdoor life, L.L. Bean. Highlights along the way included an off-season viewing of the Sebago Lake and Long Lake regions—with the towns of Naples and Bridgton at their center—a visit to Bethel, a year-round resort town within the orbit of the Sunday River ski facilities, and a winding tour among selected mill towns of the Androscoggin River valley.

ROUTE 302 TO NORTH WINDHAM ▪ ROUTES 35
AND 114/11 ALONG THE WESTERN SHORE OF
SEBAGO LAKE ▪ ROUTE 302 TO BRIDGTON AND
FRYEBURG

The Fryeburg Fair opened on a fine fall Sunday to an overflow crowd. During the week, I was told, the numbers of fairgoers would diminish substantially, picking up steam once again as the Saturday-night finale approached. So with my son, Simon, I set out on Monday morning and, driving at a leisurely pace, planned to arrive at the fair by late afternoon and spend the night camping somewhere in the vicinity. But, as we were to discover, there's really no such thing as a slow day at the Fryeburg Fair, come rain or shine. This one-week event makes the region as popular to visitors as Sebago Lake during summer vacation or Sunday River on any snowy weekend in the winter. And while torrential rains marred our night at the fair, the exhibitors, vendors, and ride operators hung on bravely until the pathways were so flooded with water that even diehard midway fans like my son decided to pack it in, and a decision was made to close the fair down at about 9:00 P.M.

Earlier in the day, as we turned onto Route 35 to skirt the bottom tip of Sebago and travel Route 114 up the lake's western side (more scenic than Route 302 on the opposite shore), we still had hopes of spending the night outdoors. A commercial campground near Fryeburg remains open till the first of November, but I prefer parkland camping. Both of our park alternatives, however, would put us at some distance from the fair, necessitating a late-night commute that would cut into our campfire time. We quickly ruled out Sebago Lake State Park, on the lake's northern end, as just too far from our destination under any circumstances. White Mountain National Forest, on the other hand, a few miles north of Fryeburg, still seemed feasible, though it would be hours yet till we would actually have to make that decision.

The truth is, I didn't just drive up one side of Sebago Lake, but all the way around it, which is how I concluded that the eastern shore on Route 302 is to be avoided, even in the off-season. This stretch of 302 is heavily commercialized and serves as a principal transit artery, linking an ever-widening ring of semirural inland suburbs with the city of Portland. I had been forewarned, by a series of investigative articles in a Maine newspaper, that Sebago and the many smaller lakes in this corner of southwestern Maine were in danger of succumbing to overutilization. This was reason enough, in my mind, to avoid Sebago in the summertime, much the way I would steer clear of the towns along Maine's southern coast during the same season. Of far greater import than one's personal convenience while motor touring is the long-range impact this overutilization portends for traditional recreational resources that Mainers have long imagined to be inexhaustible. An increase over recent years in motorboat accidents, drownings, and noise and water pollution throughout this popular lake region are stirring an unprecedented bipartisan concern for environmental regulation in Maine.

Route 114 has remained picturesque, and the traffic—in the fall at least—is relatively light. Lakeside cottages set under canopies of pine are the predominant man-made features along the roadway, and the lake itself is much more frequently in view here than on the opposite shore. The sudden arrival at Naples is unexpectedly dramatic, as Route 114 confronts the lower end of Long Lake and is crossed like a T by Route 302, which continues on through Bridgton to Fryeburg. Even on a quiet and cloudy fall day, Naples retains the latent animation of a resort town that pauses in the off-season but never slumbers. The small village center, top-heavy with attractive roadhouses like Rick's Café and a floating restaurant in an old "river queen" moored at dockside, curves around the lower lake, with all the buildings to one side of the road and only water to the other.

Nathaniel Hawthorne, who spent his boyhood in these parts, apparently thought the Naples of his day was the cat's meow. And while summers here today may be hectic and overcrowded from my point of view, I would have no hesitation in recommending this town and the Long Lake region in general as a fine choice for an autumn drive or a getaway weekend just on the strength of the area's unique lakeside setting. Literary romantics, by the way, may want to make a slight detour here and descend to South Casco along Route 302 to view the home where the author of *The Scarlet Letter* grew up. The white clapboard house, as square as a livery stable, can be found midway down the Hawthorne Road in South Casco, in front of Rodney's General Store, where I went to get Simon a root beer and myself a cup of coffee. The Hawthorne house is marked by a plaque, but it is used only as a community and garden club meeting hall and is not open to the public. I asked Rodney if any Hawthorne lore still circulated around the community, and he was not aware of any. When I went to pay for my purchases, he charged me only for the soda, saying, "I'll buy you the coffee," thinking perhaps it was a bit overcooked by then, though it smelled okay to me; with a simple gesture like that, guys like Rodney can make your day.

The 1,300 acres of Sebago Lake State Park are also located only a few minutes' drive off Route 302, between South Casco and Naples. The park's recreational facilities occupy two distinct land masses, separated by the aptly named Crooked River. The first area offers picnicking in a grove of thick-trunked and towering pines, plus swimming from a long crescent of sand along the shore of the upper lake. Some 300 campsites are located on a second peninsula, across the Crooked River, and many of these are on the lake shore or, failing that, within sight of the water. Fifteen minutes' drive beyond Naples is Bridgton, which to my eye was only slightly less appealing, lacking only the dimension of the wide waterscape in its front yard, though in fact Bridgton is surrounded by a dozen small and lovely lakes just minutes away from its village center.

By now a light but steady rain had begun to fall, and Simon lobbied heavily for spending the night in a motel, preferably one equipped with a giant color television. I agreed, but as we were still a good half hour or longer from the fairgrounds, I hoped to get us a bit closer before starting to hunt seriously for a room. I was heartened to find that most of the motels on the outskirts of Bridgton still had vacancies, so I figured we had the option of returning if we failed to find accommodations closer to Fryeburg. A long detour in an attempt to drive up Pleasant Mountain, from where, I have read, some fifty lakes may be counted on a clear day, consumed more time than I had anticipated. And, in the end, we did not succeed in finding a road to the summit. When we finally reached Fryeburg and neighboring Conway, New Hampshire, the few motels in the area were already filled. We had noticed two lodging establishments, however, back on Route 302 on the Bridgton side of Fryeburg. One was a B-and-B and the other a somewhat unappealing block of motel rooms; both still displayed VACANCY signs when we had passed them. But the motel's sign spoke of TV, so we sped back there only to discover that not only were the room fees doubled during the week of the fair, but the accommodations were simply too dismal for words, even at the normal asking price. Notwithstanding the fact that Simon characterized the place as "awesome," we went off again in a flash toward the B-and-B, and to what turned out to be possibly the only other available room in the entire area.

A young Conway native named Coreena Eaton had recently opened the
Edgewood Farm B-and-B in this rambling, twenty-one-room house that
had alternately functioned as both farmstead and inn during its 130-odd
years of existence. Coreena showed us to a room on the second floor,
which, while small, was perfectly adequate, and Simon was thrilled and
surprised to hear that the inn's public room not only contained a large color
TV, but a VCR and Nintendo with a stock of movies and games to boot.
Though we still planned to spend most of the evening at the fair, I suppose
he felt relieved to have these entertainments to fall back on, should our
plans go awry—which in fact they did. My relief was more basic, since I had
begun to dread the possibility of spending a miserable night off the side of
the road somewhere in the car, if instead of Coreena's warm welcome we
had been told there was "no room in the inn." Also, and not insignificantly,
we were charged only the normal "high season" rate for our room, not the
inflated Fryeburg Fair prices most of the town's other lodgings were
getting—because, as Coreena put it, she didn't "feel right about ripping
people off."

The rain was now coming down in buckets. Still, we hoped and expected
the downpour to stop or at least diminish to a tolerable drizzle as the
evening wore on. But by the time we entered the fairgrounds, the weather
showed no sign of cooperating with our expectations. If anything, the rain
increased in its intensity during the hour and a half we slogged up and down
the midway, eating soggy hot dogs, playing various games of chance, and
riding an attraction called the Gravitron, which provided a momentary if
jarring shelter from the relentless precipitation.

By nine, we were headed back to the inn, having failed to see any of the
exhibits (except a shed filled with rabbits) or shows for which these country
fairs are renowned. Fortunately, the TV room at the Edgewood Farm Inn
soon made Simon forget his discomfort, past and to come—what with the
prospect of drenched sneakers to look forward to on the following day. I sat
for a while in the inn's more formal parlor, commiserating with Coreena
about how she and her partner Debbie had passed their first winter in the
house the previous year, wrapped in blankets because they found it impossible to accept monthly bills in excess of three hundred dollars to heat
the place. Since the inn was open year-round, they prayed for winter
guests all the more, since then they could justify warming the entire house
and could share the comfort they needed to provide for their visitors. This
year, these two game young innkeepers will attempt to solve the heating

problem with the addition of two woodburning stoves, the only solution in Maine—I can speak from personal experience—for those who inhabit porous old farmhouses.

Route 5 to bethel and sunday river ■ Route 26 to poland springs by way of west and south paris ■ Route 136 to freeport

Simon and I awoke the next morning to a clear sky, and after eating Debbie's hearty breakfast of ham, eggs, and home fries, we were on our way, Simon having resolved his wet sneaker problem by going barefoot for the remainder of the day. To reach Route 5, which would take us to Bethel, we followed Careena's suggestion to avoid traffic around the fairground (which opened at 7:00 A.M.) and drive the old road that ran in front of the inn, Fryeburg's main street years ago, before the arrival of the railroad resulted in the town's shifting its center six miles westward to its current location. Called the Hemlock Bridge Road, and dirt-surfaced most of the way, the drive provided an unexpected vision of how this historic area looked in the mid-nineteenth century, passing many fine old homesteads along Kezer Pond and crossing a covered bridge—a rare sight in Maine—over what is called the Old Course Saco River. As we approached this narrow, time-forgotten rivulet, I noticed that a little red car parked just off the road there had Nebraska license plates, a sight almost as rare in Maine as the hemlock-shrouded bridge that the car's occupants were admiring. The driver, it turned out, was a young man whose sister, also a Nebraska native, lived up the road. He was showing the bridge to his two preschool-aged daughters, and I asked him what he thought of Maine. "It has a lot of trees," he deadpanned; spoken like a true plainsman.

The Lovells—and other nearby towns, like Harrison and Waterford—deserve more attention that they received during my tour of this area. Sometimes, as any touring motorist will readily understand, the urge to drive on is greater than the urge to stop and explore, no matter how compelling the locale you are passing through. I find that at the beginning of each day on the road, I simply want to enjoy the sights as they pass by my windshield, not because I'm in a hurry to arrive somewhere else, but because the pleasure in the act of driving outweighs for the moment the desire to linger.

When we arrived at Bethel, we initially bypassed the village and drove an additional seven miles to the Sunday River ski resort. Sunday River's reputation as a ski spa has been on the rise in recent years, thanks to the resort's location in a reliable snow belt and to its snow-making capabilities during those dry spells when Nature fails to add fresh powder to the well-packed base. Something on the order of sixty trails are etched over one face of the mountain, and ideally—or so I was informed at the base lodge where staff were busy preparing for the upcoming season—there is the potential for skiing from November till June. Back at the foot of the access road that leads up to the ski area, the Sunday River Inn offers an alternative to the fast-paced party atmosphere preferred by the downhill set, who lodge closer to the summit, mostly in condominiums. When I stopped there in early October, the inn was hosting an Elderhostel group— mostly seniors who wish to combine their touring with some form of ed- ucational structure—in this instance, attendance for a week at a variety of craft and nature workshops. Another covered bridge, preserved but no longer in use, can be seen by traveling a mile or so beyond the inn along the Sunday River Road.

Bethel is the first town of any size on the banks of the Androscoggin River, which springs from the mountains of neighboring New Hampshire, then winds through western and central Maine before joining with the Kennebec in Merrymeeting Bay, just above Bath. Best known today for the Bethel Inn—a popular country club/resort—the town is also steeped in early American history, and the local citizenry over the years has seen to the preservation of its generally preindustrial appearance. Indeed, many of the town's early Victorian buildings, including the old Opera House, have been refitted as inns, so that Bethel's reputation as a four-season touring or conference center seems entirely plausible, though—as the room rates reveal—winter is by far the town's prime time, owing to the proximity of Sunday River and Mount Abram, the other nearby center for downhill skiing. A hermetic neighbor of mine on the mid-coast spent his high-school years in Bethel, some sixty years ago, at Gould Academy. Gould today is an elite preparatory school, but in those days it also offered a full vocational program in woodworking. There my neighbor honed the skills that led him to become a leading practitioner in the restoration of some of Maine's late-eighteenth-century timber-frame structures, using only the hand tools of that era.

From Bethel back to the coast, our trip was relatively uneventful. We left the town on Route 26, and traveled a scenic road, typical of that hilly, well-forested countryside, until we came to West Paris, where the landscape along the route we followed transforms into a succession of old but reconstituted mill towns. Just outside West Paris, we did stop at Perham's, a gem and mineral store that has long been a haunt of rock hounds. Many of the stones displayed in Perham's were mined in Maine, which is rich in the variety of its mineral deposits, and especially valued these days for the quality of its tourmalines. Perham's allows rock hounds free access to its five local feldspar quarries, where they are free to pick over the tailings and collect such rocks and gems as they can discover. Perham's fascinating display of gemstones and crystals did not draw any particular interest from my still-barefoot son, who, I must confess, also does not share my love of long drives on country roads; nor would he be a "normal" preteen, I suspect, if he did. What did impress Simon was something he observed about the twin communities of South Paris–Norway, which elicited his use of the exclamation "Awesome!" for only the second time on a somewhat disappointing excursion: "a town with a McDonald's, a Burger King, *and* a Dunkin' Donuts, all within a quarter-mile of each other." Truly "awesome" indeed!

A brief detour to Poland Springs could only be justified by an odd connection the once grand, but now faded, resort has with my own house in Maine. In 1980, while on a summer pilgrimage to Maine, my wife and I impulsively purchased a homestead and some acreage that had once been part of a saltwater coastal farm. The house had been empty for twenty-five years and, while kept up to some degree, had never been modernized; there was neither electrical service nor indoor plumbing. The last resident, a man named Carl Z. Bailey, had been a bachelor farmer who apparently enjoyed the simple life. In the summertime, however, he plied his homespun trade as butcher and meatcutter at the then genteel resorts of Old Orchard Beach and Poland Springs. Neighbors who had known Carl Bailey—the name, pronounced in the thickest Down East accents, sounds more like "cow belly"—regaled us in subsequent years with many a yarn about the eccentric loner who once occupied our antique farm as if the twentieth century had never dawned.

Then one day, an old man, well over eighty and nearly blind, appeared in our dooryard. He said he had managed a nearby property some sixty years earlier and had known "old Ca'l" well, having hired him with his horse for day labor on many occasions. And did we know that "old Ca'l died a very rich man, but the town had t' bury 'im 'cause no one ever found his money. I believe that money," he added, "is still heah" and he proceeded to explain that, "knowing Ca'l, the money would a been someplace where he could get his hands on it easy," no matter what the season. Well, we had already heard several local versions of this story. It was of a genre that one typically associated, moreover, with people of strange, miserly habits and solitary ways, like those of our predecessor in this homestead. But the mysterious stranger in our dooryard added spice to his tale by claiming, "I'm the only one who knows how he got his money. He'd blackmail folk up t' Poland Springs. Seems he'd tell a fella that his wife was steppin' out, then tell the same t' her about the husband. And Ca'l got 'em both to pay him t' watch t' other." When he heard all this, Simon's eyes grew as big as saucers, and he was ready to tear the place down, convinced that a pot of gold lay concealed somewhere beneath the floorboards or in the foundation of the old stone cellar.

As for Poland Springs today, the original main house, dating from the resort's most fashionable days, burned down a few years back. Yet some five thousand guests still go there every year, stay in the remaining unpretentious accommodations where they take all their meals and play a few rounds of golf, for what may be the cheapest rates for any resort in the entire state.

Our journey over Maine roads returns now to the coast. Those who wish to stop at L.L. Bean in Freeport, and yet avoid the crush of recreational shoppers, should heed the orientation suggested in the following chapter. From Auburn, a pleasant drive to Freeport can be taken along Route 136, which follows close to the banks of the Androscoggin as far as Durham. And those who wish to continue directly on to the mid-coast (see chapter 5) may descend to Brunswick by way of Topsham along Route 196.

INFORMATION ▪ *Windham Chamber of Commerce* (892-8265), P.O. Box 1015, North Windham 04062. Information on cottages, camps, and other facilities located on the eastern shore of Sebago Lake. ▪ *Naples Business Association* (693-6765), P.O. Box 412, Naples 04055. ▪ *Bridgton–Lakes Region Chamber of Commerce* (647-3472), P.O. Box 236B, Bridgton 04009. ▪ *Bethel Area Chamber of Commerce* (824-2282), P.O. Box 121, Bethel 04217. ▪ *Oxford Hills Chamber of Commerce* (743-2281), P.O. Box 161, South Paris 04281. Information on Harrison and Sabbath Day Lake—active Shaker community and museum—is available through this office. ▪ *Lewiston-Auburn Area Chamber of Commerce* (783-2249), 179 Lisbon St., Lewiston 04240.

LAKES REGION

LODGINGS ▪ *Epicurean Inn* (693-3839), Rte. 302, Naples 04055. Open year-round. ▪ *Tarry-A-While Resort and Chalets* (647-2522), Ridge Rd., Box D, Bridgton 04009. Open mid-June to Labor Day. ▪ *Lake House* (583-4182), routes 35 and 37, Waterford 04088. An old roadhouse converted to a modern inn, directly opposite Lake Keoka. ▪ *Edgewood Farm Inn* (935-3970), Rte. 302 and Hemlock Bridge Rd., East Fryeburg 04037. A B-and-B open year-round.

RESTAURANTS ▪ *The Epicurean Inn, Tarry-A-While,* and the *Lake House* (see above) have restaurants that are reputed to serve excellent meals.

BETHEL–SUNDAY RIVER

LODGINGS ▪ *Bethel Inn and Country Club* (824-2175), Town Common, Bethel 04217. An elegant old-country resort; many rooms have fireplaces. Open year-round. ▪ *Chapman Inn* (824-2657), Broad and Church Sts., Bethel 04217. Full-service inn, suitable for grownups traveling with kids. ▪ *Bethel Opera House* (824-2312), "on the Common," Bethel 04217. The building is an attractive late-Victorian theater, converted into hotel rooms and condominium suites. ▪ *Telemark Inn and Llama Farm* (824-2211), RFD 2, P.O. Box 2100, Sunday River Rd., Bethel 04217. Llama treks in the summer and horsedrawn sleigh rides in the winter add to the fun. ▪ *Sunday River Inn* (824-2410), RFD 2, P.O. Box 1688, Bethel

04217. The quiet, family alternative to the downhill scene on the mountaintop; modified American plan and dormitory rooms available.

POLAND SPRINGS

LODGINGS ▪ *Poland Springs Inn* (998-6002), Poland Springs 04274. Near the springs of the famous bottled water, the inn has off-season weekend rates beginning at $25 a night per person, including three meals. The same package in the summer begins at $39 per person.

CAMPING THROUGHOUT THE REGION

▪ *Sebago Lake State Park* (693-6231), just off Rte. 302 between Naples and South Casco. More than 300 campsites on or near the lake; open May 1 through October 15. ▪ *White Mountain National Forest* (824-2134). Details from the Evans Notch Ranger Station, Bridge Street, Bethel 04217. ▪ *Sebago Lake Resort and Campgrounds* (787-3671), RFD 1, P.O. Box 9360, Rte. 114, Sebago Lake 04075. Full-service commercial campground, near the lake. ▪ *Canal Bridge Camping Area* (935-2286), Fryeburg 04037. Closest camping facilities to the fairground.

SOME SPECIAL SHOPS AND ACTIVITIES IN SOUTHWESTERN MAINE

SHOPS ▪ *Perham's* (674-2341), Rte. 26, West Paris. Native gemstones, minerals, and jewelry, open seven days a week. A shop on the order of a mineral museum. ▪ *Bethel Craftworks* (824-3215), Bethel. Many craft items; I was especially intrigued by the heartwood "secret boxes."

SPECIAL ACTIVITIES ▪ *The Fryeburg Fair* (935-3268), every year, first week in October. ▪ *Sunday River* (800-543-2SKI) and Mount Abram (875-2601) ski areas in the vicinity of Bethel. A dormitory offering low-cost accommodations for over 200 skiers opened recently at Sunday River. ▪ *Sabathday Lake Shaker Community and Museum* (926-4596), Route 26, New Gloucester. One of six surviving Shaker communities in the United States; several of the plain clapboard buildings—including the Meeting House and Ministry Shop—are open to the public between Memorial

Day and Labor Day. ■ *Willowbrook at Newfield* (793-2784), off Rte. 11 in
Newfield. A village decimated by fire in 1947, and reconstructed by Donald
King as a thirty-building "living museum" complex. Open May 15 to September 30. ■ *Step Falls,* a steeply descending series of cascades and
pools, is located in Grafton Notch, eight miles above Bethel on Route
26, near Newry. With a total drop of over 150 feet, it is one of the highest
falls in Maine. A twenty-four-acre preserve surrounding the falls is open to
the public.

4

MIDNIGHT RAID ON L.L. BEAN

No one in his right mind who lives near Freeport, Maine—as I do—goes to L.L. Bean during the daytime, especially on a summer weekend. The best time to go to Bean's—and most Maine residents I know are drawn there at least once during the year—is in the late evening. Otherwise you may find yourself embroiled in traffic (no one comes to Maine for that) and grumbling audibly while you hunt for a place to park within reasonable walking distance of the famous store. Bean's, primarily a mail-order company, has this single retail store ("because that's the way L.L. wanted it"), and its success is the main cause of Freeport's perpetual, and un-Maine-like, congestion. Bean's is open twenty-four hours a day, every day of the year. You might say it's the state's only bona fide round-the-clock, four-season destination. Why is L.L. Bean so popular—and, for that matter, so invulnerable to imitation? Somehow the Bean style encapsulates both extremes of Maine's genteel frontier image; it is simultaneously the outfitting Mecca of serious outdoor enthusiasts and the leading haberdasher of rugged preppy fashions for men and women alike.

From what was more or less a quiet country outlet two decades ago,

L.L. Bean has transformed into a veritable department store, expanding again just recently into new quarters—though still in its original location—that doubled the company's retail space in a single stroke. Now the store will be able to display two seasonal lines of clothing side by side. As Bean's has grown, so has Freeport. Once a typically quaint, quiet coastal village, Freeport is now the frenzied outlet capital of Maine. Every new business—even McDonald's and Burger King—is required to occupy an old house or building to help maintain some continuity with the past. But all the big boutique chains and brand-name fashion designers or manufacturers of housewares and accessories are here, having somehow acquired existing space that was adaptable to their varied purposes. I have had guests at my home who viewed Freeport as the ideal setting for an outing on a summer day, one couple scoring heavily in shoes, departing from Maine with nineteen pairs between them. In my own case, only Bean's still brings me to Freeport, and then only at night.

One evening well after dark I was driving up the coast, headed home after a long day's scouting in Portland. But when I got to Freeport, I couldn't resist doing something I'd been anticipating for a long time. Normally when I go to Bean's, it's just for an hour or so to purchase some specific item and for a bit of wide-eyed browsing in the incredible camping department. On this night, however, I decided to hang around for several hours so I could really observe something of the store's nighttime scene. Even though it was almost 9:00 P.M. on a day still deep within the off-season when I pulled into Bean's large parking lot, I ended up with one of the last two available spaces. The store, while not exactly packed, was humming with activity. Shoppers and sales clerks shuffled everywhere among the acres of clothes and sporting gear, and this nighttime crowd would have been the envy of most other stores at the best of times.

For a good while I simply wandered around the store from one department to another, amazed at the volume and variety of the merchandise. Of the boots, parkas, and tents I have long been aware, but I'd never realized before that Bean stocked such a range of nature books and trail guides, or until I stood some minutes before the flickering blue aura of a TV monitor, that professional videotapes have already been produced on a wide range of outdoor subjects. Most of the shoppers seemed to be concentrated in the camping and sporting-goods areas, while the large clothing departments were relatively quiet. No trout swam in the artificial pool at the foot of the stairs in men's wear, the speckled fish apparently having been removed in anticipation of some remodeling that would accompany the move into the new expansion just then nearing completion.

Suddenly a minor drama began to unfold in the vicinity of the "Maine Products" display, foodstuffs for the most part—maple syrup, jams, pickled beans, and porridge mixes—spread over a combination of shelves and counters. A young woman was talking earnestly through a walkie-talkie, giving a quick description of a man she believed to have shoplifted a pair of expensive sunglasses. She spoke with someone at the security desk near the front entrance, and suggested that the man might not yet have had time to leave the store. Then she rushed off in pursuit. When she returned some ten minutes later, I asked if she had caught her thief. But he had apparently slipped her net. "Who shops here at night?" I asked, introducing what must have struck her as an incongruous subject at that moment. Rather than the cold shoulder I might have expected, she gamely provided the following profile of Bean's nighttime denizens: "People come at night for a variety of reasons, some obvious. They want to avoid the crush. Some just can't sleep, more than you'd imagine. Others are just passing through. In the off-season, maybe we get ten customers per floor in the dead of night. But in the tourist season it's active all night long. People route their trips through Freeport because they know Bean's is open."

Another woman—a shopper—who had observed the hubbub around the theft, approached and asked why I was writing in my notebook. Was I a reporter or something? I confided in her the nature of my weighty mission, and we soon fell into conversation. She was there from Florida with her husband, a retired naval officer, and their two young sons, all of whom soon appeared at her side. The family had once lived in Freeport during an extended tour of duty at the nearby Brunswick Naval Air Station, and the woman was herself a long-standing observer of the phenomenon that is L.L. Bean. To her, the company had "gone commercial" after winning the Coty fashion award sometime in the mid-seventies. The prize, she recalled, went to a black raincoat, the single item, as it were, that launched the "camp look"—and with it L.L. Bean—into the national fashion market.

Inevitably, when I am in Bean's, my attention is drawn to those many novel and fascinating accessories that add a touch of efficiency or comfort to camping, backpacking, or hiking. Whether it's a lightweight, single-burner butane stove, a tiny, candle-powered lantern, a fold-up saw, a many-bladed Swiss Army knife, or one of a host of other fascinating outdoor accoutrements, no one outshines Bean's in the range and durability of its selection, or in the availability of competent staff to advise your outfitting needs without suggesting the slightest pressure to buy. I had long been searching for a suitable battery-operated tent light, one that would cast enough illumination to write by. With the help of a very pleasant fellow who patiently unwrapped and demonstrated one product after another, I found the very lamp I wanted. Then, while I experimented with a small, portable lounge chair that also interested me, the clerk turned his attention to a young man who asked to see a knife from the display case. I overheard the customer say in a genuine tone of amazement, "I couldn't imagine buying a $300 knife and then taking it into the woods."

The "factory store" is Bean's in-house bargain basement, where the company retails its discontinued items, customer returns, and "irregulars," that is, second-quality merchandise. Also, with each change of season, leftover stock—often in small sizes and heavily discounted—finds its way onto the shelves and racks of the "factory store," shoes and boots representing the items most in demand. I learned all this from a friendly salesperson who teaches "special ed" by day and spends her moonlight shift here, and who comes from a long line of Maine coast fishing families. As she and I chatted, a couple who had driven down from Prince Edward Island, where they raise livestock and grow corn and barley for fodder, joined the conversation. How long a trip was it, I asked. "Well," the man replied, "it was five hours to the border, two hours to Bangor, and two more hours to Freeport." A nine-hour car trip—just to spend a few hours shopping at L.L. Bean. They were lodged in a hotel that the woman said "smelled new," and she also observed that there had been more growth in town since their last visit. "Where will it end?" she mused without any apparent anxiety about the ultimate fate of Freeport, Maine. We all talked for what was easily forty-five minutes; no one who comes to Bean's at night seems to be in much of a hurry to get their shopping done.

By 11:30 P.M., things had quieted down considerably. But the prediction of a snowstorm for the next day—the biggest of the year, and this already mid-April—may have had something to do with curtailing the Friday-night crowd. The midnight shift was about to come on, a scaled-down team of salespersons—one per floor, I was told. But the size of the work crew actually increases overnight, what with cleaning up and restocking. Taking over in the camping department at midnight was a tall, strapping young fellow named Sam, who had just come back from two days of mountain climbing and "winter" camping in the hills of western Maine. Sam's been working on the graveyard shift for two and a half years, and loves it. "It's quiet—Sunday night is the quietest time, it's really dead then around 4:00 A.M.—but you can really talk with the customers who do come."

The most serious expeditions often get outfitted in the middle of the night, he said. In season, you get the hunters and fishermen around 4:00 or 5:00 A.M., coming in for gear. Then there are students going off to Europe, outdoorsmen en route to the wilderness in Alaska or Canada, even rock stars who show up after their gigs in Portland. But an occasional weirdo or two can really make your night, Sam said. There was one man who ran up the stairs screaming, "I'm the King of England." And the trout pool, it seems, serves as a magnet for eccentricity. One man, Sam recalled, stood there throwing twenty-dollar bills into the water, while on a different occasion, another fellow threw himself in. L.L. Bean by night: the human carnival on parade, and great conversation.

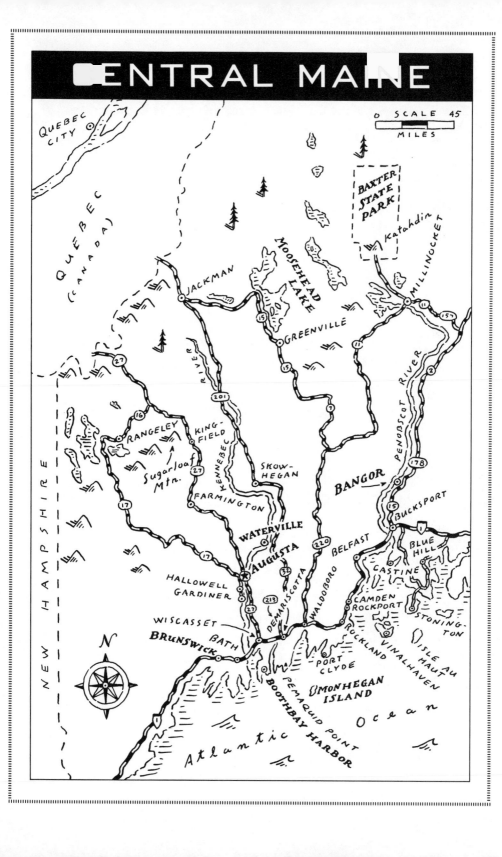

5

THE MID-COAST AT
LILAC TIME

After Freeport, we will no longer be able to avoid Route 1 quite so easily as we continue our tour up the coast. The configuration of Maine's shoreline changes radically above Brunswick. Strung between mid-coastal headwater towns at intervals of roughly ten miles are the long clusters of peninsulas whose estuarial rivers extend as much as fifteen miles seaward before reaching the Atlantic. Each of these peninsulas has its separate character and attractions, and visitors touring the mid-coast would miss much of the region's charm were they to confine their travel exlusively to a drive along Route 1.

While the tourist season along the mid-coast brings nowhere near as dramatic a change to the region as occurs along the state's southern sections, residents know that when the lilacs burst into fragrant bloom, the sightings of cars bearing out-of-state license plates suddenly increase with the same cyclical regularity we observe in the comings and goings of Nature's other migratory flocks. Lilac time along the mid-coast more or less coincides with Memorial Day, quite a bit later than the yearly appearance of that flower memorialized by Whitman in the line, "When lilacs last in the dooryard bloomed . . . ," an event he juxtaposed with the anniversary of Lincoln's assassination on the fourteenth of April. Spring comes late to Maine, but it comes in a sudden rush. Two weeks into May, the foliage is still quite sparse; by month's end, however, around Memorial Day, the lush green of summer is fully established, the ancient lilac stands lending their lavender blush to many an old dooryard, always on time to greet the first wave of seasonal visitors.

Despite the presence of intermittent rains, June is an ideal time to visit the mid-coast. B-and-Bs and other seasonal enterprises have opened their doors, touring traffic is light, and local seacoast communities have yet to swell to their inflated summer populations. The population of my own town, for example, increases from a year-round census of 800 to three times that number during July and August. Even then, there's plenty of space to accommodate all without any sense of overcrowding, a condition that is typical of most mid-coast communities in summer.

Each section within this description of the mid-coast—spread over three separate chapters—except for Boothbay Harbor, combines a headwater town with a tour of its respective peninsula appendages, and can be treated as an independent destination or as a series of leisurely digressions for those who wish to sample something at each geographic entity.

BRUNSWICK VIA ROUTE 1 ▪ HARPSWELL VIA ROUTE 123 ▪ ORRS ISLAND, BAILEY ISLAND VIA ROUTE 24

Fifteen minutes from Freeport along either Route 1 or Route 95 is Brunswick, home of Bowdoin College, one of the only institutions Maine has produced that transcends the state's essential identity as a paradigm of regionalism. But for Bowdoin, which adds a genteel dimension, Brunswick would have remained exclusively a blue-collar mill town at the mouth of the Androscoggin River, and—by virtue of a large naval installation there—a military town as well. Evidence of the town's mixed roots—Yankee and Franco-American farmers and mechanics—parallels Bowdoin's illustrious past, the latter offering the wayfarer one or two concrete cultural attractions, while the town itself is well stocked with its share of interesting shops. To put Bowdoin into perspective on the nation's literary and political canvas, one need only refer to the college's graduating class of 1825, which spawned a controversial president (Franklin Pierce), a major poet (Henry Wadsworth Longfellow), and a great novelist (Nathaniel Hawthorne). While her husband taught English there, Harriet Beecher Stowe sat in their Brunswick home and drafted *Uncle Tom's Cabin*—a book whose polemical impact on the American Civil War was equivalent to that of Tom Paine's *Common Sense* on the American Revolution. Today, two Bowdoin alumni, George Mitchell and William Cohen, serve Maine in the U.S. Senate.

But it is two other famous alumni whose adventurous lives will claim the attention of the visitor who schedules a stop at the two museums found on campus at the far end of Maine Street, Brunswick's principal avenue and the widest in the state. The Peary-MacMillan Arctic Museum exhibits displays of many of the expeditions of these two Bowdoin-trained explorers, including Peary's historic 1908 expedition that allegedly reached the North Pole, featuring photographs and original documents and equipment. Equally if not more impressive is the MacMillan collection of artifacts illuminating the culture of the Inuit natives who inhabit Labrador and Greenland. This collection is surely unique and extremely interesting as a visual introduction to the obscure customs of the Eskimos.

Bowdoin's other vest-pocket museum is housed in the Walker Art Building, a little gem of a temple devoted to the college art collection. Several small galleries contain as diverse and eclectic a selection of art as you are likely to find anywhere, from Roman antiquities to Renaissance oils to American portraiture. In this last category are four excellent works by Gilbert Stuart, including interesting studies of Jefferson and Madison. Among other American paintings and sculptures, there is some notable work by Mary Cassatt, William Zorach, and Marsden Hartley, and an enigmatic bronze bas-relief of Robert Louis Stevenson in profile by Augustus Saint-Gaudens, etched with a verse by the invalid poet entitled "Youth Now Flees on Feathered Foot," which closes with the melancholy lines, "Life is over, life was gay, we have come the primrose way." Less lyrical, but firm in their celebration of life's quotidian pleasures, are some thirty prints, oils, and drawings from the sober palette of Winslow Homer, by far the museum's most exciting treasures. The museum is free to the public, as is the Walker-MacMillan.

Just off campus, opposite the Dunkin' Donuts shop, is a museum of a different stripe, perhaps one of the more unique concepts among the period houses anywhere I know of maintained by local historical societies. The Skolfield-Whittier House, which is in fact attached to the museum of the Pejepscot Historical Society on Park Row (the service road for upper Maine Street), houses the furnishings and memorabilia of three generations of a single family who resided here from 1858 to 1925. The residence, which has a widow's walk and a pleasing warren of irregularly distributed rooms, remained in the family as a summer house until 1982, but it was never modernized. Through no conceit or restoration efforts on the part of the museum's curators, the Skolfield-Whittier House credibly reflects the presence of all three generations, largely because the inhabitants seem never to have thrown any furniture away. Even the smell of the place still conveys a lingering, lived-in feeling. The $5 entrance fee ($2.50 for children) is steep, but includes an informative, hour-long guided tour in what is a truly fascinating artifact of small-town domesticity.

Brunswick is a town I visit on occasion to shop in a few specialty stores— mostly around Christmas—or to see the kind of movie that might come to a college community, but not to one's local theater. The shop called Ask Your Mother, for example, has an imaginative range of traditional and novelty toys, and the Old Bookstore has seldom failed me in my search for some recycled classic I get a yen to place within arm's reach on my own bookshelves. Bookstores are a good bet in Brunswick generally. Macbeans has the widest general selection, and the Maine Writers and Publishers Alliance stocks more titles by Maine authors, past and present, than any other outlet in the state. In the same building that houses the Alliance offices and retail space was the Dog Ear Press (since moved to Hallowell), where I found Mark Melnicove, poet, publisher, and—in a state where cornball humor still reigns—a prince of wit and sarcasm, hunched over a computer terminal. Mark and some cronies once put out two issues of a satirical tabloid called "The Maniac Express" that leavened the somewhat Rotarian earnestness of daily repartee around the mid-coast for a week or so. With that spritz of fresh air in mind, I unabashedly sought Mark out in the hope of extracting a sassy quote.

"Why," I asked in mock reportorial seriousness, "should people come to Brunswick?" And Mark looked at me as if I were trying to sell him a used Subaru. "If you like to go plane watching," he deadpanned in reply, "you should come to Brunswick. Watch the Orions do their touch-and-goes on the airfield at the Naval Station. What they do is fly in, land, and then take off again instantly." The best place to watch, he says, is from Fat Boys, an all-fried-food, traditional drive-in complete with carhops on the Bath Road, just opposite the landing strip. Another worthwhile diversion while in Brunswick, he said, would be to visit all the places Longfellow is reported to have slept. One of Mark's office mates, a native of faraway Millinocket, mentioned that there's a real French influence in Brunswick, and in several shops like Tibeault's (whose proprietor does his own butchering) you will still hear French spoken. She also suggested a popular offbeat restaurant, Grand City, located in a department store of the same name that was formerly a W.T. Grants and retains much of the same atmosphere. But I've got another recommendation for a one-day itinerary in the Brunswick area that includes breakfast, lunch, and dinner down by the seashore.

As you turn from Maine Street onto the Bath Road, which runs along the town side of Bowdoin's campus, look for the signs indicating Harpswell Township, a long peninsula with forty-five islands—among which the three largest are interconnected by bridges—and some twenty-five miles of scenic seascape among traditional fishing and summer communities. Turn right onto Route 123 (marked Sills Drive here) where you see the giant pines, and head south past a mile or so of surburban spread until the vegetation thickens and you are well on your way into North Harpswell. Just beyond the intersection of the Mountain Road, which crosses Harpswell Sound over to Route 24 and on to East Harpswell and Orrs and Bailey islands, look for a restaurant on your right called Richard's, now occupying what was originally a one-room schoolhouse. Working in reverse, this is my recommendation for your dinner in the Brunswick area. Owner Richard Gnauck—formerly of Mannheim, West Germany—offers, in addition to daily gourmet selections, a menu of traditional German dishes that adds an element of variety to a coastal cuisine otherwise dominated by fresh seafood (I'm not complaining). These specialties, whether a platter of wursts or a portion of sauerbraten, are accompanied by all those tasty, slightly vinegary side dishes—red cabbage, dumplings, noodles, kraut, hot and cold potato salad—that give the Rhineland cuisine its distinct flavor. On Richard's beer list are a number of hearty German brews worth sampling, like the Pinkus Weizen "wheat beer" at $3.75 a pop.

Of the two inns that struck me as ideal spots for an overnight on the Brunswick coast, one is not far from Richard's. To find it, continue down

Route 123 to Harpswell Center (where you might look for a copy of *Fishy Business*, a spicy tabloid and advertiser filled with local gossip). Turn right at the sign to Lookout Point, past a small constellation of old buildings, including the Old Meeting House (1757) and the Elijah Kellog Church (1843), and a common that together define Harpswell Center. The inn, Lookout Point House, stands cheek-by-jowl with an old harbor and is the former cookhouse of a once productive Harpswell yard whose ships were familiar in ports throughout the world during the 1800s. The stately and comfortable inn, with fourteen rooms priced between $65 and $90 a night double, and open year-round, is a popular stopover for the boating crowd; as its brochure says, "It's only 1,500 miles to Florida."

Drive the remainder of the Harpswell peninsula for its scenic appeal, but come out early enough for a great breakfast on Basin's Point, at the tip of Potts Harbor. To get there, turn right off Route 123 near the Harpswell School, and take a second right at the sign announcing the Dolphin Marina, where you'll find a lunch-counter-style restaurant (open year-round) that serves an unusual à la carte breakfast, with each egg, flapjack, or strip of bacon priced separately. The food is good, and there's a view of the ocean beyond a protected anchorage where lobster-boat races take place every July. The opposite point on this peninsula is South Harpswell, where a number of artist's studios and handicraft shops can be found. On the drive back to Route 24 via the Mountain Road crossover, pick a side road or two at random, to explore one of the several quiet coves along the sound.

The drive down Route 24 to Bailey Island winds dramatically among low, bushy vegetation, quaint cottages, and seascapes brought into sudden focus by bridged inlets or indented coves, and which seem all the more wild amid the general air of domestication on a seacoast shared by native fishing families and summer folk. An unusual cribstone bridge, engineered to allow the flow of tidal waters, crosses over to Bailey Island. Just beyond the bridge on the left is a fancy, seasonal restaurant called the Rock Oven, featuring a selection of enticing platters of *fruits de mer* along with a list of crafted appetizers and side dishes. Many windows in the multiroom space frame Water Cove, over which the restaurant is perched, and at some distance can be seen a mass of land called Ragged Island, where Edna St. Vincent Millay, a Maine native, spent summers contemplating the aesthetic and psychological distance between herself and her neighbors: "Safe upon the solid rock the ugly houses stand: Come and see my shining palace built upon the sand!"

Cook's Lobster House, near Garrison Cove, serves more traditional Maine seafood specialties. A ferryboat leaves from the Cove daily during the summer, and tours the islands of Casco Bay in the vicinity of Portland. Mackerel Cove, farther down the island, also has a seasonal seafood restaurant, and a year-round coffee shop catering to local fishermen. Giant tuna boats come into this harbor regularly, and charter boats for recreational deep-sea fishing may be hired at short notice. Near land's end, a sign for the Driftwood Inn, the second of the two inns referred to earlier, leads you down a narrow lane with the unlikely name of Washington Avenue, lined with old-fashioned beach bungalows sheathed in weather-darkened shingles. The road dead-ends before a complex of large cottages of a similar look and vintage. Here are the premises of the Driftwood Inn, which stares from a rocky ledge right into the face of the ocean. The Driftwood is a rustic place, with echoes of the hunting lodge, all paneled and comfortably rugged, but with both open and screened-in porches to catch the evening sea breeze. During July and August, when the dining room opens, a weekly rate of $240 per person, American plan, is a bargain for those with a taste for simple accommodations and a dazzling natural setting. Connecting the Driftwood grounds to the Giant Steps, a rock formation true to its name, is a magical path over the rocks above the surf, where in a few concentrated moments I saw a veritable parade of wildlife, including a green snake that crossed inches from my feet and several yellow-breasted, cardinal-like birds flitting among the twisted branches of the wind-tapered bushes. Nonguests who merely wish to see the steps and walk the path may park in front of the tiny, one-story Episcopal Church on Washington Avenue, through whose windows can be seen five rows of straw-covered, ladderback seats facing a rustic altar.

Orrs Island, as you will already have observed on the way down, has considerable charm of its own, and, judging from the many pockets of fifties-style cottage motels, is a watering hole of some longevity for touring motorists. Not far beyond the cribstone bridge (returning up Route 24 toward Harpswell at a point just beyond where the houses are most concentrated) look for a roadside sign offering Homemade Candy, the much-praised, kitchen-spun confectionery of a local grandmotherly lady. An outdoor option for lodgings is the Orrs Island Campground, which offers some special tent sites strung along a half-mile of shoreline. Before departing the Harpwells, a final detour is in order down to Cundy's Harbor, off Route 24, to Holbrooks Snack Bar, for some short-order seafood dishes on the pier, the suggested lunch spot I referred to earlier. Route 24 approaches Route 1, where the local shopping mall can be found at a place called Cook Corner. Follow the Bath Road north here, just before the entrance to Route 1, and at the Gulf station turn onto the bumpy, hard-top Thomas Point Road. Follow the signs to the beach of the same name, a well-tended, privately owned strand and greenspace at the end of a small bay. Beyond the beach, the road heads to Woodward Point, but ends abruptly at a panoramic turnaround before fields, woods, and distant water, signposted politely by the farm's inhabitants, "This is the end of the town road. Please turn here." Turn and continue on the road to Bath.

BATH VIA ROUTE 1 OR THE BATH ROAD ▪ POPHAM BEACH VIA ROUTE 209 ▪ REID STATE PARK VIA ROUTE 127

The first year I came to summer in Maine with my wife and our two small children, we arrived in a truck with a massive camper strapped to the pickup bed; our old farmhouse had no plumbing or electricity, so the camper was to be our shelter for a few weeks until we could get in some power to jury-rig a cold-water tap in the kitchen and raise a new outhouse where the old one had gone horizontal. I can still remember vividly how as we neared Bath on that first trip, at the crest of the hill on the outskirts, a giant crane suddenly rose out of the tree-tops before us. For the years of our summer residence thereafter, the familiar appearance on the horizon of that crane—the landmark of the Bath Iron Works shipyard that dominates the town's skyline—happily signaled the beginning of the home stretch after our long drive from Brooklyn.

Despite being a terrible bottleneck during shift changes at BIW (midnight, 8:00 A.M., and 4:00 P.M. being the times to avoid), Bath is a town I love to pass through for its visual appeal. From the road, Bath is viewed somewhat from above. A modified skyway arches between the red-brick shops and commercial buildings of a once-elegant internationally recognized port and the modern shipyard complex—Maine's largest single industrial entity—before crossing the historic Kennebec over a great steel drawbridge en route to points Down East. The time I have spent in and around

Bath over the years has been necessarily fragmented according to the program or task of the moment. Recently I roamed the region for an entire day, retracing many old steps, mapping out the following itinerary for the touring motorist, to include several unique lodgings or campgrounds for those who wish to prolong their visit in the area.

The town of Bath itself should be your first stop, parking somewhere close to Front Street, the main commercial drag. You can drop by the Chamber of Commerce storefront, next to the old Custom House, for an orientation and a full stock of brochures on local inns and attractions. Front Street blends a variety of retailers, by no means all chichi; indeed, the general layout and appearance of the old buildings for once outshines the merchandise, a rare occurrence in such an attractive, preindustrial setting. Not that there's anything wrong with the shops. In fact, Povitch's—a traditional urban workingman's store—is my personal standby for casual clothes and accessories, as much for sentimental reasons as for taste. Three other shops not to miss—all on Centre Street in the general downtown zone—are Wood Butcher Tools, attached to the Shelter Institute where the craft of old home renovation is taught, Telltales Children's Bookshop, and the Grainery, a natural foods store.

Somewhat farther up the hill on Centre Street, near the little square with the obelisk where High Street comes in, is Kristina's, a restaurant, bakery, and community meeting spot in Bath for the last half-generation. Originally a dessert and pastry shop—the kind of place you dropped into for a late snack after a night out—Kristina's now offers five separate menus, including Saturday and Sunday brunch and breakfast, lunch, and dinner. Behind Kristina's is an art gallery belonging to Ray Shadis, a bit of a folk hero in these parts. Shadis was an activist and spokesperson for the 1980 campaign to shut down Maine's only atomic power plant, which happens to cast its dark shadow quite near Shadis's old farm in nearby Edgecomb. After helping to fight the good fight for many years—repeated referendums barely losing to a majority of citizens who feared rate increases if Maine Yankee were dismantled—Shadis retired from politics when he failed to win a seat in the state senate. I talked with the talented sculptor for a bit the morning that I dropped into Kristina's to munch a tasty cheese pastry, and soon discovered that Shadis and I shared other interests beyond a mutual distrust of nuclear power. He's a fellow backroads enthusiast, having once ridden his motorcycle from the state's remote northern reaches all the way to Waterville, exclusively over an all-but-forgotten network of dirt roads. In a very brief chat, he turned me on to a dozen odd or interesting sites to look for around the state, and these will appear in their appropriate places throughout this book.

A walking or driving tour through Bath's historic residential district is a must. The concentration of antique houses on and around Washington Street may not be the most elegant you will see along this coast, where many a prosperous ship's captain settled in splendor after a life of successful trade and seafaring; but they are on the whole among the most pristine and unaltered of such seaport architectural treasures. Bath is similarly well endowed with B-and-Bs, a number of which are located in the homes of this district, notably the Victorian mansion at 1024 Washington, and the three establishments of diverse styles and price ranges—the Packard House, Glad II, and the Levitt Family—that grace the charming back street named Pearl.

Pearl is linked to High Street, which in turn leads to North Bath, where glimpses of Merrymeeting Bay may be seen. Merrymeeting Bay was once the stomping grounds of colonial adventurers like Thomas Morton, a rabble-rouser whom the Pilgrim Puritans at first imprisoned and shipped back to England. Morton returned, however, and played an important role in developing trade with the Indians along the Kennebec during the mid-1600s. Englishmen of Morton's jolly and decidedly non-Puritan temperament named Merrymeeting in the spirit of the Robin Hood tales, and reproduced the whole outlaw band on native soil by naming their favorite Indians after the characters of Sherwood Forest. To get to Merrymeeting, turn right onto High Street, heading north until Whiskeag Road, where you turn left and proceed through a very lovely countryside of gentleman farms. During a recent June visit, the fields off these North Bath roads were brightened by a dense crop of buttercups the likes of which we have not seen for some time in these parts. (A map indicating this route can be obtained at the Bath Chamber of Commerce office.) When you pass a succession of trailer homes, look for the sign pointing to West Chops Point, where a looping road offers a few segmented vistas of the vast inland "bay" formed by the waters of five rivers—a perennial refuge, moreover, for migrating birds (and birders) along the Atlantic Flyway.

Return to Bath over the same route, staying on High Street past the town and crossing beneath the Route 1 skyway for a drive down the Phippsburg peninsula to the mouth of the Kennebec River at Popham, where one of the earliest English settlements in the New World was attempted. Along the way is the usual assortment of off-road digressions that animate these drives on the Maine coast. Minutes beyond Bath, High Street becomes Route 209, a wide, fast road designed to speed visitors to Popham Beach, the most popular attraction on the peninsula. Not far out of Bath, 209 jogs acutely to the left, following a bridge over an ample creek. The alternate route continues straight along Meadowbrook Road, leading past a large campground, but recommended primarily as a way to slow the drive and avoid the more intense beach traffic along 209 that accompanies weekends and good weather. During a brief stop at Meadowbrook Camping, I overheard one of the more amusing snatches of conversation thus far in my Maine travels. Responding to a question from a woman behind the reception counter, a pleasant-faced man in mid-exit through the door I was entering said, "I'm going off to mow where no man has ever mowed before. Why, you've never seen such boulders as where I'm going to mow." I still smile when I recall that bit of homespun humor. After leaving the campground, I tried to remain on the secondary roads indicated by the map all the way to the village of Sebasco, but became hopelessly confused and kept driving down dirt roads that were posted with No Trespassing signs, forcing me to return to Route 209 and strike for Sebasco via a short branching road marked Route 217.

Midway on 217 is the well-known Sebasco Lodge—a classic Maine coast resort of a certain scale, where vacationers come for a minimum of a week, many to play golf on the well-kept nine-hole course. Route 217 itself, which I followed to its end, narrows away to nothing in two or so miles beyond the resort, ending at a small cove where a little island is stacked with lobster traps that surround a small shingled cottage; at least one lucky fisherman has held on to his piece of earthly Eden against the covetous winds of development that blow so strongly in these waters. Another curiosity about this stretch of macadam is that the houses—most of which are fairly old—don't really appear until quite near the cove, a particularly unambiguous reminder that settlement on the Maine coast began at water's edge and only gradually moved inland as roads were built and extended.

Returning along Route 217, I hesitated at entering the drive to Sebasco Lodge. Maine's grand resorts, still relatively numerous and quite popular, run a bit contrary to this book's focus on more intimate and remote lodgings, away from the madding crowd. Sometimes, however, reportorial curiosity disables an operative but as yet unrigid bias, as in this case, prompting me at least to explore the grounds and catch a glimpse of the lodge's shorefront view over Casco Bay. Near the water, I slowed my car to a crawl behind a group of men in shirtsleeves, each of whom carried a briefcase and a large pad of graph paper—engineers, perhaps, on a working group vacation, though their way of clogging the road made me think of sheep on a country lane. Beyond this point, I noticed that the road did not end at the wharf belonging to the lodge, but continued down a peninsula lined with summer cottages, at the end of which I was thrilled to discover just the kind of inn I *am* interested in passing along to my readers.

The Rock Gardens Inn is one of those few places that actually are as pretty as they appear in the slick color photos of their promotional brochures. The ensemble of cottages, with one or two larger houses, creates, without affect, the feeling of a cozy seaside colony. Just as I arrived, a half-dozen painters were setting up their easels, about to make subjects of the gardens and the sea, so beautifully blended into the inn's general atmosphere. These painters were participants in one of the five-day art workshops that the inn sponsors during what amounts to its off-season before the Fourth of July and just after Labor Day. From July 12 to August 19, the Rock Garden books guests for a minimum stay of one week at a daily rate averaging roughly $70 per person, including breakfast and dinner. Ironically, my own visit coincided with that of a man doing research for the Mobil Travel Guides, prompting the obviously spirited innkeeper, Ona, to inquire in mock exasperation, "Why don't you guys call ahead?" Ona explained that several of her family members are painters—thus the inn's art's connection—then she led us on a brief tour of the cottages. I was curious to observe how my colleague's modus operandi differed in relation to my own; while I focused on the inn's scenic qualities and its general air of competent sophistication, he inspected the sheets.

The other marvelous overnight setting in the vicinity—a campground in this case—can be found on Hermit Island, reached via Route 216 just a bit farther down the peninsula from Sebasco. The 255-acre island, two-thirds of which is wooded, is studded with sites for tent camping only. It also has seven beaches and the usual washing and toilet facilities, although there is no electricity. Almost as ideal as Hermit Island are the oceanfront campgrounds strung along Popham Beach on the final stretch of Route 209. The beach itself is a state park, complete with lifeguards, open daily from 9:00

A.M. till sunset (admission $1 per person). All told, there are seven miles of beach at Popham, overlooking many small, rocky islands close to shore in a chilly sea of moderate surf. The road ends at Fort Popham, a stone ruin dating from the Civil War, which once guarded the west bank of the Kennebec River. Spinney's, a seafood restaurant here on the point, is a popular seasonal eatery with some guest-house facilities. The original Popham colonists settled on the opposite end of the cove from the fort in 1607, leaving for Virginia the following year after a disastrous winter. A narrow road leads to a small parking lot near the old colonial site, and from there a path winds up the hill to Fort Baldwin, which comprises three abandoned gun emplacements and bunkers that were manned during the First and Second World Wars. The highest of these offers an excellent view over the river mouth.

Return to Bath on the scenic Parker Head Road; then, after having rejoined High Street on the southern outskirts of the town, turn toward the river and continue along the lower end of Washington Street. Maine's Maritime Museum is located along this strip (just south of BIW and Route 1), and is definitely worth a stop; indeed, you will require at least two to three hours, or more, to do the museum justice. This is the single most important institution in the state that preserves the story and the artifacts of Maine's rich seafaring heritage. Formerly located in the old Sewel House, near the center of town, the museum recently opened new quarters near the restored nineteenth-century Percy and Small Shipyard, finally joining the museum's two principal exhibits on a single ten-acre park at the river's edge. Just up from the museum, look for the Cabin restaurant, which serves the best pizza I have eaten in Maine, a state not known for this specialty that seems to diminish in quality beyond a ten-mile radius from the streets of New York.

It is now time to cross the Kennebec over the long Carlton Bridge, and explore the Georgetown peninsula along Route 127, an area far more sparsely settled than Phippsburg across the river. The ride along this route is actually best from June on throughout the summer. My impression of this drive during the leafless season was not favorable, but a revisit in the late spring led to a totally opposite visual experience. Also, I had never driven to Five Islands before, where Route 127 terminates at a working fishing wharf, with the requisite lobster-and-clam shanty to service the summer trade. The sweet little harbor seen from this wharf is filled with pleasure boats at anchor and ringed by five small, spruce-covered islands. I happened to observe the contents of a large fish tray while walking on this dock, and saw two giant fish heads staring back. One, I was told, had belonged to a mako shark weighing some 150 pounds; the other—not much larger—was severed from a tuna of more than twice that weight. Incidentally, for those who may be tempted to stay over, there is a B-and-B in Five Islands called the Coveside.

The access road to Reid State Park turns off just before Five Islands, and leads past the Audubon Society–run Josephine Newman Sanctuary to a mile-and-a-half stretch of ocean beach with a bit more surf than at Popham. This beach is generally less crowded than Popham, but parking here can be at a premium on weekends during the summer dog days. Before returning to Route 1, I suggest a brief detour to view the mouth of the Kennebec River from this side, which can be done by driving down to Bay Point, a fishing hamlet of the simplest dwellings where a native population obviously clings to some simpler vision of the maritime past. The fort and the little community at Popham stand out very clearly on the opposite bank, but none of the summer houses one sees from that side are at all visible as you stand within this little settlement at Bay Point. In fact, this entire access road has a great flavor of a forgotten time, lined as it is with old saltwater farmsteads, a tiny stone schoolhouse tucked to one side, and the fields ablaze with wildflowers—lupine, Indian paintbrush, daisies, and buttercups mixing their colors as if the whole world were nothing but a giant Impressionist landscape.

A culinary stop one might wish to consider on the return to Route 1 is the Osprey, a restaurant of some repute at the marina in Robinhood, a coveside community just above Georgetown. While I haven't eaten there myself, I understand that the menu has a classic French accent that fills one with great expectations. The turnoff to the marina, which I approached from the south, coming up from Five Islands, is a little confusing. A sign appears with an arrow pointing to what one assumes is the next right turn, which in fact is someone's long asphalt driveway. I am sure I was not the first one to surprise the lady of the house as she perused the contents of her mailbox at midday. "I've reported that sign a hundred times," she said with an air of resignation. "People come up here all the time, and they'll never do anything about it." When I suggested, tongue in cheek, that she and her husband might stage a midnight raid on the sign, we both shared a chuckle, but she said, "Oh, we're too old for that." The actual road to the Osprey is the second right (not counting a dirt road), just before the green garage building with the many ranks of antlers over the door bays.

Our tour of the mid-coast continues in Chapter 7; what follows here is another inland digression, to the Rangeley Lakes and the Blue Mountains.
The directory for the mid-coast can be found at the end of Chapter 9.

6

THE RANGELEY LAKES AND THE WESTERN MOUNTAINS

I have fashioned here a digression from mid-coastal Maine that both orig-
inates and terminates in Wiscasset. Along the way, we take in several
towns of the lower Kennebec and Androscoggin valleys before encircling the core of western lakes and mountain district over a network of
scenic roads, and returning to Route 1 to continue our travels up the coast.
Wiscasset is the next village "down" the coast from Bath following Route
1 north.

Lake-saturated, mountainous western Maine has evolved in recent years
into a "four-season resort area," or so says the advertising hype generated
by local chambers of commerce and the tourism mavens in Augusta. Actually, the term "four seasons" *is* a slight exaggeration, considering the
dismal weather that generally plagues the state in the springtime. But this
region, where the scenery is so magnificent it borders on the mystical,
comes closer to providing a year-round, multipurpose tourist spa in Maine

than any other recreational area in the state, with the possible exception of the Bethel region, slightly to the south. The prime times for visits to Maine's Rangeley lakes and environs are winter and summer, with a fair amount of movement occurring during the fall shoulder as well. Depending on conditions for spring skiing, April, May, and June are usually the cruelest months, though fishermen for whom the weather is no obstacle may take umbrage at this assessment. Downhill and cross-country skiing and snow-mobiling are the principal winter attractions; hiking, camping, fishing, ca-noeing, and vacationing in general draw the summer crowds; and "leaf peepers" and Sunday drivers keep the restaurants and inns afloat during the transition between the hot and cold seasons.

Maine's western lake and mountain district would itself be a fitting sub-ject for a full-blown guidebook. In addition to a half-dozen incomparable, interlocking bodies of water (Rangeley, Mooselookmaguntic, Kennebago, Upper and Lower Richardson, and Aziscohos lakes), there is the vast mountainscape, summed up as follows by reporter Bob Cummings, writing for the *Portland Press Herald:* "Saddleback is the southern terminus of the largest block of 4,000-foot mountains in the state. Bigelow lies thirty-six trail miles to the north across the Carrabassett River Valley from the multiple high peaks of Crocker Mountain, Sugarloaf Mountain, and Abra-ham Mountain, which together form the Saddleback-Bigelow mountain mas-sif. It is a land of cascading streams, spectacular waterfalls, and wild ponds." In a word, it's a knockout!

GARDINER AND HALLOWELL VIA ROUTE 27
FROM WISCASSET

Route 27 just outside the village of Wiscasset, on the Bath side, is usually a busy road, a commuter route from towns along the mid-coast to the state capital in Augusta. During off-peak hours, however, Route 27 is an easy enough road to travel. And just beyond Dresden Mills—about a fifteen- to twenty-minute drive from Wiscasset—you will come to a store, Troop's Variety on Telegraph Hill, that is the best-kept secret in the town of Pittston. Troop's Variety is currently owned by a former Londoner named Barb and her husband, Pete

Kaiser, who worked his way through jet mechanic's school in Germany as a butcher and, when he could find no job in his chosen field, became a *kanditor*. What is a *kanditor*? "Pastry chef," I suppose, would be a reasonable translation, a trade given as much respect during the course of German history as any other ennobling craft or art. *Kanditors* traditionally were viewed as sculptors in flour and sugar, and Pete Kaiser can indeed craft those one-of-a-kind skyscraper cakes you sometimes see at weddings and similar high ceremonial shindigs.

The sojourner up Route 27, however, should think of Pete Kaiser as a baker, and you'd better schedule your stop at Troop's Variety for a Friday morning. A fairly serious allergy prevents Pete from baking more than one night a week, and even at that, he must don a high-tech helmet equipped with a respirator to get the job done. But the result: incredible aromas when you enter the store, rising from soccer-ball-sized ryes and pumpernickels, torpedoes of Italian and French bread, buttery loaves of challah, and croissants, raspberry and apple turnovers, cinnamon twirls, and fudge brownies, all of which make Troop's Variety a rare treat in this part of Maine—but only on Friday mornings. By noon the stock of baked goods is usually depleted, the locals knowing a good thing too when they find it. At other times you might be tempted by another item Barb and Pete keep in stock: a full line of Schaller & Weber German-style prepared meats and sausages.

GARDINER

Route 27 crosses the Kennebec River at Randolph, and a detour into Gardiner is recommended. The A-1 Diner was the first Gardiner landmark that caught my eye on a recent visit there. And even though I had finished my awful on-the-road breakfast of two cups of coffee and a box of plain doughnuts only minutes before, I felt compelled to sit in the diner for a half hour or so, just to soak up the ambience. But first I took a short stroll down Water Street, Gardiner's principal avenue, lined with shops and restaurants galore. The impression this walk provided was that some high energy was afoot in this town. Johnson Hall, an old theater, is back in operation; AN ERA RETURNS, said the sign, PERFORMANCES AND CLASSES. *Understanding Rocks & Fossils,* and similar titles concerned with gems and crystals, revealed the New Age emphasis of the Maine Circle Bookshop. A restaurant called 151 Water Street looked nice enough to consider for my wife's "big" birthday coming up, while traditional Maine was well represented by a branch of the irreplaceable Reny's, where the orange vests and hats of the fall season (to ward off hunters' bullets) were the focal point of the display window.

The clincher that a migratory wave of some sort had made Gardiner its Maine *pied-à-terre* was, I thought while sipping coffee back at the A-1 Diner, the unobtrusive sign on an office door that identified the state's Autism Society. This reference brought to mind *Einstein on the Beach,* the work of unusual sophistication that minimalist dramaturge Robert Wilson staged in New York over a decade ago, the association due, I guess, to Wilson's work with autistic actors. It was Sunday morning, and the A-1 was hopping. Four or five young women—not a soul over twenty-five, I would venture—were running the show with aplomb, seating and feeding the hungry customers, many of whom were on their way to the Common Ground Fair in Windsor, this being the event's final day. Breakfast fare was the food of the hour, but the menu also showed some interesting pasta and Greek and Mexican dishes. When one of the young women broke a saucer, two nice old gents of retirement age chuckled to each other after one made the comment, "There go the profits," not unlike in Portugal when a waiter breaks a glass and the whole café crowd yells *"Paga!"* to no one in particular. The radio had just finished playing one of my favorite tunes by Dire Straits when I walked back to the kitchen to ask the cook—a young male— what I had stumbled into. "Just a diner," he replied.

A few miles up the road, still Route 27, is Hallowell, and many vistas of the Kennebec present themselves on the drive between these two towns of the lower river valley. Of all the rich human sagas this river has witnessed over the years, the most elaborate occurred when a spirited, impetuous general, Benedict Arnold, led his ill-fated expedition of Continentals up the Kennebec to Canada, hoping to find the British off guard in Quebec. Everyone has this idea that Maine is the place of the "square deal," of the shrewd but unstintingly honest Yankee trader whose righteous upbringing would prevent his giving you poor value for your dollar even if he were tempted to do so, and so forth. Well, some Mainer in 1775 took Arnold to the cleaners, but good. The fleet of bateaux that Arnold had commissioned by a boatbuilder down by Randolph got him and his troops about halfway up the river before the seams gave out. This and other disasters that scuttled Arnold's expedition militarily did not, however, cause the intrepid general to abandon fully the pleasures of civilization during this rugged wilderness trek. Even courtship, legend reports, had its place, as Arnold's adjutant, the flinty Aaron Burr, is said to have romanced nightly at his commander's table an Indian "princess" of exceptional beauty and intelligence.

Speaking of civilization, Hallowell, like Gardiner, is an outpost of unexpected social entertainments, home of the Speakeasy Pub, for example, "where party animals come to graze." This, folks, is a rare—dare one suggest the term—singles bar in Maine for grownups, who are not supposed to go out and party once they've moved to the state, the move being viewed initially by most newcomers as *the* solution to wanderlust, rather than just another stumbling step in the quest for the perfect life-style. Hallowell has its own Water Street, and there you will find a smoke shop called the Maine Pipesmoker. Talk about an anachronism; the Pipesmoker's owner has covered his walls with eight-by-ten autographed glossies of the stars, a lot of "real men" types with the cigar habit who express in their personal inscriptions on the black and white prints a certain sentiment for this shop. At the opposite end of town is Slates, a giant café decked out like a bohemian salon, and doing a land-office business this Sunday morning with the brunch crowd. From the wall of a building across the street from Slates, history sanctions Hallowell's preservationist trend, in the form of a faded sign advertising HIGH GRADE COAL, FLOUR, GRAIN & HAY.

ROUTE 17 TO JAY ■ ROUTES 140 & 108 TO MEXICO VIA DIXFIELD AND RUMSFORD

Regrettably, we must forgo the opportunity to get hopelessly confused within the state capital of Augusta, of which Hallowell is a virtual suburb, trying to discover whether or not anything there is worth stopping for. Since becoming a resident of Maine, I have often been in and around Augusta to accomplish a variety of practical chores, but have yet to find a reason to go there if I didn't have to. We will turn diagonally west from Hallowell, traveling along Winthrop Street, found at the north edge of town. When Winthrop intersects Route 202, we'll turn left for a brief distance, and then right onto Route 17.

The road to Jay begins with frills and ends up in towns where fish is still sold wrapped in old newspapers. Through Redfield and Fayette, the setting is one of modern country living, material for a photo essay in a magazine like *Country Journal*. There are beautiful lakes not far above the Route 17 turn-off. Farther up the road are Chisholm and Livermore Falls, twin mill towns that seem to be holding their own. But in Jay the air is foul from the belching stacks of the paper mill, an intrusion to the nostrils made the more noxious to me by the residue of ill feeling in Jay generated by a modern episode in successful union-busting. In recent years, the strike in Jay was big news in the local papers, sometimes from day to day, until the union was finally brought to its knees—a sad day, say I, for the American labor movement.

At Jay, we temporarily leave Route 17 for Route 140, and a chance to follow the Androscoggin River as it bends around Canton, then flows up through Dixfield and on to Rumsford and Mexico. I drove this way in the early fall, and found the journey from here on—seen as a pure act of motor touring—one of the most scenic drives I've ever taken. Without question, the time of year contributed to my exuberance; the leaves were not in full bloom, but the colors were nothing to sneer at. With such displays of color and terrain as those I enjoyed during this drive, anyone can be a Van Gogh in his own eyes. The retina is all the canvas you need as your eyes paint the imagination with an infinity of flaming autumn landscapes over low ground and high, in clearings and enclosures, and by bodies of water, still and flowing. I gazed in dumb amazement and could write nothing at those moments because the words were so inadequate to express the depths of my feelings in the face of such beauty.

Turning onto Route 140 from Jay, one's contact with the Androscoggin—Maine's third largest river—is almost immediate, and I was instantly struck by the river's virginal appearance. The riverscapes I enjoyed from here forward were truly pastoral; you could imagine a movie like *Tom Jones* being shot along this segment of the Androscoggin. About two miles before Canton, another road marked only FR 20 (FR standing for "fire road"), enters from the right. But on the map (the DeLorme *Maine Atlas*) this was further identified as the Dixfield Road, and I could see that it paralleled the river on the same side I was traveling, though my road, Route 140, would soon cross to the river's opposite shore at Canton. There I had planned to leave Route 140 and ascend the river toward Rumsford along Route 108. Then, also on the map, I spotted the Pinewoods Road, which runs closer to the Androscoggin than does Route 108. Such dilemmas as this wealth of choices creates for the leisure motor tourist are easily resolved. I would weave my way over all of these roads, and if that meant covering the same ground twice over several stretches, well, so much the better.

So first I followed my initial plan in part and drove to Canton on 140, then rode on 108 only as far as West Peru. There I recrossed the Androscoggin into Dixfield, doubling back via Route 2 to the Dixfield Road (aka FR 20) and finally back to the junction with Route 140, where I began this slightly baroque digression in the first place. A major scene change takes place along the horizon above Canton. From here, as you head north and west, you leave the coastal plain behind, and the river valley starts its climb up the foothills into Maine's majestic western mountains. This sense of a dramatic transition in topography is the background against which this network of river roads is set. The Androscoggin River truly deserves some Whitman to sing its praises. Unfortunately, even the poet today is a post-industrial creature, hurtling over the landscape like any typical traveler in a motorized vehicular capsule, and lacks the biorhythms of true vagabond-age necessary to contemplate life much beyond the bottom line.

And while one's celebratory mood may be dampened by the times, yet the spirit may still soar for a span of fifteen minutes or so on a very special country lane called the Pinewoods Road. Again I traveled that stretch of 140 back toward Canton, only this time, just after crossing the river over the little green bridge, I took the first right turn, and stayed to the right at a fork in the road. Soon the river reappeared, and I drove a narrow strip near the water's edge beneath a most colorful cover of autumnal trees. I have seen photographs of the old lanes that existed in Maine well into the 1930s, before road widening and paving became a virtual national pastime. Now that I think of it, I grew up watching the American highway system being built. Most of the Pinewoods Road, however, has escaped the rev-olutionary change of scale that our whole society faced almost en masse when the country accelerated from World War II right onto the fast lane of economic prosperity. The Pinewoods Road—long domesticated, but little altered for a century, at least in scale—is what remains of the slow lane, so you'd better check it out soon.

■ ■ ■

The Pinewoods Road emerges on Route 108 above Canton, and this time, rather than cross over to Dixfield, I drove straight on and soon approached the outskirts of Rumsford, where the stacks of a mill puffed clouds of white pollutants against the sky that were no more offensive, to the eye at least, than the low-lying and innocent nimbus. Rumsford is a full-sized town, with a long line of shops on Main Street. Italians must have come to Rumsford once in significant numbers, for the Sons of Italy stage an annual fair here. Rumsford was also once quite a mill town, or so the old Hotel Harris would lead one to believe. I walked into the Harris, which is now a residential hotel, and stood in the unexpectedly ornate lobby next to an old man who was watching a Red Sox game on TV. The hotel, he said, "was built for the big shots over to the mill who used to come here in the old days." Lingering for a minute to watch the Sox catcher Rick Gedman take two beauties right down the fat part of the plate, it was easy to see why he was batting only .213 near the end of September.

ROUTE 17 ALONG THE SWIFT RIVER AND ON TO RANGELEY STATE PARK

In Mexico, a much smaller town than Rumsford, we reconnect with Route 17 for the final leg to the Rangeley Lakes and the Saddleback ski area. Pinewoods Road provides a unique, if brief, exposure to autumn's finery, whereas this stretch of Route 17 is the "leaf peeper special" that I referred to with such rapture earlier in this chapter. I don't think it took me an hour to drive from Rumsford to the state park campgrounds, located on the south shore of Rangeley Lake, and that included at least three stops at particularly dramatic or sweeping scenic overlooks. But who was watching the clock? So visually intoxicating was the scenery that it seemed to neutralize the passage of time. As I drove along, my eyes were filled with an uninterrupted ensemble of dancing colors projected against a distant rim of alpine peaks. Running through this picture like a silver thread, the shallow, stone-bottomed Swift River undulated in and out of view through every dip or twist in the terrain or break in the treeline. By constantly shifting its angle to the sun, the winding road would manipulate the lighting, now softening, now brightening the scene, creating a cinematic effect as if a film of extraordinary depth and texture were being screened along the horizon. At a point called Height of Land, each of the scenic details that, until then, had been strung out in some linear fashion were gathered into a wraparound visual crescendo of natural harmony and three-dimensional grandeur. From here, the great Lake Mooselookmeguntic can be seen in its entirety, with its prominent island called Toothacker floating on the near end like a treeclad carrier at its mooring. A succession of overlooks lines the descent of the hill, bringing both lake and island by stages into closer focus but diminishing in equal spurts the windswept panorama until we are returned to solid ground once again.

By about four that afternoon, having followed the sign from Route 17, I pitched my tent in a virtually empty Rangeley Lake State Park. Only two or three other camping parties were there and willing to brave the possibility of subfreezing temperatures predicted over that night. Since I had my pick of the sites, I selected a dramatic setting right at the edge of the lake. The air had turned blustery, and a brisk wind blew choppy waves over the surface of the water that filled the lake's basin right to the brim along the shoreline. I planned to spend the remainder of the daylight hours absorbing such scenes throughout the general area, and then select a restaurant in the village of Rangeley for that evening's dinner. But first I decided to gather up kindling from the floor of the surrounding woods and construct a campfire that would be ready for the match on my return to the site, both to lift the outdoor chill and to provide some cheery illumination on what promised to be a cloudy, moonless night. Fortunately, some previous camper had left a stack of dry wood at a vacated site that I could easily ignite with the brittle faggots I'd recycled from a fallen pine bough; ironically, the only other ingredient I lacked was paper to set my little pyramid ablaze—an easy enough commodity to scrounge, however, when I got to town.

Driving down the South Shore Road in the direction of Route 4 and Rangeley village, I spotted various clusters of tourist cottages, and began to regret my decision to rough it in a sleeping bag that night. Figuring it wouldn't hurt to check out a place or two, and assuming I could find a reasonable off-season deal in a comfortable cabin with a woodstove or a fireplace, there could be little lost in having to return to the park and break camp. But the accommodations I saw not only were shoddy but overpriced, especially when one considers the paucity of demand during that time of year; clearly, much of the cottage trade around Rangeley Lake is a seller's market. And in fact during both the warm and the snowmobiling seasons, you had better make reservations long in advance if you want your digs located either on the lake or in the immediate vicinity of the village.

Until well after dusk, I drove around the lake, and explored up and down the various back roads that crossed my path. And while this is not an area I personally would plan to vacation in at the height of the winter or summer festivities, it is one of the more serene and grandly scenic places in Maine to spend some time during the lull periods between the seasons. I found, moreover, that at least in early October, there was still considerable activity in the diminutive village; a large, multiservice inn at one end of town offered resort-style comforts and evening entertainment year-round, while all four or five of the local restaurants remained open as well. Only the lodge, somewhat off the beaten path on nearby Saddleback Mountain, was closed at that time, I was told, and would remain so until the advent of the ski season. The most animated of the night spots that evening in Rangeley was a tavern called Mike's Sports Bar, where a crowd sat before several TV screens watching an NFL football game in progress. I joined the group at the bar, and ate a light meal of chili and a sandwich while cheering on the hapless Jets, even though I am no fan of the sport and in general hardly ever see a game from one season to another. Somehow, though, both the game and the buzz of conversation among the bar's other patrons provided all the company I needed, the perfect complement to a day of pleasant touring and to my monastic choice of a cold, companionless night at a solitary campsite.

ROUTE 16 TO STRATTON ∎ ROUTE 27 NORTH TO COBURN GORE ∎ ROUTES 27/16 SOUTH TO KINGFIELD

The return itinerary to the coastal region for this chapter actually documents an excursion separate from that narrated above. What follows is an account of an overnight trip, primarily along Route 27, that my wife, Carol, and I took during the early winter, with the town of Kingfield our primary destination. We also made a brief visit to Rangeley, and while it was only two months later in the season than my solo journey up Route 17, the village seemed more bedded down than it had at the beginning of October. But this was merely an inevitable pause for breath—akin to a commercial break on television—before the downhill skiing and snowmobiling seasons would turn the town topsy-turvy again from Christmas till the April thaw. It was now the first week of December, and our approach to Rangeley had been on Route 4, following the narrow, rock-strewn bed of the Sandy River.

The leaves still clinging to the trees had lost their fall coloring and would soon be hidden by the first cover of snowfall. The sky already had its snow face on, but the river still ran, thin and swift. In a week, perhaps three at the outside, all these residual details of the autumn landscape would be bleached to their skeletal essence. A new visual paradigm would reign over the next seasonal cycle, with its own peculiar complexities to fathom, despite its deceptively minimalist appearances. In a month, all these lakes and rivers would be frozen solid, ready byways and bridges for the thousands of miles of interconnecting trails that allow snowmobile enthusiasts to travel all the way from Pennsylvania to Quebec, inn- and restaurant-hopping as they go.

We merely drove through Rangeley that day and on to Stratton via Route 16, a stretch of road surrounded by lumber company lands. The woods were mostly second growth, healthy adolescent conifers roughly fifteen to twenty years of age—paper on the hoof, so to speak, being grown for the twenty-first century. The squiggly South Branch of the Dead River accompanied the roadway in places and provided some relief to the monotony of the immediate scenery in the foreground, but my wife, to improve the scene, suggested "it would be nicer if the river were on the right." Stratton, home of the picturesque Dead River Historical Society, isn't much of a town, but on its outskirts is a natural endowment in the form of gigantic Flagstaff Lake and the 30,000-acre Bigelow Preserve that offers innumerable recreational options for all seasons—camping, hiking, fishing, and cross-country skiing, among others. The succession of high peaks rising off to the east is Bigelow Mountain. The Appalachian Trail, in fact, crosses over the mountain's 4,150-foot-high West Peak summit, and then follows a dramatic ridgeline along neighboring Little Bigelow Mountain en route to the upper Kennebec River valley and beyond.

At Stratton, we decided to take the drive all the way to Coburn Gore, on the frontier with Canada. Shortly, just south of Eustis, we passed a truly magnificent and memorable natural sight, the so-called Cathedral Pines, all the more exceptional in this day and age for the rarity of such ancient timber stock in the Maine woods. These giant white pines are botanical monuments that have been allowed to survive, and my only complaint is that they were sadly so few in number and that this daunting file of towering arboreal ancients was gone from view all too quickly. I suppose we should be thankful that any such species have survived the many decades of environmental plundering that span the dark epoch from which the nation is only now emerging. Still, these pines were by far the highlight of this half-hour to forty-five-minute excursion to the border, which also passes long, unbroken stretches of lumber company growth, undoubtedly of greater touring interest at the height of the fall foliage season.

For us, it was an ambience of desolation. Like most commercial wood-lands, it was ragged and unkempt, yet lacked the spontaneity and wildness of the virgin forest or the formality and shaping of its opposite, a great wilderness park. Traffic to the border, light for the most part, was domi-nated by large trucks, the intimidating kind that haul seemingly precarious loads of logs and pulpwood to the lumber and paper mills. Suddenly, Coburn Gore appeared, a gas station and a border crossing. The guard spoke to us first in French. As we crossed into Canada, the snow began to fall—another turn of the weather dial as we proceeded northward. After three miles we arrived in the small, French-speaking village of Woburn, of little touristic interest other than to underscore how distinct the housing stock can be from one side of an international border to another. The Canadian town had a prefab appearance, as if it had been built by Fisher-Price; it lacked any sense of continuity with history, not to mention the harmony of scale that characterizes the more vintage communities throughout the neighboring regions of Maine.

STRATTON TO KINGFIELD ON ROUTE 27/16, VIA THE CARRABASSETT VALLEY AND SUGARLOAF MOUNTAIN

Driving back from the border en route to Kingfield, we had no reason to stop at the main attraction in this area that draws thousands of visitors to the Carrabassett Valley each winter. Below Stratton, the appearance of an occasional sporting-equipment "chalet" and numerous old-fashioned lodges only vaguely hints at the intensity of the downhill skiing scene to be found just off the road at Sugarloaf USA, a village-sized resort of condominiums, restaurants, and night spots, spread over the base of Maine's second-highest mountain. Even if we skied—which we don't—there was not enough snow on the mountain at that early date to tempt even the most fanatic downhill daredevil. Not that Sugarloaf USA is exclusively a wintertime resort. A small fortune has been invested there over recent years to underwrite the creation of warm-weather facilities—like an eighteen-hole golf course—so the posh accommodations and fancy eateries need not stand idle while the entrepreneurs around the Rangeley Lakes soak up all the region's summer tourist trade.

The fact is, whatever the season, a place like Sugarloaf USA just isn't our style; we aren't into golf or condos either. But admittedly it is owing to Sugarloaf USA's existence and proximity that Kingfield, where we were bound, has evolved into such a little pocket of cosmopolitanism, providing for those who do ski—or simply tour, as we do—the lodging and culinary alternative to the homogeneous and up-tempo resort scene on the mountain. The reputation of one fine Kingfield inn had even filtered down to us on the coast, and we chose it as the base for our overnight getaway. Quite by chance, we had scheduled our arrival at the Winter's Inn with just enough time remaining in the late afternoon to discover and enjoy Kingfield's singular cultural institution, the Stanley Museum.

The museum honors the genius of the Stanley twins, F. O. and F. E., inventors of the Stanley Steamer, and their sister Chansonetta, a pioneer photographer of the *verité* genre, whose work anticipated other female giants of photography, such as Berenice Abbott, by a full generation. By the time the Stanley brothers launched their steam-powered auto, they had already left their native Kingfield for Newton, Massachusetts, owing to the success of a previous invention, a coating machine that speeded production of dry photo plates. It was this process that truly made their fortunes when it was purchased by the industrialist George Eastman, of Kodak fame, before the turn of the century. The museum is not so much a large collection of objects—there are indeed several steam-driven cars on display, as well as violins and other stringed instruments crafted by the twins, plus a collection of Chansonetta's remarkable photographs—as it is a repository for the written record that documents many episodes in the lives of a little-remembered but exceptional Maine family.

The Stanley twins also left their mark on Kingfield proper in a more tangible way, we were told by Michael Thom, owner of the Winter's Inn, at the time of our visit. (Under new management now, the establishment's name has been slightly modified to the Inn on Winter's Hill.) The stunning Georgian Revival mansion that today houses the inn, Thom informed us, was designed by one of the Stanley brothers in the 1890s for a friend named Amos Winter, whose son later went on to found Sugarloaf. It was almost twenty years ago that Thom bought what was then the virtually abandoned and dilapidated Winter mansion, and began the arduous task of restoration. He tells the story of how one day, Amos Winter, Jr., wandered onto the building site and said, "Anyone who'd buy this place has to be either rich or a goddamned fool." When Thom subsequently opened the inn with a gala party, he invited Amos, whose first comment after giving the place a quick scan was, "Now I know you're not rich." This is Maine humor at its best; only a crotchety, dyed-in-the-wool Yankee can set up a joke that simmers for two years before he delivers the punchline. In fact, the inn Michael Thom created on Winter's Hill—with its panoramic view of the surrounding alpine landscape—was one of the most delightfully decorated and comfort-able lodgings I have ever stayed in; one hopes his gracious touch has been continued by the current owners.

Two of Kingfield's other inns are also well regarded, namely One Stanley Place and the Herbert Hotel, only the latter of which we actually visited at its prominent location on Main Street. The thirty-three-room Herbert, first opened in 1918, was the elegant whim of a local pol. In the early eighties, it was restored to its original gilded state and reopened by a former public-relations man from Ohio. Today, according to *New England Monthly* mag-azine, the Herbert, "with its terrazzo marble floors and finely crafted oak woodwork, is the centerpiece for a reborn village here in west central nowhere." The restaurants at both the Herbert and One Stanley Place are also highly spoken of.

KINGFIELD TO WISCASSET ON ROUTE 27, VIA FARMINGTON AND THE BELGRADE LAKES, WITH A SIDE TRIP TO WATERVILLE

When Carol and I left Kingfield the following morning, we spent the day slowly making our way back to the coast. During our brief stay, we had barely scratched the surface of the area's possibilities. This was to be the case with many of the more remote areas I would visit in the course of researching this book. It is the logic of this work that each episode of motor touring described leaves more to be discovered on some future drive than could ever be reasonably digested on any single excursion. Not only are there the many roads and attractions not chosen along a given itinerary, but—even assuming a minimum of transformation in a given locale between visits—the eye is so selective that fresh discoveries are revealed with each repeated drive over the most familiar routes. The secret of a great car ride is to strike a balance between the desire to stop and explore and the continuity of the forward momentum inherent in the act of driving.

I mention this because, as we left the Winter's Inn, Michael Thom armed us with the three- to six-hour "after breakfast" motoring itinerary he provided guests who were spending several days in the vicinity. His outline of a drive down Route 142, to choose one example, made our mouths water, but our priority before returning home that evening was to call at the Colby College Art Museum, outside of Waterville, and this required our heading off in an opposite direction. We did take a brief detour at his suggestion in New Portland, a town just south of Kingfield originally bestowed on the citizens of Portland (then Yarmouth) in compensation for losses suffered from the destruction of the town by the British in 1775. Like those in New Portland, many of the homes and outbuildings we had seen in this northern country had steeply pitched roofs, covered with metal panels rather than the asphalt or fiberglass shingles used on the more gently pitched roofs of our own coastal region; the greater volume of snowfall here was the obvious explanation for these peculiar architectural features. But there was no such obvious explanation for the presence in New Portland of so many domed and turreted buildings, though generally such idiosyncrasies are the whims of a single builder whose ideas were in fashion at a given moment in a locale's development.

Our purpose in New Portland, however, was not to admire the local architecture—which was unavoidable in any event—but to glimpse an even more unique man-made feature of the town, the so-called Wire Bridge, said to be the last of its kind surviving in New England. A side road from the center of New Portland (called the Wire Bridge Road, but unmarked, as I recall) leads down through a "hill-'n'-holler" neighborhood—more reminiscent of Li'l Abner's Dogpatch than of the Maine outback—toward the Carrabassett River, to an old suspension bridge whose caissons are sheathed in shake shingles. When first constructed in 1810, the newfangled structure—a radical departure from the familiar wooden bridges of the day—was known locally as "Fool's Bridge." But Colonel Morse, who designed it, believed that no conventional bridge would be capable of long surviving the high water of the Carrabassett when swollen by the spring freshets.

In Farmington, a two-street town with its own branch of the University of Maine, we found a large, well-lighted café and decided to drop in for a bite to eat. After our break, we walked around the town, and in contrast to the somewhat tweedy, professorial crowd at the café, the people sitting around the counter at the local drugstore looked as if they hadn't been disturbed since the 1940s. But the two eccentric, elderly ladies with whom we visited briefly at the neighborhood thrift shop were as familiar to us now as the wives of old farmers in our own community who belong to such rural institutions as the Grange and the Fortnightly Club. Thus, despite its college-town patina, Farmington still seems very much rooted in a kind of mixed agricultural economy that is typical of towns throughout central Maine—at least those not located near major rivers where water power added an industrial edge to former market centers turned mill towns. Farmington, too, has had its share of factories over the decades—mostly related to food processing and lumbering—but, at least visually, it lacks the factory dimension of a real river town. It retains, however, the sociological completeness one associates with shire towns—the homes of the prosperous at one end of town, the dwellings of the less fortunate at the other.

Leaving Farmington in the direction of New Sharon, Route 27 is like a paved path over a long, wide corridor of flatlands cutting through the surrounding hills, a picture-perfect valley where farms and fields are the dominant features of the immediate landscape. Pastures are set off by cedar posts leaning seven ways to Sunday, strung with single strands of electrified wire to stimulate the memory of any critters who momentarily forget the boundaries of their confinement. Also notable at the time of year we were passing through were the scores of idle tractors and other farm machinery scattered helter-skelter around outbuildings and sheds, left outdoors to confront the elements until needed again the following spring, when the first stages of cultivation would begin anew. For the most part, this agrarian setting prevails until one arrives at Belgrade, a pretty little town flanked by lakes. The foothills had by then faded in the distance behind us, and planted trees close to the road's shoulder narrowed the paved surface near the small wooden bridge on the edge of town. For a short stretch the effect was very parklike, but also highly domesticated, with a pleasing combination of cabins and estates lining the roadway. Like the China Lake area on the opposite side of the Kennebec River, the Belgrade Lakes fall within the orbit of Augusta, and are traditional spas for vacationing families and sport fishermen.

Route 11, below Belgrade, offers direct access into Waterville, where we had planned a stop at the small art museum on the campus of Colby College. We arrived at the college by following signs to the town's northwestern suburbs after crossing under the overpass of Interstate 95. For us, the museum's principal draw was its unique collection of John Marin watercolors, probably the largest permanent exhibit of Marin's paintings on display anywhere. One of the early greats of American modernism who exhibited at the famous Armory show of 1913 in New York, Marin spent considerable time in Maine and was enamored of both the ruggedness of nature here and the plain solidity of the coastal villages. Because of the airy watercolor medium in which he worked for the most part during his life, Marin's lyrical, evocative paintings do not reproduce well and really have to be seen in their originals to be fully appreciated; thus our excitement at having this priceless resource here in Maine, and our reason for the brief digression this day from our more direct homeward trail along Route 27.

I had briefly visited Waterville on a prior occasion. A fortuitous encounter that first time with the president of Colby College while dining downtown at the Unicorn Restaurant—where I ate very well, incidentally—led me to visit the Marin collection here. To this date I have not fully exploited Waterville's cultural offerings. During that first visit, I did become aware of its Summer Music Theater, six-plex movie house, and several hot night spots for dancing on the outskirts of town. I did perceive, moreover, that Waterville is not a place to gobble up in a single visit, but to savor repeatedly in response to the impulses—culinary, intellectual, and aesthetic—it can uniquely satisfy.

■ ■ ■

Thus our journey through western Maine comes to a close; travelers may proceed as we did, retracing their steps along Route 27 to Wiscasset. From there you may pick up the thread of our mid-coast expedition at Boothbay Harbor.

INFORMATION ■ *Kennebec Valley Chamber of Commerce* (623-4559), P.O. Box E, University Dr., Augusta 04330. ■ *Rangeley Lakes Region Chamber of Commerce* (864-5571), P.O. Box 317, Main St., Rangeley 04970. ■ *Sugarloaf Area Chamber of Commerce* (235-2100), P.O. Box 2151, Carrabassett Valley 04947. ■ *Western Maine Mountains Chamber of Commerce* (897-5434), P.O. Box 11, Jay 04239. ■ *Mid-Maine Chamber of Commerce* (873-3315), P.O. Box 142, 131 Main St., Waterville 04901.

INNS AND RESTAURANTS ■ *Slate's* (622-9575), 167 Walker Street, Hallowell. An animated eatery, minutes from Augusta. ■ *Rangeley Inn* (864-3341), Main St., Rangeley 04970. ■ *The Inn on Winter's Hill* (265-5421), Box 44, Kingfield 04947. Now featuring Julia's, a restaurant specializing in New England cuisine. ■ *The Herbert* (800-MAINE-800 or 265-2000), P.O. Box 67, Main St., Kingfield 04947. A large menu with familiar favorites and an extensive wine list. ■ *One Stanley Avenue* (265-5541), Kingfield 04947. Reputed to be number one among the many fine restaurants located throughout cuisine-conscious Carrabassett Valley.

CAMPING ■ *Rangeley Lake State Park* (864-3858), entrance on South Shore Rd. between routes 17 and 4 on the southern shore of Rangeley Lake.

RESORTS ■ *Saddleback Ski and Summer Resort* (864-5671), P.O. Box 490, Rangeley 04970. ■ *Sugarloaf USA* (800-451-0002 or 237-2200), RR 1, P.O. Box 5000, Carrabassett Valley 04947.

THE MID-COAST: BACK ROADS TO BOOTHBAY

BOOTHBAY HARBOR VIA A CIRCUITOUS,
BACKCOUNTRY ROUTE

The most direct way to get from Bath to Boothbay Harbor is to continue on Route 1 via Wiscasset, a town that bills itself—undeservedly, in my opinion—as "the prettiest village in Maine." Personally, I avoid driving through Wiscasset during the daylight hours from Memorial Day to Labor Day, when the town becomes a terrible bottleneck. The alternate route suggested here adds roughly fifty miles to the journey onward (and untold hours, depending on your schedule and mood), but it passes through some of the most extraordinarily comely countryside on the inland fringes of the Maine coast. Thus, you can either accept the inevitable stop-and-go traffic on Route 1 around Wiscasset (by no means the last place you will encounter such conditions from here on Down East, the approaches to Boothbay, Camden, and Bar Harbor are capable of being equally congested in the high season), or you can surrender to the lure of the back roads, lock in the cruise control at thirty-five miles per hour, and go explorin'.

The alternate itinerary mapped out here requires not only a leisurely approach to touring, but a degree of alertness on the part of both driver and designated navigator. Also a good map. I use and recommend *The Maine Atlas and Gazetteer*, available for about $10 from bookshops and drugstore newsstands throughout the state. One can get lost or disoriented quite easily, however, following unfamiliar country roads, in which case it's best just to stop and ask directions from such local folk as happen to be about, and who generally know these roads the way Natty Bumppo knew James Fenimore Cooper's Atlantic forest. Getting a bit "lost" on these back roads is really part of the experience, leading not uncommonly to some agreeable discovery or human encounter. Be forewarned, however, that one byway included on this itinerary is an old dirt road that, although relatively well surfaced, some might consider rough going. But even here, an alternative "long cut" over hardtop road presents itself, and takes you only a few more miles out of your way—which is the whole point of this digression in any case.

DAY'S FERRY, DRESDEN, WHITEFIELD, HEAD TIDE, ALNA, AND SHEEPSCOT

After crossing the Kennebec at Bath, turn left onto Route 127 North, executing another left in a mile or so onto Route 128 at the sign announcing Day's Ferry (1740). This little stretch along the right bank of the Kennebec is full of surprises. Savor first the display of old homes from the Middle Colonial period, which testify to the longevity of the Kennebec valley's link to the early Old World settlements. The very first of the European seadogs and explorers in these waters knew of the Kennebec, having centered their trade in what is today Augusta, and by implication they thereby assured the survival of the Plymouth Pilgrims and the early Massachusetts Bay Colony in general for many years. The Kennebec opened its wide mouth to the sea and disgorged the first great cargoes of furs, sassafras, and other forest surplus that the Indians exchanged for metal goods unknown among them before the white man came, while the profits of this trade went to London to satisfy creditors who had financed the Puritan colonizations.

The old homes in Day's Ferry are worn but well preserved, their contours aging harmoniously with the hilly land that slopes everywhere toward the banks of a very visible Kennebec. Note the fairly unique presence of many brick houses cut to the same forms as their wooden brethren. Brick kilns were once almost as commonplace as mills in these parts, the mud in the region having properties suitable for the fabrication of good red bricks. Not too far along Route 128, a dirt road comes in from the left, and a large sign beckons a welcome to the Chop Point School. There is a protocol to be observed when it comes to driving down dirt roads; they often double as residential driveways. Deciding whether or not to risk inadvertently invading someone's privacy is a judgment call. The "welcome" sign removed the usual onus, so I plunged down the road, cruising bumpily along for two miles till I arrived at a little campus of wooden buildings perched on a green knoll above the spectacular, unspoiled shores of Merrymeeting Bay. Since it was late June, school was out, but a summer camp was in progress. I walked about unannounced until Peter Willard, the director, signaled a friendly hello from across the grounds. Peter said that the school and camp were a nondenominational Christian establishment, attracting young people from all over the world. Himself a Protestant, he said a third of his campers were Catholics, and there were also several Jewish children. Peter's message is for the kids to think of Jesus as a role model, sort of a healthy father image, he said. Visitors are indeed welcome—the view alone is worth the digression—and Peter encourages you to stop for a cup of coffee or a picnic, or even to camp overnight.

Our next stop on Route 128 is Goranson's farm, where a vegetable stand is open roughly from Memorial Day through the end of October. Look for the red barn on the right farther on down the road. During this drive I was taken, even surprised, by the scale of farming still being practiced by the sides of this road, and Janis Goranson provided the explanation: "The whole Merrymeeting Bay is one big floodplain. That's why there's so much flat ground, and it's sandy too, perfect for farming. Up in Whitefield [where she and her husband have a maple syrup operation] they have all the rocks; we have all the sand down here." The Goranson farm was purchased by Janis's parents after the family moved from farm country in northern Maine, where her grandparents had settled as Swedish immigrants. At this farm on the outskirts of Dresden, some forty acres are planted in a large variety of vegetables—corn and potatoes being the cash crops—plus another twenty-five acres in hay, a lot of production for a small Maine coast farm. Most of the Goransons' vegetables are sold at the stand and at various farmers' markets in places like Brunswick and Damariscotta. In October, hordes of people come here to buy their winter potatoes, five and six hundred pounds at a time. Also available along this route are apples and cider in the fall and blueberries in late July and August.

Literally next door to the Goranson place are the wide strawberry fields of the Emil Popp farm, where you can pick your own fruit. Janis told me that Emil had passed on, but his wife, Olive, and a son still run this dramatically functional and beautiful berry farm that sits up a dirt drive a mile or so off the main road. Farther up Route 128, just past Dresden's old brick school-house, a junction in the road with Route 197 offers several more touring choices. My solution was to take all of them. First I went left on 197, and drove over the long but narrow steel bridge into Richmond, a handsome river town. Then I returned and continued north on 128 above this junction for a half-mile or so until the well-marked entrance to the Pownalborough Court House appeared on the left. This is indeed a historic site, Maine's oldest courthouse, a plain but stately three-story Federal structure, built prior to the Revolution (1761) and open to the public during the summer months. Artifacts of life along the Kennebec are on display, including an exhibit on ice harvesting; as a young lawyer, John Adams once pleaded a case before the Pownalborough bar.

From here, drive the remaining mile or so till the end of 128; the Kennebec again comes into view and the farmscapes are breathtaking. When the road joins Route 27, turn to the right and follow Route 27 into Dresden Center, a four-cornered hamlet with a church and a convenience store called the Dresden Grocery. Just opposite the church—a funny-looking, gray clapboard affair, with double entryways on the flanks and a squat, Romanesque bell tower—you will see an unmarked asphalt road. Turn left here. This is the Blinn Hill Road, and almost immediately on the left is the Mathom Bookshop, a converted shed next to an old white farmhouse. It is this road I mentioned at the beginning of this chapter as the somewhat tricky stretch of this journey; more about that after we drop in on Lewis Turco, poet, literary critic, teacher, and bookbinder, who summers here and helps keep old titles in circulation through his book business.

Lewis teaches creative writing at Oswego University and has managed to publish some twenty-five books, including many volumes of poetry. We exchanged books. I gave him my Frommer's *Chicago,* by no means my magnum opus, but a good little travel guide, and he presented me with a lovely chapbook of poems entitled *American Still Life.* Since I am a former writing teacher myself, and sometimes poet, we found we had a lot to talk about. The Mathom Bookshop was also a treat, and despite its name, from J.R.R. Tolkien, meaning "useless treasures," it was full of good reads and literary gems; I didn't get out without making a nice purchase. In fact, Mathom books is part of a network called Maine Antiquarian Booksellers, so if old books are your thing, pick up—from Lewis Turco or elsewhere—a copy of their directory listing more than eighty book dealers throughout the state.

The ride back to Route 1 from this point, for me, was strictly scenic and thoroughly relaxing. True, what with all the stopping and chatting, it took hours longer to get from Bath to Boothbay. But—and this is certainly a plus in my mind—for long stretches hardly another car passed me by. This, I stress, was in late June. Now I continued down Blinn Hill Road until a fork where the blacktop went off to the left, and a dirt road came in on the right. By all means, stick to the asphalt if you want a hard-surfaced road all the way to 218, our next target route. My preferred way (probably best attempted only in the dry season, unless your vehicle has four-wheel drive, and staying always to the right), will take you over dirt along the Bog Road past Pinkham Pond, and finally over a stretch my *Maine Atlas and Gazetteer* designates as the Rabbit Path. (If this sounds complex, a brief consultation with the atlas map will provide graphic relief.) Near the pond, I sighted a pheasant hen shooing her chicks across the road one by one, while I waited like a motorist idling at a school crossing. This network of roads emerges on Route 218 just above Head Tide. From here you can follow 218 north to Whitefield, a shabbily attractive rural backwater of a few odd buildings, then loop back along Route 194 East; these two routes accompany opposite banks of the Sheepscot River, a tranquil country stream that widens into what was once an active cargo port in Wiscasset.

Actually to enter Head Tide, you must turn right from Route 194 after descending a relatively steep hill. The cluster of red-and-white-trimmed buildings, listed on the National Register of Historic Places, is hard to miss. These well-tended buildings, despite standing empty (many apparently for sale), still manage to exude a feeling of life within. The little bridge over the Sheepscot, the dam and fish run seen upriver, the path along the banks behind the old country store, the white church on the hill, all add up to an especially lyrical setting, a fitting birthplace for the hamlet's best-known son, the poet Edward Arlington Robinson. On sultry summer days, a dip in the local falls can provide welcome refreshment. Continue down Route

194, through Alna and into North Newcastle, known locally as "cow shit corner," as the uncensored sign on Russell's general store and gas station bears witness. Turn right onto this unmarked road, which forms a T with 194, between Russell's to one side and the Newcastle Repair Shop to the other, and drive on through Sheepscot's delightfully scenic farmland before returning to Route 1 opposite O. W. Holmes, purveyor of gravel. You can now turn right, head back toward Wiscasset, and exit off Route 1 onto Route 27 south, the approach to Boothbay Harbor.

THE BOOTHBAYS AND SOUTHPORT ISLAND

Boothbay Harbor is a mecca of summer tourism. One local resident—very much a partisan of the town and its environs—described it as "very commercial during July, August, and the first two weeks of September." Crowd-lovers love Boothbay Harbor during this season for its glitter and intensity, and especially for the popular Windjammer Days, a yearly celebration in mid-July that attracts a dozen great sailing boats to the picturesque harbor, punctuating with their dramatic billowy presence three days of public festivities. The off-road trekker can also find a quiet corner within the Boothbay region, even during the peak of the touristic invasion. You need not actually enter Boothbay Harbor, the core of commercial activity, to savor the unexpected scenic delights of the ragged constellation of points, peninsulas, and islands that make up the greater Boothbay region.

Several old-fashioned resorts survive from the days when Boothbay was a major port of call for the Boston and New York steamers. For the most part, these sprawling cottages recall a style of leisure fashionable at the turn of the century—albeit adapted to our own times—each commanding a superb sea view or coveside vista in some relatively sequestered spot well removed from the carnival atmosphere of the harbor village. In keeping with the spirit of this book, the itinerary here takes the form of an orientation drive through the Boothbay region that avoids the seasonally congested areas, while highlighting a few choice retreats along the coastal periphery.

We have entered the region from Route 1, following Route 27 south. The initial stretch of road passes through Edgecomb's discreet development. But once the line to Boothbay is crossed, the endless caravan of motorists who have passed this way over the years is reflected in the low common denominator of the roadside honkytonk establishments. In all, it is a tasteless strip steamrollered into its current chaotic form by the forces of unenlightened private interest. Trapped here in the crawling traffic, in the face of such a vision of crass commercialism, one might be tempted to flee the region and miss the unique beauty to be found just minutes off this unsightly road. Initially, we will avoid a fair segment of the strip, and perhaps some of the seasonal crush, by turning right onto Lakeside Drive opposite the great common at Boothbay Village (separate from Boothbay Harbor, located farther along Route 27), just before the circle where the tall statue of the Union soldier stands. (For on-the-spot orientation, I suggest you stop at the Chamber of Commerce information booth on the right as you head south, perhaps a quarter-mile before this turnoff.)

Take the second right off Lakeside Drive and follow signs toward Barters Island. At the first bridge, proceed toward Sawyer Island, where the road wanders near the shoreline. The view here of a misty bay, crowned by the Isle of Springs, explains where words would fail the source of the Boothbay region's enduring appeal to generations of visitors and summer residents. One's feeling of a special, almost mystical beauty, if anything, intensifies when you leave Sawyer Island and accompany an even more intimate view of this anonymous harbor along Samoset Drive until it reconnects with Lakeside Drive a mile or so below.

Turn right onto Lakeside Drive, and then right again on Route 27 south soon thereafter, crossing the swing bridge to Southport Island, a Maine coastal community of a traditional sort with many craggy corners to explore, and a few choice possibilities for accommodations. My first digression on Southport was a point of land off Ebenecook Harbor that juts into the Sheepscot River opposite Five Islands. To get there, having crossed the bridge, continue on Route 27 down the west side of the island, and turn onto Dogfish Head Road at a little Civil War monument occupying a diminutive traffic circle in front of a somewhat frilly-looking market. Several roads wind around this Southport appendage, one leading to the Pink Cottages at the tip of Dogfish Head, housekeeping units with decks overlooking a wide and working harbor. The Beach Road leads to a charming crescent of piled rocks along a cove used for local swimming. Down a bit farther on Route 27, turn into Cozy Harbor, where the Hendrick's Head

Light adorns the view of the Lawnmere Inn and Restaurant, which has the air of a civilized outpost and fine grounds that end at water's edge. Route 27 then melts without transition into Route 238 at Southport's tip, called Newagen, where the old seaside resort of the same name occupies a spit of land connected to the mainland by a drawbridge. Innkeeper Heidi Larsen seems to have infused the enormous Newagen Seaside Inn with some of the intimacy of a B-and-B combined with the scale and facilities—tennis courts, swimming pools, acres of ground—of a resort. Running up Southport's east side, Route 238 reconnects with Route 27 back at the swing bridge where Robinson's Wharf, a popular chowder and lobster restaurant, overlooks Townsend's Gut.

The next leg of our Boothbay excursion takes us through the harbor village itself. It is hard to imagine that a greater number of shops, restaurants, and dockside motels could be squeezed into what was once a simple fishing village with an exceptional harbor. Parking is, of course, a problem in the village during the season, but commercial lots are available. I drove on to the Spruce Point Road, just beyond the village, and a single house caught my eye because among all the bright and trite promotional images that beckon the consumer's purse in Boothbay Harbor, this was one of the few that in my view retained an element of distraction and individuality: Emma's Guest House and Cottages. Emma apparently left the stage some years back, and now she tends to her guests like an eccentric den mother in her homelike setting, where there's always a pot of coffee brewing throughout the morning. The little cottage behind her house would make nice digs during the cusp of the season for anyone wanting to be lodged near the harbor, one of the few locales on the mid-coast for night prowling in several cabaret-style bars. At the end of Spruce Point Road, past the gates of a private community, is the Spruce Point Inn, the kind of self-contained resort you come to for a weekend or a week. The inn looks over Linekin Bay and has the comfortable feeling of a somewhat provincial country club, with a pool, plenty of tennis courts, and ample grounds spotted with cottages around a fine old main building. It is the food that gives the Spruce Point Inn its edge of distinction; or at least I can speak from experience about the Thursday-night buffet, a culinary tour de force staged weekly by the inn's very talented chef.

The drive to East Boothbay and beyond to Ocean Point along Route 96 also should not be missed. East Boothbay is what Boothbay Harbor once was, a working harbor with a still-healthy boatyard industry. In general

appearance, the peninsula over which Route 96 extends seems more affluent than Southport, more of a summer colony. The Five Gables, a newly
renovated, highly polished inn of some sixteen rooms, occupies what was
formerly a kind of boardinghouse of double that capacity for theater people in town for summer stock, a Boothbay cultural staple for many decades. The Five Gables is pricey, but each room has a fireplace, and a
typical gourmet breakfast prepared by the innkeeper, a graduate of the
Culinary Institute, might be bacon, cheese and potato pie served with
baked apples. Another East Boothbay resort called Ocean Point, more
family-style and a regular stop for tour buses, also happens to have the
most spectacular shoreline setting of any inn I visited in this region
where lodgings in general have magnificent water views. The final mile of
the approach to Ocean Point should be filmed as a video and played
nightly by insomniacs, for the coastline here has a magical and dreamy
quality capable of inducing a feeling of well-being and visual satisfaction
that is hard to match. Near the end of a seaside lane that winds and
climbs among the tightly packed summer cottages is the Ocean Point Inn,
large and informal, with simple rooms and a reputable restaurant—a bona
fide retreat at land's end if ever there was one.

NEWCASTLE VIA THE RIVER ROAD

Midway on the return toward Route 1 along Route 27, a sign
indicates the way to Newcastle along the River Road, a
meandering back road that should be driven with some caution, as a number of blind, ninety-degree curves make the
road potentially hazardous. The ride, however, is a lovely one, past many
graceful farms that line the banks of the Damariscotta River. In recent
years, several B-and-Bs have been installed in old sea captains' houses near
the end of the road, but the perennial favorite lodging remains the Newcastle Inn, one of the oldest roadhouses in the area. Room furnishings at
the inn have a collected look, and public rooms—the sunlit porch all in
wicker, and a parlor with a stenciled floor—also have an unstudied charm
about them that reflects a choice of taste over fashion. The public is wel-

come at the inn's small and popular dinner seating, with a set menu for $28 per person. Reservations are an absolute must.

Beyond the row of B-and-Bs, River Road passes through the somewhat undefined center of Newcastle, curving right into Damariscotta, and straight on over Route 215 to Damariscotta Mills, a very special setting of early dwellings scattered tightly over the high ground above the Great Salt Bay. It was here that the novelist Jean Stafford and her husband, Robert Lowell, once lived. In his poem "The Mills of the Kavanaughs," Lowell recalled an early settler,

> "Who gave the mills its lumberyard and weir
> In eighteen hundred, when our farmers saw
> John Adams bring their Romish church a bell,
> Cast—so the records claim—by Paul Revere."

That church is Saint Patrick's, Maine's oldest Catholic Church, and a lovely chapel in brick on a shady plot just beyond the hamlet. Noteworthy also in the Mills are a very pretty inn at the edge of the mill pond (Millpond Inn) and a fine fabric shop (Alewives Fabrics), located in the space of the onetime general store.

The directory for the mid-coast can be found at the end of chapter 9.

OFF TO MOOSEHEAD

MOOSEHEAD AND RETURN TO DAMARISCOTTA
VIA SECONDARY ROADS

After ten years in Maine, I'd never been to the Moosehead Lake Region. The time was more than ripe for a visit. School had already been out for three weeks, and still two weeks remained before my son's camp was to begin. What with two writers in the house under deadline pressure, and a soon-to-be-ten-year-old with "nothing to do," a bold gesture was in order. By the Fourth of July, I was nearing the end of my chapter on the mid-coast, revisiting what are for me local haunts in and around Damariscotta. And I thought, Why not use Damariscotta as a jumping-off point for a journey to Moosehead Lake that would also embrace a wide swath of central Maine, taking Simon along for a little father-son camping in the bargain?

Early one Friday morning, we left Damariscotta on Route 215, which we had chosen from among many potential routes on our road map. Ultimately we traveled almost 700 miles before returning four days later with a pocket full of special memories.

DAMARISCOTTA MILLS TO SKOWHEGAN VIA ROUTES 215, 32, 137, AND THE EAST RIVER ROAD

Route 215 actually begins in Newcastle, just before the bridge that crosses onto Damariscotta's Main Street, also known as Business Route 1. Route 215 winds through Damariscotta Mills (also referred to in chapter 7) like a country lane before beginning the climb inland toward the mountainous regions to the north and west. Small livestock holdings line this often tree-shaded road. Here in a dell, you might see twoscore cattle watering themselves at the edge of a pond, or a line of sheep walking Indian file across a muddy barnyard. Glossy snatches of Damariscotta Lake are visible from time to time along the eastern horizon. Shortly, Route 215 empties into Route 32, which itself soon joins with State 17 for a stretch before it too branches, heading toward Windsor.

Just beyond this junction is Cooper's Mills, an otherwise anonymous spot where one stop, Elmer's Barn, is almost obligatory for zealous admirers of curios and collectibles. The accumulation of junk can be both a form of recreation and an obsession, which it is for Elmer in spades, and on which he has capitalized with aplomb. His barns and buildings are filled to overflowing with every imaginable species of tool, household item, stick of furniture, and gewgaw fabricated in America over the past hundred years. More and more, though, Elmer has turned to antiquing, and several showrooms on the premises are almost of museum caliber, displaying many thoroughbreds of country furnishings retrieved from the last century. Among the artworks not to overlook is an excellent sculpture of the portly entrepreneur himself, cut life-size by chainsaw from a sawlog and painted with Elmer's most reticent expression. Behind Elmer's is downtown Cooper's Mills, a few sober houses by the quiet banks of the Sheepscot River.

The next landmark we took note of as we roved onward along Route 32 was the Windsor fairgrounds, where every September Maine's largest countercultural fair, Common Ground, attracts organic farmers, craftspeople, and antiques dealers from all over the state. Windsor also was once the summer residence of Clara Barton, founder of the American Red Cross, and it is the gateway to the mostly private "camps" that encircle Threemile Pond and the long-domesticated China Lake. The word *camp* here refers to an old Maine usage, originally meaning a rustic cabin near water and off the beaten track, used in summer months by the whole family and during those times when menfolk require solitude and go off fishing. We departed from Route 32 and drove near lakeside on combined routes 9/202 through the little town of China and onward to Winslow by way of Route 137.

Winslow is the sister city of Waterville, that oasis of culture in central Maine discussed in chapter 6. Of a slightly more bohemian cast than relatively mainstream Waterville is our next destination, Skowhegan, a refuge for 1960s back-to-the-landers. But Skowhegan is also a crossroads for Canadian tourists streaming down from Quebec and New Brunswick on their annual pilgrimages Down East, mostly to Old Orchard or Bar Harbor. To approach Skowhegan from Winslow, we drove the East River Road, which is a bit tricky to find, but considerably more scenic and untrammeled than the alternative, Route 201 on the opposite—or Waterville—side of the Kennebec. Simply stay on the Winslow side and continue straight past the Scott Paper Company mill. The in-town stretch of the river road is uninspired, but before long the city is left behind, and countryscapes once more proliferate, an aesthetic my young son failed to appreciate, having buried his nose in a book from the moment we left home some two hours earlier. But his company, while silent, was in some ways all the more pleasing as we occupied our respective spaces without strain or conflict.

Along this stretch of road, Bonnie's Diner had a special appeal, the kind of look that signals good, home-style cooking. I stopped there for a coffee refill and eavesdropped on the two women behind the counter, who were discoursing on the subject of rhubarb pie, a perennial spring delicacy in Maine, where it appears on the menus of many diners of this sort throughout the summer, thanks to the miracle of freezing. The real countryside of rolling farmland began to open up beyond the underpass of Route 95, not to mention several powerful prospects above the Kennebec—still quite wide this far north—that appear unexpectedly at high points along the road. On an impulse, I turned off at Pishon Ferry onto Route 23, unable to pass up a visit to a town named for the promised land of Canaan, which turned out to be a hamlet of antiques shops astraddle Route 2, the northernmost east-west artery in all of Maine. While Simon went in search of a youngster who we saw disappear behind a barn on a dirt bike, I popped into the Avid Collector, a shop specializing in the somewhat zany Roseville pottery, made by hand in Zanesville, Ohio, from the early 1900s until only recently. As to why there are so many antiques shops here, I was told that Route 2 is the principal alternate to Route 1 for Bar Harbor–bound folk. And Canaan is the halfway point between Augusta and Bangor, an hour's drive from either city.

We returned to the river road, rejoining Route 2 just outside of Skowhegan, where a nice-looking greenspace called Coburn Park, a twelve-acre picnic area set above a bend in the Kennebec, warranted a quick look, which we accomplished by driving the loop road within its confines. In the town itself, most of the shops can be found on three streets—Madison Avenue and Russell and Water streets—that form a triangle. We planned to camp out near Skowhegan on a friend's land, and went off to meet her now at K *art*, a collectively run art gallery on Madison where she both exhibited work and tended shop in her turn. K *art*, as Abby Shahn explained, "is like K mart with the *m* shot off. It's an outlet for artists in several ways," she added. "For their art, and for their lawn-sale pick. We're all nutty pickers. The idea was, maybe the lawn sale stuff would support a gallery." Possibly, but as she also warned, "Don't be surprised if the store isn't here or has moved by the time your book comes out." Simon and I hung out at K *art* for an hour or so, mostly in the back room, which is the gallery, set up like someone's living room with a couch and armchairs. Local people kept dropping in to visit with Abby, and the trade in the store up front wasn't bad either. The place has a lot of character, and some art with a punch, like Abby's friend Fang's "art in a bag," a kind of loose collage wrapped in plastic, each work a satirical statement on modern society, but not in any literal or obvious sense. Fang and Abby co-host a show on the Colby College radio station (90.5 FM) in Waterville called "Sounds Around the World." It features a selection of international music with a special emphasis on contemporary African music.

Abby's father, Ben Shahn, was himself a kind of political satirist, a foremost muralist and, to paraphrase one art historian, a pictorial reporter of the social realist school, perhaps the most subtle and soulful of the Americans who pioneered that tradition. Certainly his famous painting of labor organizer and pacifist A. J. Muste, where the aging Muste appears totally at ease among a group of youthful longhairs in a Greenwich Village setting, suggests that the generation gap of the sixties was not only undesirable but perhaps exaggerated as well. Ben Shahn had once taught at the Skowhegan School of Painting and Sculpture, a well-known art colony located off Route 201 north of the town, where lectures by visiting artists are open to the public on weekends during the summer. Abby settled up here more than twenty years ago, when many social activists fled the cities of the northeast to gain survival skills on the land in the face of a political Armegeddon that many felt was then imminent. Now a successful painter herself with a show on New York's Madison Avenue to her credit, Shahn remains spiritually close to the movement that first brought her to Maine.

While Simon remained in the shop to gab with Abby and her friends, I roamed around Skowhegan, a small town for all intents and purposes, judging from the limited sidewalk life, but a major transit point through Maine, as attested by the stream of traffic that crisscrossed the streets from three directions. Skowhegan does have a movie theater in town, however, and, on its outskirts, one of the three remaining drive-in movies in the state, an option, I thought, for the evening's entertainment. Other than the movie house, the other business that caught my eye was a corner tavern and restaurant on Water and Madison called Bloomfields, just a few doors up from K *art*. This is the obvious meeting place and night spot in Skowhegan. Back at K *art*, after agreeing to meet Abby later at her old farm, Simon and I drove off for some more exploring.

Traveling north from Skowhegan on the East Madison Road, we stopped at the junction with the South Solon Road to inspect the old Meeting House, whose walls and ceiling are covered with frescoes of biblical themes, done by artists of the Skowhegan school of the fifties. The fine allegorical representations are quite stunning in this sparse, otherwise unadorned Yankee temple filled with box pews. The original iconoclastic congregation doubtless would have been scandalized by this blatant display of Romish trappings that are nonetheless thrilling to the sojourner who happens to pass this way.

At the Meeting House we turned to the left and, after several miles, rejoined Route 201, where we headed north into Solon. In recent years Solon has attracted an assortment of craftspeople, counterculturalists, dropouts, and progressive politicos. Land once was relatively cheap here, and logging companies still pursue their anachronistic clear-cutting operations, making instant wastelands of the surrounding woods and spewing herbicides to prevent the recurrence of broad-leafed vegetation rather than the desired evergreens needed for the manufacture of paper. The town of Solon is a crossroads with a blinking light, a convenience store, and a defunct hotel of the old style—a great wood-framed building, where a restaurant and tavern were closed down recently, owing to one of those small-town political epics in which neighbor is pitted against neighbor.

To the left at that blinking light are combined routes 210A/16, which we will follow later. To the right, the unmarked French Hill Road leads past a concentration of homes that have an oddly institutional look, as if they were once dormitories and workshops with some past connection to a rural religious sect. Beyond is a network of dirt roads, which my son and I unwittingly explored while trying to find our friend Abby's land. The roads are rough going, and recommended only for the genuinely curious and vehicularly well-equipped. In this rural outback are the remnants of old communes with colorful names like Creep City. The hip clans still keep the faith and gather in the old slate quarry at West Athens for their annual Fourth of July dose of theatrical social criticism. Originally called the Arm Pit Theater and now the In Spite of Life Theater, this year's spoof was on the *Exxon Valdez* oil spill.

After finally settling in to Abby's one-room cabin, we managed to peek into her studio for a quick tour. Her latest work, which recently played well in New York, is in the abstract-colorist style, powerful images of shattered forms entitled *A Walk Through Babylon*. Now she is working on a series of gesso panels inspired by Indian petroglyphs like those found on rock ledges along the Kennebec in Solon. That evening, we drove off, following Abby toward a friend's house, and her car suddenly stopped in the middle of the road. Dusk was settling. A sunset against a background of trees and mountains enveloped us in an air of extraordinary beauty, which Simon described as a "ladder in the sky, where each step is a different color." Abby jumped from her car and pointed to the treeline on the side of the road. There a yearling moose, with its comic jaw a veritable caricature of itself, stood eyeing us with indifference before scampering off into the woods. Later we returned under a crescent moon in the clearest starlit sky I had seen all summer, and were treated to another display of wildlife as a large deer bounded before our headlights.

SOLON TO JACKMAN VIA ROUTES 16 AND 201

The next morning we made an early start, intending to head toward Bingham on Route 16, which runs along the opposite side of the Kennebec from Route 201. Turning from the intersection in Solon onto Route 201A, we drove past the Popsicle factory, where the mounds of stacked white birch logs in the adjacent yards are whittled into ice-cream sticks, tongue depressors, and paint stirrers. We might have stopped for a tour had it not been Saturday and the factory closed down. At the sign for the Evergreens Campground we turned in, because we had heard a good breakfast was served there. The Evergreens has several cabins plus some forty tent and RV sites strung along the banks of the Kennebec under a cooling canopy of conifers. This is definitely where we would have stayed the night under other circumstances, having made sure to secure our site through a prior reservation. The Evergreens is saturated with history. As early as 9,000 years ago, it is said, these shores were a camp for Indians during their annual spring fishing for landlocked salmon. Many stone artifacts—some on display in the lodge—have been unearthed here over the years. Not only is the campground beautifully situated, but the lodge houses a restaurant serving breakfast, lunch, and dinner, food well spoken of locally and moderately priced. Nature again provided the entertainment as we sat on the outside deck and, over corned-beef hash and sunny-side-up eggs, watched a single merganser instruct a flock of some thirty fuzzy ducklings in how to negotiate the river currents.

Initially, riding on Route 16 to Bingham is like a drive through the park, green and quiet, but a bit farther on, the road is sparsely inhabited by poor folk in trailer homes with an occasional farmhouse or manor standing out like an outpost of baronial prosperity. A road descending to the river leads to a view of Caratunk Falls, across from Benedict Arnold's Landing, a natural portage around the falls used by the heroic traitor en route to Quebec on his failed expedition in 1775. A bridge crosses back to Bingham, a town of metal-roofed buildings with the whiff of a frontier logging center still hovering in the air. The town was named for William Bingham, who, though his fame is now obscure, founded the nation's first bank and was one of the most powerful capitalists during the early years of the Republic, and proprietor of over two million acres in Maine.

On Route 201 again, hordes of Canadian motorists, headlights still ablaze by midmorning, went parading by from north to south. In our direction there was only a trickle of traffic. At Caratunk we left the main road again, where the Appalachian Trail crosses Route 201 and skirts Pleasant Pond, which on the map looked like a promising spot to check out. Not a mile on, a large moose blocked our way, straddling the center of the road and munching something off the surface of the asphalt. She seemed not the least bit concerned with our presence and we happily stopped to watch her for as long as she was willing to linger. Before long, a few other cars halted, several people emerging with their cameras clicking away. Suddenly a calf trotted out from behind a thicket to join its mom, to the general approbation of the grinning bipeds, and Simon—a great animal person—was able to walk to within arm's length of the pair, a gesture the cow took as the cue for their exit back to the safety of the woods. Words failed us—my son and I—and we too could only beam and celebrate our good fortune with a resounding "high five." Pleasant Pond looked pleasant indeed, and we stopped to look over a B-and-B called the Dew Drop Inn, but found no one at home.

From Caratunk to Jackman is whitewater country. More than a dozen outfitters line the road in and around the Forks. Rafting on either the Kennebec or the Penobscot—both of which flow from or through Moosehead Lake—is timed to coincide with the release of tons of water from various dams upstream. A typical one-day expedition involves four to five hours of exciting rafting. Right around the Forks we saw the first of a series of road signs that stretch from here to the Canadian border, each alerting motorists to moose crossings for the next fifty miles. In fact, soon after the first sign, I saw a young bull moose, antlers just beginning to bud, feeding in a culvert by the side of the road. I was beginning to wonder if all these sightings had been somehow programmed by the Moosehead region tourist industry: trained guides stalk the moose at dawn, sedate them with tranquilizer darts, and prop the woozy creatures by the side of the road for the benefit of the gullible tourists. But in my heart, I knew that we were just damned lucky.

I have to say that Jackman was something of a disappointment. We stayed there overnight and had planned to camp out for free on paper-company land, an accepted practice assuming you have filled in a fire permit at the ranger station north of town. But so much of the land around Jackman has a barren look for lack of thick woods, or is just plain unsightly owing to the mounds of slash—boughs and tops trimmed from the pulp logs—that we decided to stay in a commercial campground on the Moose River. This turned out to be a good decision, since the pool table, swimming pool, and video games somewhat compensated Simon for the chore of having to listen to me *ooh* and *aah* about the scenery for the previous two days. We also sighted a number of other somewhat domesticated critters around the campgrounds, including a phlegmatic woodchuck who stared at us quizzically as if he had materialized from a fable by Aesop or a story by Joel

Chandler Harris. I half expected to hear him grunt "ayup" when he left in disgust and slouched off behind a hedge. We did make the drive to the border, a stretch of road lined by many hardwood trees, and said to be a favorite excursion during the fall. And I must say this for Jackman; we saw moose everywhere, and these were the last sightings of that gangly, delightful beast we were to experience on the entire journey.

ROCKWOOD AND GREENVILLE VIA COMBINED ROUTES 6/15

With Simon grumbling at having to be awakened early on yet another lazy summer morning, we broke camp in a hurry in order to reach Rockwood by 8:30 A.M. to catch the Float Boat ferry to Mount Kineo. Roughly halfway between Jackman and Greenville, Rockwood is definitely the base I will choose for my next visit to the Moosehead region. Rockwood occupies the banks and hillsides adjacent to the Moose River, and possesses the romantic image of a north-woods town that is entirely missing in its two much ruder and more visibly commercial rivals. Not that Rockwood lacks a touristic dimension; the town is surrounded by many excellent, so-called remote resort camps. But Rockwood retains a backwater feeling that is supported by its unique placement midway up the west side of Moosehead Lake and its relative isolation along a route less traveled than those that lead directly to both Jackman and Greenville. And like these two, Rockwood is considered a "four-season" destination: summer—family vacations; fall—hunting and foliage; winter—snowmobiling and skiing; spring—fishing.

On entering Rockwood, we found a shady spot to leave the car in the church parking lot, and crossed the road to the dock behind the Moose River general store. There, skipper Carol Swanson awaited us with her Float Boat, engines already idling, for the one-mile crossing to Mount Kineo. Readers of Thoreau's *Maine Woods* will recall that the author and his companion stopped here during one of Thoreau's visits to Moosehead Lake, and climbed to the top of the almost 1,000-foot rock face that is a topographical signature of the region. Already in Thoreau's day—the mid-nineteenth century—there was an inn located on Kineo, a way station for loggers, trappers, hunters, and the occasional adventurer-naturalist. Such was the traffic that flowed this way, taking the lake steamer from Greenville to the North East Carry—a land portage to the upper Penobscot River—and thence onward into the wilderness broken only at great intervals by a logging camp or the clearing of a north-woods settler.

Later, at the turn of the century, Kineo was developed by Swiss entrepreneurs who dubbed the region "the American Alps," and built what for years remained one of the most fashionable summer resorts in the nation, but which, by the 1950s, had fallen into decay. Today, all that remains of that era is the golf course, a dozen "cottages," and the Annex—a grand old building itself scheduled for demolition. The golf course and cottages have already been fully rehabilitated and sold to private individuals by a modern generation of developers who bought the "island" and are planning to build there a kind of golfing community in the wilderness. Mount Kineo is no longer literally an island, accessible only by water. A causeway now connects it to the mainland, and a logging-company road provides a circuitous route to Greenville, an hour and a half's journey primarily over dirt roads.

Within minutes we were putting down the Moose River, past colorful cabins and seaplanes moored at dockside, and soon entered the waters of the legendary lake rimmed by an extraordinary vista of mountains and sky. On our boat, available both as a shuttle service and for historical cruises, we were joined by a couple from Georgia and their four young children, all of whom planned to hike to the top of Mount Kineo, an activity normally accomplished—up and back—in three and a half hours. Two paths lead to the top, one a gentle climb through the woods, the other a more challenging ascent along the facing ridge. Simon and I would have time for neither, but we did have over two hours to walk and explore before the next scheduled return of the shuttle boat. Our first stop was a cottage where Timberland Management—Mount Kineo's new owner—has installed a B-and-B and restaurant called Kineo House, open year-round for the convenience of property buyers visiting their houses under construction on Mount Kineo, and to accommodate tourists. From the B-and-B we went off in search of the paths that lead up the island.

We were supposed to follow the shore path right beyond the end of the last cottage, but instead we climbed the steep clearing that rises to one side of the cliff. Realizing our mistake when we reached the top of the field, we decided to descend to the shore through the woods, rather than retrace our steps. This was a fortuitous choice, leading to some interesting discoveries, the first being a chubby white-tailed deer who sprang before us and ran off in the direction we were headed, thereby indicating an existing animal thoroughfare down the wooded slope, where the footing was none too steady on a surface of loose rocks. Next we stumbled upon the "awesome" sight of intricate rope ladders rising high into the tall evergreens, which we later were told belonged to Outward Bound, the wilderness training school. It was all I could do to keep Simon from scurrying up the rigging, finding it necessary to apply the wet blanket of parental caution to his unwarranted bravado. Once on the shore, we walked for roughly another ten minutes to the ranger's cabin, where the easy path that leads to Kineo's summit is visibly marked. On our return we could not find any exact marker indicating where to begin the more difficult ascent, but it was fairly obvious that one simply begins to climb—hand over hand, if necessary—at the point where the treeline meets the mountain's naked rock face.

Back on the mainland, I took Carol Swanson's advice to visit a nearby resort called the Birches, and found the place much to my liking. As a lodging camp, the Birches merely expands on the Rockwood themes of natural beauty and laid-back atmosphere. The convivial owner, John Willard, gave me a quick tour of the lodge, with its massive stone fireplace and homey but elegant dining room, and then we walked off to peek into one of the cabins, all very rustic and comfy-looking. I should also note that the Birches' sporting and recreational facilities, including those for whitewater rafting, seemed first rate.

For the next half hour we drove south along routes 15/6 toward Greenville, getting some sense of the development that reportedly is rapidly transforming the west side of the lake, though most of the subdivisions indicated by slickly painted signs were well off the road, hidden behind the trees and closer to the water's edge. The center of Greenville sits right at the southern-most cove of Moosehead Lake, and comprises a few stores and tourist shops and an attractive-looking restaurant with a deck over the water, made festive by bright umbrellas shielding many outdoor tables. To the rear of the Indian Store is the wharf where the steamship *Katahdin*, the floating Moosehead Marine Museum, is moored when not making excursions on the lake. After setting up our tent at Stevens Point on Spencer Bay, up the east side of the lake (a road here leads to Baxter State Park via Repogenus Dam), Simon and I returned to Greenville and booked passage on the *Katahdin*'s two-and-a-half-hour afternoon cruise, which took us back within close proximity of Mount Kineo, where the water, at 240 feet, is the lake's deepest point.

To appreciate fully the grandeur of Moosehead Lake, you must see it from the water. Many vistas of the lake seen from the shore are equally spectacular, but invariably segmented and narrow unless, of course, the lake is seen from high ground or from the air. From the middle of the lake—cruising on a boat like the *Katahdin*—you see vast stretches of Moosehead in silhouette, the shoreline still remarkably unspoiled. At one time there were as many as fifty-five steamships that cruised these waters; today, only the *Katahdin* remains, having been rescued from decay and restored as a floating repository of Moosehead's colorful history. Over his loudspeaker, our skipper told of the *Katahdin*'s role in the last log drive in the United States, when, in 1976, the steamship towed 6,000 cords of floating pulpwood, covering some thirty watery acres. As I sat on the bow, napping dreamily on the clear, sunny afternoon, or taking in some terrain feature pointed out by the captain, Simon went off by himself. Suddenly I heard his voice booming over the loudspeaker, "Hi, Dad." And I turned to see his best cherubic smile shining through the window of the bridge, his hands firmly on the helm, steering the *Katahdin* homeward.

To get to our campsite on Spencer Bay required a bumpy ride down a pitted dirt road almost seven miles long. As is the case with all these paper-company roads, log-carrying trucks have the right-of-way, and the drivers are not shy about claiming that right. At one point we waited in our car for a half hour while a truck that straddled the center of the road finished taking on its load. And we were lucky we hadn't arrived earlier, instead of when the truck was already three-quarters full. These drivers, I should point out, are not bound by normal traffic or safety regulations on these private roads, so tread lightly when you see them coming; they are not by nature a cuddly lot. And while our campsite on the end of this long and slow access road was undeniably remote, it was anything but private, being all but filled to capacity with RVs and other tenters, and totally lacking in amenities—including a camp store—despite its considerable distance from Greenville. If the campground had a single redeeming feature, it was its location facing Spencer Bay, where at dawn I was awakened by the wild, haunting chants of the loons and saw the glimmering, disembodied forms of Big and Little Spencer mountains through the morning mist rising out of the placid water.

HOMEWARD VIA THE ROADS OF CENTRAL MAINE

We might have stayed another day in Greenville, and had actually contemplated doing some rafting and taking a ride on a seaplane (or "float plane," as they are known locally), but the balmy weather we'd enjoyed till then gave way to a series of violent thunderstorms. So we broke camp and started for home over a network of roads different from those we had taken to get here. Despite these disappointments, Simon's spirits remained high, and I felt no pressure to accelerate our pace, being quite content to continue touring through more unknown territory in central Maine until we reached the coast. The route I had mapped out would take us somewhat east of the Kennebec, bringing us out on Route 1 directly opposite the incomparable Moody's Diner in Waldoboro, the next town east from Damariscotta, where we had begun our trip.

MONSON, GUILFORD, DOVER-FOXCROFT VIA ROUTES 15, 6, 16

As the rain continued to trickle or pour in turns, we wound our way from Greenville to Monson, another center of bohemian life in central Maine. Stopping there at the Appalachian Station, a combination lunch counter, café, thrift shop, and way station for hikers and locals alike, I tried to get some information on the whereabouts of the nonagenarian photographer Berenice Abbott, having the vague intention of calling on her. I knew that Abbott lived near Hebron Lake off Blanchard Road on the outskirts of Monson, and we drove up that way, past a small public beach and boat landing. But I decided to abandon the quest for another trip, it being time to end our adventure, not begin another episode. Monson, by the way, has its own small theater company, Browns Head Repertory, at that moment performing several plays throughout the area, including something called *North of the Waldo Patent*, apparently a historical retrospective about the early settlements in Maine, north of what is today Route 2.

Just above tiny Abbot Village, we crossed the Piscataquis River and followed its path toward Guilford—a mill town—where we stopped for lunch in a pizza shop. (Simon's response to my disapproving glance after he spilled tomato sauce all over his clean white sweater was, "What? They didn't put it on tight enough.") Two fliers posted on the shop's counter are worth mentioning for their insight into the region's cultural life. The one from Central Maine Tactics advertised the "Game to Survive." For $15 "you get 50 shots of paint, a splatmaster gun, 4 hours playing time, and a free drink." The other announced the "Li'l Miss America Pageant" for girls from infancy to age 14—"beauty, swimwear, westernwear, photogenic & talent divisions." In Guilford, at Evelyn's Pastry Shop, we also sampled the very rich "whoopie pies"—a gooey regional concoction sandwiching a creamy filling between two saucers of chocolate cake. Guilford wears its blue collar twenty-four hours a day, manufacturing interior wall fabrics in its rambling red brick mill. Sangerville, across the river, is known as the birthplace of the man who invented the machine gun, Sir Hiram Maxim, knighted by Queen Victoria for this and other dubious "contributions to effective warfare." Farther down the road, at Dover-Foxcroft, another of central Maine's predominantly industrial towns, we made two brief de-tours: first along Route 153 to Sebec Lake, where the Peaks-Kenny State Park offers picnic and camping facilities, and next to the Blacksmith Shop Museum on the Chandler Road near town, the way being indicated by several road signs. The shop, built in 1863, is another of those wonderful, unattended historical museums of which Maine has a fair number. Much of the shop's original equipment, the hearth and anvil included, is on display, as are numerous iron products wrought by the resident smiths over the years.

DEXTER, PITTSFIELD VIA ROUTE 23 AND ROUTE 220 TO WALDOBORO

From Dover-Foxcroft on, neither Simon nor I was in the mood to stop and explore much. We'd had a good trip and were now ready to head home. But the three hours of driving still before us evolved very comfortably into a pleasant ramble on back-country roads, totally devoid of the tedium we might have experienced on a stint of the same duration along some speedy interstate. One section of the route we followed, moreover, was so appealing that I decided to cover it separately, and it is described as a postscript to this chapter. Route 7 took us from Dover-Foxcroft to Dexter, a town billing itself as "The Center of Maine's Future," and it is a tidy burg with a number of spruced-up red brick buildings and the definite look of a place on the move. Dexter also has a Reny's, part of a chain of small-town "department stores" that many Mainers depend on to keep the kids in clothes and for their own accessories and work duds, as well as for all kinds of household odds and ends.

When leaving Dexter, we switched to Route 23, and from a hilltop just out of town, a panoramic view of the surrounding farmlands was spread before us. From here we also spied a sign that Simon felt justified a brief stop: "Spring of Life Farms—Tropical Birds." Inside the house of a family soon moving to the Midwest, we saw many cages filled with colorful parakeets, hopping finches, and talking cockatiels—including many nests brimming with newborn, featherless chicks that Simon thought looked like naked, miniature turkeys. The stop was serendipitous; for you to see this breeder's flock in the future, you'll have to roam the back roads of Missouri. Route 23 zigs and zags through several crossroads settlements and the small town of St. Albans, before arriving in the old tanning-mill town of Hartland, a place that looks a bit worn about the knees and elbows, but is not without its visual merits. Here we elected to follow Route 152 to Pittsfield, "A Nice Place to Live and Work," according to a sign on the municipal outskirts, and then on Route 69 toward Detroit—where a horseshoe tournament takes place every Saturday—to pick up Route 220 south, the very byway that is the subject of the aforementioned postscript.

About Route 220 there will be more to say below, but before completing our journey, Simon wanted to stop at the camp he'd soon be attending, which also happens to be located just off this long and scenic road. We had visited Meg and Peter Kassen at Hidden Valley during the past winter to see firsthand the camp we had heard raved about by New York friends whose daughter had attended one of last year's four-week sessions. For one thing, Hidden Valley is the only camp in the country with a herd of llamas, and in some ways this bright, solid, and gentle animal is the perfect symbol for this unique camp, which seems to embody those very characteristics. During our brief visit now, Simon once again gave me a tour of the Ropes, a network of tightropes, trapezes, and similar aerial apparatus mounted in the woods that is one of the favorite activities of all the campers here. Strapped into harnesses and capped with helmets, the children get the opportunity to perform many exciting airborne feats under conditions of total safety. We took a short walk around the camp, observing the children in their various activities, and I gauged from Simon's enthusiasm for the place that we had chosen well. "Only ten more days before your session begins," Peter told Simon encouragingly as we were leaving. We still had a forty-five-minute drive ahead of us before reaching Moody's, where we ate what was only our second restaurant meal during the four days we had been gone. Later the next afternoon, at home, Simon and two of his mates were sulking around with that "nothing to do" look on their faces again. Both Carol and I refused to budge from our computers to take them to the local swimming hole. In five minutes they appeared in our study, marching and chanting, "Beach, beach, beach—take us to the beach," each with a rapidly scrawled protest sign held above his head: "Unfair" and "We Protest." Carol relented, and I thought of Peter's parting words: "Only ten more days. . . ."

ROUTE 220 REVISITED

What better time to revisit Route 220 then the day Simon was to be dropped off at the Hidden Valley Camp. Since this was to be our son's first prolonged separation from his family, we were all a bit nervous about the transition. But Simon makes friends easily, and within an hour or so after arrival, we were summarily dismissed with barely a peck on the cheek. So off we drove up Route 220 as far as Detroit, and then turned back to retrace our steps a bit more systematically. We had, of course, just covered the full length of the road while driving north from Route 1, and impressionistically the road's appeal held up nicely, as we simply chose to enjoy the background without being overly focused on the details. On the return, we planned to stop and wander as our moods dictated.

The land and dwellings just south of Detroit have a shaggy look, another reminder of the contrast in economic health between the interior and the coast. A string of tumbledown farms suggested images prevalent on network newscasts a few years back, when it seemed that every night the

eviction of some poor farm family in the Midwest was broadcast to underscore a regional crisis in banking and agriculture. The hardscrabble Maine
farmers never had the credit to get too far out on a limb, though; they
endured in the spirit of Bob Dylan's words. "When you got nothing, you got
nothing to lose." Out of this ethos a native reticence has evolved, rife with
suspicion toward people "from away." It's a dull topic, but one we have
been harangued with repeatedly since moving here from Brooklyn. (And
you can't be more "from away," existentially, at least, than that!) We got
the rap again at Ted's Dickerin' Den, hearing for the umpteenth time about
how the rich out-of-staters have bought up the coastline, etc.—we being,
in Ted's eyes, I guess, palpable examples of this breed. We were also
potential customers, but like a lot of Maine natives Ted was true to type.
The opposite of an unctuous car salesman, he couldn't dissemble if he
wanted to. Ted had great stuff at his trading post—"a little touch of everything," as he put it—books, furniture, tools, rustic farm implements,
and so forth. We spied a vintage Hotpoint electric range like the one we
have in our own kitchen; ours cost a dollar at an auction, while Ted had his
priced at $350. The true market value is probably somewhere in between,
and that's no doubt where the "dickerin' " comes in.

Before long, as we traveled on, the hard edge was honed from the
surroundings, replaced by another scene still more Midwestern than Maine-
like: small-scale but prosperous dairy farms, with silos and gambrel-roofed
barns surrounded by acres of corn for fodder. At Cooks Corner we were
tempted to strike out for North Dixmont, but then decided to hold off
leaving 220 until Thorndike, where we'd swing over to Brooks instead.

Unity Pond is a big feature on the map before Thorndike, and we drove
the road into the town of Unity, but could neither catch a glimpse of the
water nor find an access road leading to it. Then, on the way out of town
I spotted a sign with small lettering indicating Unity Marina Camping. A
short way down a dirt road brought us to the lake and a no-frills campground, a family place run by nice people who will charge you a buck to park
if you want to take a dip.

Back on 220, the long white buildings of Bryant's Stoveworks next
caught our eyes, so we pulled into the parking lot. The large showroom of
woodburning and combined-fuel ranges and stoves was open, but—this
being Sunday—unattended. No doubt the owners have their security meth-
ods, but one wanted an attendant for other reasons, someone to query
about the remarkable stoves, player pianos, and such other delightful odd-

ities as an old hand organ. Our stop here easily absorbed thirty minutes, part of which involved walking among the long files of dismantled stoves piled up behind the shop.

The rail line from Belfast used to stop here in Thorndike, and the old main street, a half-block long, still follows the tracks that parallel the more modern Route 139. The scene is vintage Bonnie and Clyde. Now the passenger train exists as a tourist ride out of Belfast, and runs only as far as Brooks, except in the fall, when it travels farther inland to allow views of the colorful foliage. Brooks is a town of some parts, with a smokehouse selling native beef jerky among other meat products, and Gallagher's Gallery, a little restaurant where you can eat a pot-roast dinner for about $6. At Gallagher's, some country tunes wailed from a radio offstage, and a large color photograph stuck out from the wall in the dining room, depicting a young marine with a "pleased as punch" expression standing betwixt a beaming Ronald and a demure Nancy Reagan before a stone fireplace that could only have been at Camp David.

On the return, we departed from Route 139 and elected the Brooks Road to get back to 220. As remote as this road is, development here is beginning, and on the initial stretch the few homes are cut from the surburban mold, suggesting that the countryside hereabouts may be serving in part as a bedroom community for not-so-distant Bangor. Dairy farms and silage crops occupy the land farther on, as the road follows a high ridgeline that offers a wide circumference of spectacular vistas above the treeline. We rejoined 220 via a short segment of Route 137, climbing to another summit, this along the Knox Ridge at Knox Corners, where stood both a convenience store with a gas pump, and a short-order restaurant with outdoor tables and a great view encompassing nearly a full-circle panorama.

More high ground provided the real find of this trip. At first, the road leading to Frye Mountain, a state wildlife-management area, suggests nothing auspicious. A sign announced a tower somewhere ahead, however, so we kept driving, and when a second road entered from the right, we followed it, trusting that the neon red marker blazed the correct trail. Offset from this junction is a little cemetery, very well maintained, but there are none of the familiar old farmsteads in the vicinity, and this is strange. The grave markers date the local settlement from as early as the mid-1700s, and the names are those of our own neighbors, who come from the same English yeoman stock. Farther on, we noticed a succession of symmetrical breaks among the trees—old house lots, we concluded, the structures probably demolished when the state acquired the land, the lots now appearing as overgrown, yet still treeless fields. When this road ended at a T with a perpendicular road, we followed the same colored marker to the left and pulled off to the side at a sign that pointed to a footpath leading to the tower. The fifteen-minute climb is gentle enough, though we were ill shod and mostly went barefoot. At the summit, the well-kept tower was unmanned, enhancing our sense of discovery, and the valley below appeared remote beyond its location.

South of Knox Corner, there are fewer farms with expansive pastures. The hills roll more tightly and the ambience turns sylvan as the road tunnels beneath the overhanging oaks that line its sides. Each crossroads has a colorful name—So-and-So's Corner—and its own constellation of buildings, a church and perhaps a shop or two. Washington is the only village of any size we will pass before reaching Route 1 again, another backroad town in keeping with the genre, but likewise distinct in style and layout. We made our final stop for the day at Morse's Sauerkraut in North Waldoboro, which has added the subtitle "Kraut House" to its name, and now sells Reuben sandwiches with side orders of baked beans and pickled beets, as well as tubs of unbeatable homemade sauerkraut, beet relish, and dried beans by the pound, among other country products. If you want to know where the cabbage for the kraut comes from, just look across the road and you will see.

SKOWHEGAN-SOLON

INFORMATION ▪ *Skowhegan Chamber of Commerce* (474-3621), Russell St., Skowhegan 04976.

CAMPING ▪ *The Evergreens Campground & Restaurant* (643-2324) Rte. 201A, Solon 04979. Shady setting by the Kennebec on ancient Indian fishing grounds. Open year-round with full restaurant facilities, catering to hunters and snowmobilers as well as summer vacationers.

FOOD/NIGHTLIFE ▪ *Bloomfields Café & Bar* (474-8844), 40 Water St., Skowhegan. Corner tavern, restaurant, and meeting place in Skowhegan.

SPECIAL EVENTS ■ *Skowhegan State Fair* in August, and the *Common Ground Fair* in September at Windsor, Maine.

THE MOOSEHEAD REGION

INFORMATION ■ *Greenville Chamber of Commerce* (695-2702), P.O. Box 581, Greenville 04441.

RESORTS/CAMPING ■ *Attean Lake Resort* (668-3792), Jackman, Maine 04945. Upscale and isolated island resort on Attean Lake. ■ *Moose River Campgrounds* (668-3341), P.O. Box 98, Jackman 04945. ■ *The Birches Resort* (534-7305), Richmond 04478. Popular and classy Moosehead Lake camp for all seasons. ■ *The Maynards in Maine* (534-7703), Rockwood 04478. Another rustic camp on the Moose River, in the same family for three generations. ■ *Hillside Gardens* (695-2768), P.O. Box 437, Greenville 04441. A B-and-B in the beautifully landscaped former manor of a gentleman farmer, just outside of Greenville on Blair Hill, off the Lily Bay Road (called the Scott Paper Road when you get several miles beyond Greenville). ■ *Casey's Spencer Bay Camps* (695-2801), Stevens Point, Greenville 04441. A scenic setting off the Lily Bay Road, down a long dirt road. ■ *Sim's Sportsman's Hideaway* (534-7370), P.O. Box 368, Rockwood 04478. Actually across the lake near Mount Kineo, about twenty miles from Greenville on the Scott Paper Road.

SPECIAL LAKE EXCURSIONS ■ *The Float Boat* (534-7582), a shuttle and cruise service to Mount Kineo, owned and operated by Carol Swanson, a former whitewater rafting guide. Runs May through October from behind the Moose River Store in Rockwood. ■ *The Moosehead Marine Museum* (695-2716), opposite the municipal parking lot in Greenville. Principle feature is the *Katahdin,* a restored lake steamer offering a variety of cruises.

WHITEWATER RAFTING ■ More than a dozen outfitters offer a great range of rafting and resort activities along the Kennebec and the Penobscot. A full listing of outfitters can be obtained from the Greenville Chamber of Commerce, but here are two names to start with: *Wilderness Expeditions,* at the Birches (534-2242), Rockwood; and *Northern Outdoors* (663-4466), the Forks.

SEAPLANE RIDES ■ Float planes, as these craft are called in the Moosehead region, are as common as taxicabs in a big city. You can hire their services for sightseeing or transportation to one of the more remote camps on the lake or to the Allegash Wilderness area to the north.

SKIING ■ *Big Squaw Mountain* (695-2272 or 800-VIA-MSHD), Greenville. A four-season mountain resort.

ROUTE 201

CAMPING ■ *Unity Marina Camping* (948-3457), Unity 04988.

FOOD ■ *Morse's Sauerkraut* (832-5569), Route 220, Waldoboro. Bulk homemade kraut plus Reuben sandwiches.

ANTIQUES ■ *Ted's Dickerin' Den* (257-4493), Route 220, Detroit. Nice selection of one-of-a-kinds. ■ *Bryant's Stoveworks* (568-3665), Route 220, Thorndike. Cookstoves, parlor heaters, player pianos, and old gas and electric ranges.

9

THE MID-COAST
AFTER THE
FOURTH OF JULY

DAMARISCOTTA VIA BUSINESS ROUTE 1

amariscotta itself can be seen first as a postcard village on the approach through Newcastle, occupying the hillsides that surround the opposite bank of the river. I ought to acknowledge that this is my own shire town, so to speak, the closest municipal center to my home for weekly shopping. Since I know Damariscotta's shops more intimately than those of other towns in Maine, I can pass on with some confidence the names of several unique establishments. Delfa Erickson's Bread Basket, for instance, is the ideal spot for lunch or for a pastry and coffee break any time of day. Delfa, who came here from Brazil, a land of endless summer, now gamely inhabits these chilly environs, daily baking a wide variety of breads and sweets, and catering the tasty specialties of her native land for private dinners. The craft shop not to be missed in town is Damariscotta Pottery, which belongs to potter Rhonda Friedman, who says of her work, "It celebrates my limitations with abandon." The rest of us celebrate her amazingly cheerful and functional plates, mugs, platters, and so forth. You can hardly enter a friend's home for miles around without spotting almost immediately some characteristic object from Damariscotta Pottery.

Where would we be without the Maine Coast Bookstore? This local purveyor of reading matter stocks everything from coffee-table books and titles on Maine to best-sellers, excellent children's books, and Penguin novels. Victorian Stables seems to be the favorite place for gifts in jewelry and Maine-made craftwork among a good half-dozen local women of my acquaintance. The owner of Weatherbird, Dierdre Barton, calls her shop "a natural store," and stocks a little bit of everything, from French scents, imported beers, natural-fiber clothing for women, home accessories, and raffia bags from Africa, to locally made pâtés and other charcuterie, packaged and canned foodstuffs, and organic produce. Also not to be neglected in Damariscotta is the Chapman-Hall House on the corner of Main and Church streets. This authentically restored 1754 saltbox Cape now serves as a museum.

Business Route 1 reconnects with regular Route 1 about three miles beyond the town center, neither of which, incidentally, is the way of departure for my Damariscotta itinerary. Midway on this business route, though, and worth the digression, are several other culinary and cultural attractions, all concentrated in a tight grouping just beyond the Biscay Road. On the left is Rising Tide, a food co-op open to the public and offering a superb selection of bulk and packaged natural foods: grains, cooking oils, produce, tofu, tamari, honey, maple syrup—everything in the "health food" spectrum. Two gifted cooks provide Rising Tide with great vegetarian lunches these days, and there's even a communal table for those who wish to eat there rather than take out.

Directly across the field is Round Top Farms, with the town's favorite ice-cream stand and a farmhouse recently converted into a nonprofit center for the arts, where various programs of music and the visual and performing arts will be scheduled throughout the year. By 1991, founder Nancy Freeman hopes to have her old cow barn renovated and ready to house the Portland Symphony Orchestra for a Down East version of Tanglewood-style summer concerts, and ultimately for productions of opera as well. Finally, look for the stalls of the Farmer's Market in operation every Friday in the parking lot of the American Legion building across the street. You will not believe the quality and variety of some of the products created by the local cottage industry. There is a cheesemaker, a maker of condiments, an herb lady, a woman named Mille who raises and sells fresh lamb and sheepskins, and several vendors of glorious flowers and vegetables, baked goods, and quilts.

Damariscotta seems to be a popular pit stop for tourists bound by way of Route 1 for more distant Camden and Bar Harbor, or who make the detour here for a glimpse of the most popular lighthouse in Maine, at the tip of the Pemaquid peninsula. And, of course, the town is also the home of Reny's, the versatile bargain department store chain, and proud possessor of a shabby old movie house, atop the Yellow Front market, where films are shown Friday, Saturday, and Sunday nights. But Damariscotta also serves its fair share of overnighters with many B-and-Bs, like the Glidden Inn, conveniently right in town. And there are more inns along routes 129 and 130, which lead down the peninsula from a road that enters just in front of the large, white-steepled church on the hill, across from the Chapman-Hall House. Initially the two routes follow the same road and branch their separate ways abut three miles from town. First we will follow Route 129.

Barnaby Porter's Ax Wood Products is right at this junction, a tidy constellation of little buildings with the air of a forest business created by elves. There, Barnaby and his helpers mill out benches and sawbucks, and lots of other functional wooden stuff with nice, simple lines. The office has a kind of cracker-barrel atmosphere, and Barnaby keeps the woodstove well stoked in the wintertime and loves to chew the fat. My own parents and others of our visitors often stay at the Brannon Bunker Inn, a pleasant B-and-B in the Walpole section, down on the right a couple of miles from the junction. But the real payoff for motorists who divert their path from Pemaquid and follow 129 is a visit to the unspoiled fishing village of South Bristol and the yachting basin at Christmas Cove farther on. The former has a dockside seafood shack, and the latter boasts a restaurant and bar on a harbor discovered by Captain John Smith one Christmas Day in the very early 1600s.

To return to Route 130, take the Harrington Meeting House Road to the right at the four corners, about five miles up on Route 129 from the swing bridge in South Bristol. Central to the community life of old Harrington Parish in colonial days was the beautiful meeting house you will see halfway along this road. A modest exhibit of local history culled from the contents of neighboring attics and barns is displayed in the choir loft on summer afternoons, when the church is open to the public. Where the Harrington

Road curves almost at a right angle, another road enters from the right (a somewhat dangerous intersection, actually), leading to Pemaquid Harbor, where the Fisherman's Co-op sells live or cooked lobsters, and the dock is ideal for mackerel fishing in late July. The Harrington Road itself merges with Route 130, just past the Riverview Market, the perfect little country store for dry goods, groceries, and the daily paper.

Turn right onto 130 past the Little River Inn, and drive on until you come to the Corner Stop gas and convenience store, then turn right again in the direction of the Colonial Restoration, site of one of the earliest fortifications and settlements in North America. The circular stone fort overlooking spacious Pemaquid Harbor was re-created from the original plans, and it is open during the summer. If you walk around the nearby grounds, you will notice various archaeological excavations; these digs have exposed the foundations of soldiers' barracks that date from the late seventeenth century. When you're leaving the site, rather than turning back toward 130 via the road you arrived on, continue straight at the stop sign just beyond the drive that leads to the Restoration. After a short curve or two, the entrance to Pemaquid Beach, a small, protected harbor strand, will appear on the right. Continuing straight on, this same road loops back to 130, coming out farther south in the little commercial center of New Harbor, and from there proceeding down to Pemaquid Point.

The stretch of Route 130 leading to Pemaquid Point has become distressingly overpopulated with gift shops in recent years—shades of Boothbay Harbor, I fear, casting the situation into perhaps an exaggerated light, but the trend is unfortunately factual and not merely the product of my preservationist imagination. Still, Pemaquid Point is one of the great spots on the coast for confronting the raw power and breadth of the northern seas, especially during stormy weather. (Venture onto the rocks with extreme caution, however, especially when near the water. Waves here have, on more than one occasion, washed visitors to a tragic end.) The famous lighthouse is more than just a pretty face; it contains a little fisherman's museum that is a genuine education for landlubbers on the ways and means of local fisherfolk from the dories and hand lines of simpler times down to the present lobster boats loaded with electronic instruments. Lodgings are available nearby in two attractive establishments, the Hotel Pemaquid—where a welcome fire warmed the parlor on the chilly, foggy day of a recent visit in July—and the Bradley Inn, which also boasts a dining room.

ROUTE 32 TO WALDOBORO

There is no need to return to Damariscotta to proceed on our ramble up the coast; Route 32 provides the perfect exit route from New Harbor, emerging after providing several miles of entertaining touring near the village of Waldoboro. You have already passed the center of New Harbor on Route 130, and now you will see the harbor itself, a safe haven for draggers, lobstermen, and deep-water fishermen from several nearby and less protected ports during the winter months, when many local harbors ice over. With something equivalent to magnetic attraction, your car will be drawn into the parking lot at Shaw's Wharf, formerly Small Brothers, and long a traditional seaside stop for seafood lovers who pass this way. Since purchasing the restaurant, Mr. Shaw has expanded the operation considerably—notably by adding a long outdoor bar that faces the harbor and that looks for all the world like a variation of a neighborhood tavern *au naturel*. Comments Mr. Shaw, "You wouldn't believe the business I'm doing here. I used to have a place in Cape Cod with 60,000 cars passing a day, and I didn't do the volume I'm doing here. Not that we're expensive. We don't have an entree over $10. But there're so many things to chose from that people think nothing of spending fifty or sixty bucks."

Lovers of lobsters without the trimmings will find a budget alternative just next door at the New Harbor Co-op. Rob Cushing, who manages the collectively owned clearinghouse for the local lobster catch, hopes to expand the co-op business in the next year or so to include picnic-style seafood dining. For the moment, though, you can still take out your lobster and clam dinner, live or cooked. You can also purchase any number of items from the rugged, quality marine paraphernalia that Rob stocks in the co-op store, including first-rate boots and foul-weather gear, gaff hooks, and heavy-duty line. Opposite Shaw's, and up the road a bit, is the Gosnold Arms, once a summer boardinghouse for Smith College girls, owned and operated by their dorm mother. Today the Gosnold is a modern inn and restaurant, though I am told that many of the original Smith students still manage an annual visit after fifty years. In addition to rooms in the main building, there are several cottages right on the water, plus moorings for three visiting vessels. At $98, double occupancy, including breakfast and any selection from the extensive dinner menu, the Gosnold Arms is a rare deal.

Now sit back and prepare yourself for a wonderful ride up Route 32, with or without the stops I have described within this itinerary. If there is one road I would freeze in amber as the attainment of my ideal of the Maine aesthetic, this is the one. The variety of houses—and, by extension, the individual domestic fantasies each reflects—is, for me, spellbinding, and I never tire of driving the full length of Route 32 to savor this experience. It's true that changes occur here as anywhere, and I might like to roll the film back a certain number of frames to the time I first encountered this road. No doubt, there are many with a deeper claim to the area who would turn things back even farther. For all that, it remains a special place and a wonderful drive.

In all the times I've driven this road, I have not made many stops, seeing it primarily as the scenic alternative for making certain local rounds. I recently corrected this oversight while in the process of developing a suggested Route 32 itinerary. Leaving the wharf in New Harbor behind, I slowly cruised through Chamberlain, a Shangri-la of summer cottages lining both sides of the road above picturesque Long Cove and past a little wildlife sanctuary, named for the naturalist and writer Rachel Carson. Then comes a stretch of country lane lost in time, and I leave it to you to appreciate personally and spontaneously this peaceful domestic landscape of lower Round Pond, pointing out only that if the shaded Georgian house turned sideways to the road doesn't melt your heart in a manner that cheap sentiment could never express, you are no true romantic. My one interruption hereabouts was a long-overdue visit to the Carriage House, where cabinetmaker and antique dealer Roy Gillespie has a barn filled with stacks and stacks of recycled books. Best of all, Gillespie's shop is open year-round. "This is where we live," he said. "If someone comes to the door, we let him in."

Down the road, past the "Welcome to Round Pond" sign, and just after the cemetery, a road with a dual entrance borders the yard of a genteel, three-story yellow home. In the carriage house to the rear, Kathy Mack fabricates decorative floor cloths like those used by refined citizens since colonial days. (Thomas Jefferson installed a stenciled floor cloth in the White House dining room during his tenancy. When they retired to Mount Vernon, Martha and George Washington did the same there.) The cloths are of heavy cotton canvas that is hemmed, coated with background paint, hand-decorated with some design in typically repetitive, checkerboard fashion, and stiffened with eight coats of varnish. Most stunning, to my eye, were the traditional designs, like the Quaker "Tree of Life."

Past the King Row, a line of spacious white Colonial homes, each an odd, rambling form owing to the addition of sheds and workshops, is Round Pond's core, where in a beige mansard-roofed house my son's Yankee ancestors lived respectable, cosmopolitan lives in a town that once boomed with a granite quarry and a half-dozen fish-processing plants. On a corner opposite this house is a magical Cape cottage so well crafted both in scale and materials as to require a quick eye to discover that it is of recent vintage. In this house built by their son, Charles, Bryan and Freda Holme conduct a seasonal antiques business, though you might at first imagine you've mistaken the Open sign and stumbled into someone's living quarters. Each piece of furniture, each lovely object distributed throughout the house seems to occupy its proper domestic space. The Holmes, who are British, seem to share an eye for home comfort that combines whimsy and refinement, and their shop is as much an outlet for expressing their talents as it is a business.

At right angles to the Holmes' cottage, down the road toward the harbor, is the Granite Hall, where Sarah and Eric Herndon keep what I guess is categorized as a gift shop, but one with especially high standards of quality and selection. Upstairs, in a space that served Round Pond in former days as a movie house and dance hall, is a sampling of unusual antiques, and racks and shelves of fine woolen knitwear; the ground floor is given over to vats of penny candies and bins of clever toys—some of timeless vintage, others hip and zany—plus soaps and scents, pottery, Maine edibles in cans, jars, and sacks, Christmas ornaments, cards, books, jewelry, and much, much more. And on an outside porch, there's an ice-cream counter for cones, sundaes, and frappés.

Many worthy artisans keep studios in their homes, and these invite your passing curiosity along Route 32, yet the road reflects not a hint of commercialization. Rather, it nurtures an updated version of the agrarian dream, complete with its cottage-industry economy. From Round Pond, I rode slowly onward, in the direction of Muscongus some miles beyond, stopping next at the Audubon Society offices at the end of Keene Neck Road, which is clearly marked. Beyond the nature trail, the Audubon folk run an ecology camp offshore here on Hog Island, accepting fifty adult campers each summer who wish to study the wildlife. Route 32 rolls merrily on through Bremen to a township settled in the 1740s, during the thick of the Indian Wars, by indentured Germans brought here from the Palatine Electorate along the Rhine.

In the early eighteenth century, Samuel Waldo, a well-to-do merchant adventurer from Boston, and of German background through his father's line, engaged in a series of clever legal maneuvers whereby he obtained vast tracts of Maine acreage, land that came to be known as the Waldo Patent. Waldo, who was also a brigadier general in the colonial militia and a hero of the 1745 campaign against the French fortress at Louisburg in Nova Scotia, established a colony of German Protestants at Broad Bay, now the town of Waldoboro. The Waldoboro phone book still reveals a significant number of German surnames belonging to descendants of those pre-Revolutionary settlers, Mainers who are today visibly indistinguishable from their neighbors of Scottish and English backgrounds. Yet Waldoboro continues to take pride in its unique heritage, a chapter of which is preserved in the Old German Church (1772) on Route 32, a mile before Waldoboro village. The church, surrounded by the graves and tombstones of many generations of German inhabitants, retains much of its original character and simple beauty, and may be visited during July and August.

Not far from the German Church, a small sign marks a long driveway to the Fox Fern herb farm, where Margaret Smith conducts periodic garden tours among her herbal plantings of some two hundred varieties, and sells seedlings in the spring and dried preparations and potpourris until Labor Day. Within the village of Waldoboro itself, which you may enter before reaching Route 1 by turning right after the stop sign in front of an obvious and active convenience store, are a number of shops, B-and-Bs, and a restaurant. While we will leave town via Route 220 south, a brief detour in the opposite direction to the Waldoboro Historical Society Museum is recommended. This museum comprises a variety of buildings and artifacts. There is an authentic one-room schoolhouse, a shed filled with rare antique fire engines, and a main building that houses several rooms typical of the early nineteenth century assembled from the contents of local homes, and a veritable crush of farm implements and machinery, as well as photographs and documents of the same period. At the corner of Route 220 and Route 1 stands Moody's Diner, a Maine institution in the "good eats" tradition. Our path, however, now takes us in the opposite direction, following Route 220 down the peninsula to Friendship.

ROUTE 220 TO FRIENDSHIP • THOMASTON VIA
ROUTES 97 AND 1 • PORT CLYDE VIA ROUTE 131 •
MONHEGAN ISLAND

It's hard to sing the praises of yet another of Maine's scenic coastal byways without suffering some apprehension about sounding repetitious. In defense, I cite some conventional wisdom of the "Poor Richard" genre: "If the shoe fits, wear it." The shoe definitely fits Route 220 south (as it does the northern segment of the same road, described in chapter 8. The charm is evidenced first in Waldoboro itself, and in the buildings on the edge of town, along 220. The button factory on the banks of the Medomak River, once lined by the ways of shipbuilders, is a throwback to the era of mill-town industrialism. The homes are quaint, and one former shipbuilder's house—on a hill where the vegetation is consciously overgrown in counterpoint to the more manicured grounds of its neighbors—is now a pleasant bed-and-breakfast called Medomak House.

The notable visual attraction of this road is the general landscape, especially the many sweeping vistas of Broad Bay that can be seen as you motor along. About midway down the peninsula is a side road—called Timberland on a street sign, but Cove Road on the map—that penetrates a somewhat privileged backwater, but privileged more in the sense of the residents' enviable natural setting than their relative individual affluence. The first mile or so of this road appears unpromising. Then begin the water prospects, which blend into a lush panoply of vegetation, and you begin to get that uneasy feeling that you have ventured onto private land. But the desire to strike toward the sea drives you, and suddenly the hard road ends and a rutted gravel causeway crosses to a tiny island with a cabin half its size, and a sign proclaims the "Town Landing." A canoe would be the ideal vessel to launch here for exploring this fairy cove embellished with bald rock ledges and conifers of the deepest, healthiest green around a pool of iron blue water.

Two points of interest on 220 itself in this vicinity are the Barn, a B-and-B where the hostess will make you blintzes from scratch for breakfast if you ask her, and, just beyond, the workshop and informal showroom of Gerritt VanDerwerker, a potter whose work has an Oriental flavor, delicate in line but functional and by no means outrageously priced. A second side road, to Martin Point, seems to go on forever. Old farms appear, a horse stands immobile beneath a shade tree in a muddy summer field. Then the woods close in once more, and reveal in jigsaw-puzzle pieces the cabins and cottages of a long-established vacation colony. A clay court enclosed in an old framed fence of wood and wire suggests the *noblesse oblige* of a Ralph Lauren ad. Tennis, anyone?

Land's end on Route 220, on the other hand, yields Friendship, a relatively nongentrified village with a working harbor sheltering what one local claimed is the second-largest fishing fleet in the state, and a wonderful B-and-B that looks over it. The Harborview is run by two men with a flair for entertaining. Flowers adorn the outdoor patio with its background of nearby coastal islands. Overall, the Harborview possesses the kind of atmosphere that makes it a suitable getaway retreat any time of year.

Route 97 skirts Cushing, another working harbor, and joins Route 1 a few miles west of Thomaston. Thomaston had its glory days as a center of shipbuilding, but today the town is often bypassed by travelers bound for Camden and points east, who elect the Route 90 shortcut just beyond Waldoboro. Thomaston is the home of the Maine State Prison, the institutional mass of bricks you first encounter as you enter the town. In contrast, some of the most elegant and individualistic of Maine's grand houses from the days of prosperous world trade also line the main drag here as well as several side streets, like Knox Street, to single out a particularly exquisite example. Thomaston also has its strip of red brick commercial buildings, its "downtown" of local services where the White Swan Café offers excellent fare, a rare discovery to be cherished in Maine's primarily barren culinary landscape, and reason enough to visit this town.

When I first stopped there, the White Swan was between meals and closed down, as it is from about 3:00 to 7:00 P.M. on the days when dinner is served. Day waitress Janet, who studies art and photography in Rockport, let me in nonetheless and served up a savory cup of hazelnut coffee. Later I returned to eat and visit with the owner and chef, Joanne, who hails originally from Terre Haute, Indiana. "Ah," I commented, "the birthplace of Eugene V. Debs" (the American socialist and labor leader whom Woodrow Wilson imprisoned during World War I for his pacifist views). "Debs's niece was my social studies teacher," she rejoined, "and Jimmy Hoffa and Hoagy Carmichael were also from there." The meal was as good as the chat. The black bean vegetarian chili, and a well-dressed salad of mixed greens and other ingredients, made my palate sing and my stomach happy for a little more than five bucks, which is about the most you can ask from any restaurant meal.

As you leave Thomaston, you can see a surreal ensemble of structures

juxtaposed along the town's eastern horizon, where Montpelier, the reconstructed mansion of the nation's first Secretary of War, General Henry
Knox, is incongruously set against the looming mounds and millworks of the
Dragon Cement Plant, lately owned by Maine's Passamaquoddy Indians.
When Knox was the lord of the original version of this manor, an exact
model of which was constructed as a public-works project during the Depression, he had achieved control of the Waldo Patent by marriage to one
of Samuel Waldo's granddaughters. Knox and Waldo family memorabilia,
plus the image of grand living reflected by the mansion's interior scale,
make this an engaging museum to browse in.

Route 131 South crosses in front of Montpelier, leading to one of the
more popular summer day-trip destinations along the entire coast, Monhegan Island, reached by regular mail-boat service from Port Clyde. Route
131 is not as visually stimulating as Route 220, on the neighboring peninsula
across the St. George River. But the journey down this peninsula can be
heightened, not to mention lengthened considerably, by following a series
of back roads linked together under the names Wallston, Turkey, and
Glenmere, the latter of which comes out at Port Clyde. Port Clyde has
become something of a parking lot for summer residents on Monhegan,
whose year-round population of roughly 70 swells to 600 from Memorial
Day to Labor Day, among whom, it is said, are many painters. There had
to be someplace for all those artists to park their cars, forbidden on the
island. Year-rounders, despite Monhegan's touristic invasions, still cling to
a vision of a simpler past, thus leaving the island largely roadless and in
places nonelectrified.

The cost of day-tripping to Monhegan has soared dramatically in recent
years, and round-trip passage on the mail boat now costs $20 for adults.
The inflated fare reflects a kind of ironic ambivalence, a desire to get the
most the market will bear while limiting the daily flow of casual visitors,
who, residents loudly complain, overrun the island and disturb their solitude. Such limits by price tag, of course, also inevitably follow social and
economic lines, and don't necessarily diminish the crowds, but simply render them more homogeneous in class and type, contributing to a stifling
preciousness that has made in-season visits to Monhegan unpalatable from
my point of view. Who, after all, but the pushiest or most stubbornly
principled individuals want to go or be somewhere they're not wanted?

For the final leg of this mid-coast sampler, we will visit the pleasant
village of Tenant's Harbor, located on Route 131, two or three coves

upland from Port Clyde. You would not have passed Tenant's Harbor on the way down, assuming you had followed the detour I sketched out above. Just as I rounded the curve, coming into Tenant's Harbor, I spotted a pretty blue house that turned out to be a B-and-B called the Bufflehead Inn. Down by the actual harbor, however, is an inn that a guest named Kate from Springfield, Massachusetts, described as ideal for "soul renewal." She was sitting on the porch when I arrived at the East Wind Inn, writing in her journal. We fell into conversation and I learned that she had just completed five days of cruising out of Rockland in a windjammer called the *Nathaniel Bowditch*. The best part of sailing on these old schooners, Kate remarked, is "going out to find the wind and letting it take you wherever it wants."

INFORMATION ■ *Brunswick Area Chamber of Commerce* (725-8797), 59 Pleasant St., Brunswick 04011. ■ *Bath Chamber of Commerce* (443-9751, which includes information on Wiscasset), 45 Front St., Bath 04530. ■ *Boothbay Harbor Region Chamber of Commerce* (633-2353), P.O. Box 356, Boothbay Harbor 04538. ■ *Damariscotta Chamber of Commerce* (563-8340), Main St., P.O. Box 13, Damariscotta 04543. Also the *Damariscotta Region Information Bureau* (563-3175), located on Church St., a seasonally operated booth for information, brochures, and maps.

BRUNSWICK AREA

LODGINGS ■ *Driftwood Inn* (833-5461), Bailey Island 04003. Open May 20 to October 15. ■ *Lookout Point House* (833-5509), Harpswell 04097. Open year-round. ■ *Brunswick Bed & Breakfast* (729-4914), 165 Park Row, Brunswick 04011. A graceful Greek Revival town house with five guest rooms, next to the Pejepscot Historical Society. ■ *Stowe House* (725-5543), 63 Federal St., Brunswick 04011. A restaurant and large motel unit in the house where Harriet Beecher Stowe wrote *Uncle Tom's Cabin*.

CAMPING ■ *Orrs Island Campground* (833-5595), Rte. 24, Orrs Island 04066.

RESTAURANTS ■ *Richard's* (729-9673), North Harpswell. Open year-round. German and fine dining. Lunch and dinner. ■ *Dolphin Marina*

(833-6000), South Harpswell. Open year-round, 8:00 A.M. to 8:00 P.M. daily. ▪ *Rock Ovens* (833-6911), Rte. 24, Bailey Island. Seasonal. Seafood and fine dining. Dinner only. ▪ *Cook's Lobster House* (833-6641), Bailey Island. Seasonal. Seafood. Breakfast, lunch, and dinner. ▪ *Mackerel Cove Restaurant* (833-6656). Open mid-April to mid-October. Seafood. Breakfast, lunch, and dinner. Also a year-round coffee shop. ▪ *Holbrook's Lobster Wharf and Snack Bar* (725-5697), Cundy's Harbor. Outdoor lunch and dinner in season. Lobster and short-order seafood.

SHOPS ▪ *Ask Your Mother* (729-1542), 49 Pleasant St., Brunswick. Toy and hobby shop. ▪ *Grand City* (725-8964), Grand City shopping plaza, Brunswick. Department store and informal restaurant. ▪ *Hobe Sound Galleries* (725-4191), 58 Maine Street. Snappy new art gallery. ▪ *Old Books* (725-4524), 136 Maine Street. Several rooms on the second floor are filled with classic titles. ▪ *Maine Writers and Publishers Alliance* (729-6333), 19D Mason St. A distributor and retailer of books about Maine and by Maine authors. ▪ *Macbeans Bookshop* (729-6513), 134 Maine St. College bookstore with large inventory.

MUSEUMS ▪ *Bowdoin College Museum of Art* (725-3000), Bowdoin campus. Open daily except Monday. Free admission. ▪ *Peary-MacMillan Arctic Museum* (725-8731), Bowdoin campus. Open daily, except Monday. Free admission. The museum staff can book passage on the boat that visits Peary's Eagle Island retreat, off Harpswell, during the summer months, leaving from Mackerel Cove. ▪ *Pejepscot Historical Society Museums* (729-6606). These include the Historical Society (free), 161 Park Row; the Skolfield-Whittier House ($5 for adults, $2.50 for children), located next door; and the Joshua Chamberlain Civil War Museum, 226 Maine St., currently undergoing repairs and open by appointment only.

SPECIAL ▪ *The Topsham Fair*, located in Brunswick's twin town across the river, is a real down-home country fair that takes place each year during the first week of August. One of the best around.

BATH AREA

LODGINGS ▪ *1024 Washington* (443-5202), Bath 04530. The name and address of this attractive ship captain's home turned B-and-B are the same.

Open year-round. ▪ *Levitt Family* (443-6442), 50 Pearl St., Bath 04530. One of three B-and-Bs on this charming back street near downtown. Open year-round. ▪ *Glad II* (443-1191), 60 Pearl St., Bath 04530. Open year-round and very affordable. ▪ *Packard House* (443-6069), 45 Pearl St., Bath 04530. A 1790s captain's house, and most elegant of Pearl Street's all-season B-and-Bs. ▪ *Fairhaven Inn* (443-4391), North Bath Rd., Bath 04530. Off the beaten track, on the road to West Chop Point, and open year-round. ▪ *Rock Gardens Inn* (389-1339), Sebasco Estates 04565. A very special place overlooking Casco Bay, a half hour from Bath. Seasonal. ▪ *Coveside* (371-2807), Five Islands 04546. At the mouth of the Sheepscot River, in the tranquil village of Five Islands. Seasonal.

CAMPING ▪ *Meadowbrook Camping Area* (443-4967), Bath 04530. Minutes from Bath on the Phippsburg peninsula. ▪ *Hermit Island* (443-2101), Small Point 04567. Tent camping only, on a private island with seven beaches that fronts the ocean.

RESTAURANTS ▪ *Kristina's* (442-8577), 160 Centre St., Bath. Nouvelle meals and bakery. ▪ *Spinney's* (389-2052), Popham Beach. Informal seafood restaurant, also a guest house. ▪ *The Osprey* (371-2530), Riggs Cove, Robinhood. French and fancy. ▪ *The Cabin* (443-6224), 552 Washington St. Good pizza and Italian sandwiches. ▪ *Montsweag Farm* (443-6563), Woolwich, on Rte. 1 between Bath and Wiscasset. Family-style restaurant.

SHOPS ▪ *Raymond Shadis Art Studio* (443-1637), 158 Centre St., Bath; behind Kristina's. Gallery, plus custom sculpture and ironwork. ▪ *Telltales Children's Bookshop* (443-1093), 27 Centre St., Bath. ▪ *Morris Povich Men's Shop* (443-4842), 143 Front St., Bath. ▪ *Wood Butcher Tools* (442-7938), Shelter Institute Building, 38 Centre St., Bath. The Shelter Institute, a self-help-oriented school for those who want to learn the skills of housebuilding and home repair, with self-help books available. ▪ *The Grainery* (442-8012), 36 Centre St., Bath. A very good health-food store and lunch spot. ▪ *C.N. Flood* (443-4573), 619 High St., Bath. Antiques. ▪ *Antique Music Boxes* (882-7163), 18 High St., Wiscasset.

MUSEUM ▪ *Maine Maritime Museum* (443-1316), 243 Washington St., Bath; south of Rte. 1, just beyond Bath Iron Works.

SPECIAL ▪ *Architectural Tours*. A brochure for a self-guided walking or driving tour of historical Bath can be picked up at the Chamber of Commerce storefront. ▪ *Downeast Flying Service* (882-6752), at the Wiscasset Airport off Rte. 144 in Wiscasset. "Why wait for a plane, when we have one waiting for you?" said the man in the lounge of this diminutive airport right out of the Smilin' Jack tradition of the American romance with small planes. Scenic overflights or charters to anywhere.

BOOTHBAY HARBOR REGION

LODGINGS ▪ *Spruce Point Inn* (633-4152), Boothbay Harbor 04538. Resort-style inn on a quiet, scenic point not far from downtown Boothbay. Open mid-June to mid-September. ▪ *Emma's Guest House* (633-5287), Boothbay Harbor 04537. Reasonably priced rooms or efficiencies in a private home at the edge of the harbor. Year-round. ▪ *The Lawnmere Inn* (633-2751), Southport 04576. A classic, classy inn since 1898. Seasonal. ▪ *Newagen Seaside Inn* (633-5242), Cape Newagen 04552 (on Southport Island). Full-scale resort with intimate service. June through September. ▪ *Pink Cottages* (633-5181), Dogfish Head Rd., Southport 04576. Housekeeping cottages overlooking a serene but active harbor. Seasonal. ▪ *Five Gables Inn* (633-4551), Murray Hill Rd., East Boothbay 04544. Newly renovated, swank rooms with fireplaces; gourmet breakfast. Mid-May through mid-November. ▪ *Linekin Village B-and-B* (633-3681), Rte. 96, East Boothbay 04544. Three rooms available in an old house with a front porch and rockers; open May 1 to mid-October. ▪ *Ocean Point Inn* (633-4200), Shore Rd., East Boothbay 04544. Pleasant tourist facility in a spectacular setting. Seasonal.

RESTAURANTS ▪ *The Spruce Point Inn, the Ocean Point Inn, the Newagen Seaside Inn, and the Lawnmere Inn* have dining rooms open to the public. Guests at these inns are generally on the American or modified American plan, particularly during the height of the season. ▪ *Robinson's Wharf* (633-3830), just across the drawbridge in Southport. Seafood. ▪ *The Carriage House*, Rte. 96, East Boothbay. Tasty grinders.

SPECIAL ▪ *The Windjammers* sail into Boothbay Harbor in the second week of July, signaling the start of a three-day festival. ▪ *Monhegan Island*

Cruises (633-2284) with Captain Bob Campbell from Pier 8, Boothbay Harbor.

DAMARISCOTTA REGION

LODGINGS ▪ *Newcastle Inn* (563-5685), River Rd., Newcastle 04553; traditional roadhouse with a gourmet dining room. ▪ *Mill Pond Inn* (563-8014), Damariscotta Mills 04553. Very picturesque location, and not far from town. ▪ *Glidden House* (563-1859), Glidden St., New Castle 04553. Comfortable lodgings only seconds from Main Street, Damariscotta, in Doris Miller's home. ▪ *Bristol Inn* (563-1125), Upper Round Pond Rd., Bristol Mills. Located near a popular local swimming hole with canoe rentals. ▪ *Brannon Bunker Inn* (563-5941), Walpole 04573. Quiet spot down Route 129, en route to South Bristol fishing village. ▪ *Little River Inn* (677-2845), Rte. 130, Pemaquid 04558. Near historic Fort William Henry restoration and Pemaquid Beach. ▪ *Bradley Inn* (677-2105), Rte. 130, New Harbor 04554. Attractive rambling Victorian inn and restaurant near Pemaquid Point. ▪ *Hotel Pemaquid* (677-2312), Rte. 130, New Harbor 04554. A century-old resort hotel, completely renovated and minutes from Pemaquid Point. ▪ *Gosnold Arms* (677-3727), Rte. 32, New Harbor 04554. Special harbor setting and very reasonable for room with meals. ▪ *Briar Rose B-and-B* (529-5478), Rte. 32, Round Pond. Large, mansard-roofed home near pretty Round Pond harbor.

RESTAURANTS ▪ *The Newcastle Inn, the Bradley Inn, and the Gosnold Arms* all have dining rooms open to the public for dinner only. ▪ *The Bread Basket* (563-1737), in the Nathaniel Austin House just off Main St., Damariscotta. Bakery and coffee shop, also serving breakfast and lunch, including dishes occasionally with a tasty Brazilian accent. ▪ *Rising Tide Food Co-op* (563-5556), Business Rte. 1, Damariscotta. Excellent vegetarian lunches. *Harborside Grill* (644-8751). The local scene in spades. ▪ *Farrin's Lobster Pound* (644-8500), Rte. 129, South Bristol. ▪ *Cove Side Restaurant* (644-8540), Christmas Cove, South Bristol. ▪ *Shaw's Fish and Lobster Wharf* (677-2200), Rte. 32, New Harbor. Seafood galore and a great view. ▪ *Dot's Bakery* (529-5770), Rte. 32, Round Pond. Homemade-style donuts, pies, and pizza. ▪ Also, for retail lobster, cooked or live, try the fishermen's co-ops at South Bristol, Pemaquid Harbor, New Harbor, and Round Pond.

SHOPS ▪ *Damariscotta Pottery* (563-8843), Notley Square, Damariscotta. Hand-painted, Matisse-like, and functional pottery; Barbara Bush bought an elephant here for George. ▪ *Weatherbird* (563-8993), Notley Square, Damariscotta. Owner calls the shop a "trading company." Quality foodstuffs and dry goods. ▪ *Maine Coast Book Shop* (563-3207), Main St., Damariscotta. Choice reads. ▪ *Victorian Stables* (563-1991), Water St., Damariscotta. Smart crafts and gifts. ▪ *The Holmes* (529-5788), Rte. 32, Round Pond. Country antiques and folk art chosen with the eye of a stage designer; also Bryan Holme's extraordinary illustrated books on cultural themes from advertising to children's literature. ▪ *Granite Hall* (529-5864), Rte. 32 (set back from the Holmes, toward the harbor), Round Pond. Classy novelties, penny candy, Maine products, woolens, etc. ▪ *Carriage House* (529-5555), Rte. 32, Round Pond. Stacks of books, plus prints, cabinetry, and collectibles. ▪ *Pemaquid Floorcloths* (529-5633), Rte. 32, Round Pond. Stenciled and varnished floor cloths of heavy canvas.

SPECIAL ▪ *Round Top Center of the Arts* (563-1507), Business Rte. 1, Damariscotta. Daily performances, workshops, children's programs, and open-air music featuring the Portland Symphony. ▪ *Damariscotta Farmer's Market*, Business Rte. 1. Open Fridays, 9:00 A.M.–1:00 P.M., from May to October, rain or shine. ▪ *Damariscove Island Preserve*, a natural environment, "long, rolling, and treeless" maintained by the Nature Conservancy (729-5181), 122 Main, Topsham. Access is by boat; occasional excursions are organized by the Conservancy.

WALDOBORO/THOMASTON

LODGINGS ▪ *Snow Turtle Inn* (832-4423), Old Rte. 1 and Rte. 32, Waldoboro 04572. A good place from which to make the Route 32 excursion in reverse. ▪ *Medomak House* (832-4971), Friendship St. (Route 220), Waldoboro 04572. At the opposite end of Waldoboro from the Snow Turtle Inn and near the village center. ▪ *The Barn* (832-5781), Rte. 200, South Waldoboro 04572. Midway to Friendship. ▪ *Harbor Hill* (832-6646), Friendship 04547. Attentive innkeepers and a nice terrace view over the harbor. ▪ *Bufflehead Inn* (372-8502), Rte. 131, Tenant's Harbor 04860. A cute inn named for a species of duck. ▪ *East Wind Inn* (372-6366), Tenant's Harbor 04860. Open all year, with facilities for meetings; perfect off-season retreat, corporate or otherwise.

CAMPING ▪ *Saltwater Farm Campground* (354-6735), Cushing. Appropriately remote.

RESTAURANTS ▪ *Thomaston Café & Bakery* (formerly White Swan Café) (354-8589), 88 Main St., Thomaston. Fresh baguettes daily and baked goods to order. Breakfast and lunch all year. ▪ *Moody's Diner* (832-7468), Rte. 1 (junction with Route 220). The quintessential diner. ▪ *Pine Cone Public House* (832-6337), Friendship St., Waldoboro. Open from early spring to late December. Water view from the dining room and deck; good local reputation.

COTTAGE INDUSTRIES ▪ *Fox Fern Herb Farm* (832-4721), Rte. 32, Waldoboro. Workshops, garden tours, and herbs for sale. ▪ *Natural Goat Milk Cheese* (832-5136), Friendship St., Waldoboro. ▪ *Unison Designs* (832-6649), Waldoboro. Hand-painted, wearable art.

SPECIAL ▪ *Old German Church and cemetery*, Rte. 32, Waldoboro. A unique story and unspoiled architectural relic. Open daily in July and August. ▪ *The Waldoboro Historical Society Museum*, Rte. 220, Waldoboro. Charming, informative museum of local history and artifacts. ▪ *Foggy Ridge Gamebird Farm* (273-6466), Warren. Smoked gourmet birds by the pound, plus a preserve for bird hunters. ▪ *Union Fair*, Union; Rte. 235 north from Waldoboro or Rte. 131 north from Thomaston. Agricultural fair held annually since 1869; midway and harness racing, too. Usually late August. ▪ *Friendship Sloop* (633-4780). A sail on the *Eastward*, a unique Maine coastal sloop, with Captain Roger Duncan.

10

'ROUND PENOBSCOT BAY: THE WESTERN SHORE

ROCKLAND TO VERONA VIA ROUTE 1

enobscot Bay is the grandest of all of Maine's harbors, studded with islands beneath the graceful vigilance of the tree-clad Camden Hills. The waters of this vast basin wash the shores of a dozen coastal towns and villages that are among the most appealing and varied in the entire state. The working harbors of Rockland and Stonington flank the bay like bookends. In between are the classic summer spas of Camden, Castine, and Blue Hill, sedate Rockport and artsy Lincolnville, and the coming hot spots of the future, Belfast and Searsport. Deer Isle is the one island in the bay accessible directly by car, but Islesboro, Vinalhaven, North Haven, and Isle au Haut, among others, can only be reached by ferry or mail boat. Route 1 passes through the towns of the bay's western shore, and for once is true to its claim of being a coastal byway; the water views are frequent and never far from the beaten path. The eastern shore—in which I have included locales like Blue Hill that front Blue Hill Bay as well—is covered in a subsequent chapter.

ROCKLAND

O ur approach to Rockland is on routes 131 and 73 from Port Clyde. If you approach Rockland from the west on Route 1, however, you might be excused for your initial impression that it is the ugliest town in the entire state. After Thomaston—beginning with the dusty moonscape of the Dragon Cement plant—the western outskirts of Rockland only get worse.

Entering from the south via Route 73, you miss the bleak western outskirts and directly encounter Rockland's downtown, a half-mile strip of charming red brick commercial buildings, filled with a wide spectrum of shops and businesses. Main Street runs one way east (that is, toward Camden down the coast), while a parallel street one block north returns traffic in the opposite direction. Rockland, a large market town, a successful port and harbor, and a center of county administration, is in every sense the legitimate gateway to the Penobscot Bay region. Yet the town is often bypassed by eastbound visitors who skirt both Thomaston and Rockland by way of Route 90, which links Warren (just beyond Waldoboro) and Camden directly.

Despite being snubbed by a fair stream of coastal visitors, Rockland still gives the impression of being one of the busiest towns in these parts. For one thing, those who live, summer, or vacation on the islands of Vinalhaven or North Haven routinely pass through Rockland to the ferry terminal located on the eastern end of town. But Rockland's deeper, more cosmopolitan significance as a regional center is underscored by the presence of local bureaus for the state's two largest dailies—the *Portland Press Herald* and the *Bangor Daily News*—and its own FM radio station, all of which are located on the town's principal thoroughfare. Several of Rockland's shops also add a quiet patina of sophistication without departing from the realm of the practical; no yuppie boutiques here. There are three bookshops, each with a slightly different focus, and The Store, an emporium for kitchenwear and cooking paraphernalia that would be the envy of Greenwich Village.

Nor are the opportunities for culture lacking in Rockland, thanks to the existence of the Farnsworth Museum. The Farnsworth is a shrine to the work of Andrew Wyeth, who has long summered in nearby Cushing. Or at least, from my perspective, the Wyeth work—which includes samples from the palette of the artist's teacher and father, N. C. Wyeth, and that of Andrew's son, Jamie—represents the Farnsworth's most original and impressive acquisitions. Contrary to popular misconception, the Farnsworth does not count Wyeth's *Christina's World* in its collection; that work hangs in New York's Museum of Modern Art. A small sampling of canvases by other well-known artists who painted in Maine occupies a separate gallery and includes works by Soyer, Hartley, Marin, the Zorachs—husband and wife—and Louise Nevelson, who grew up in Rockland from the age of five after her parents immigrated from Russia following the failed revolution of 1905. The museum has a public art library with a grand piano used occasionally for musical recitals. Adjacent to the museum, and also open to the public, is the homestead of Lucy C. Farnsworth—the museum's benefactress—which preservationists consider one of the finest Victorian homes in the country.

It should come as no surprise that Maine, a state with many lighthouses, boasts a museum devoted to these romantic beacons. The Shore Village Museum, several blocks up from Main Street on Limerock Street, is housed in the still-active headquarters of the Grand Army of the Republic, a veterans' organization dating from the Civil War and kept going by descendants of combatants in that conflict. Rockland's Grand Army building was torn down, but the current structure approximates the original and dates from the same period. Most of the artifacts within pertain to lighthouses, with much brass and glass in the form of lenses and nautical instruments. Albums of old, pastel-colored postcards with lighthouse motifs caught my eye in particular, as did the display of sardine can lids, numbering several score. A very soft-spoken woman named Rita, who helps staff the museum, showed me into the little library that houses what must be a rare collection of volumes on the Civil War—written mostly from the Northern perspective, as I gathered from the title of one large set of books, *War of Rebellion: Official Records*. For the better part of a half hour, I talked with Rita about the "state of the world," and had one of those rare, spontaneous, and intelligent conversations one can sometimes have with a perfect stranger.

ROCKPORT

Feeling that I had at last discovered the "real" Rockland, not just the "ugly quarter" where I had hitherto confined my visits to the Motor Vehicle Bureau or to shopping for storm windows, I decided to push on. The outskirts on the opposite end of town, going toward Rockport and Camden, are much softer in appearance, though lined with the usual cutesy tourist traps and motels, one of which, the Strawberry Hill Motor Court, has a certain folk charm. A cluster of little white cottages with views of the sea are drawn close together in the old Puritan fashion, as if they still expected an attack by "savages."

Though I had passed this way many times, I had never actually been to Rockport, and in fact there is no sign to indicate the way. I had therefore come to believe that Rockport was an empty municipal entity with no discernible center. On this occasion I was looking more carefully to test my hypothesis, and not far beyond Rockland I spotted a sign that read "Main Street," indicating an unassuming asphalt road that ran between two islands of modern commercial buildings. This I followed around several bends toward the shore until I came to a small group of old storefronts that looked out on a cove labeled on my map as Rockport Harbor. So, I thought, there *is* a village of Rockport. And then my less-than-reliable memory suddenly recovered a few forgotten facts. Rockport is home to the Maine Photographic Workshop, hardly an anonymous institution by a long shot. Some of my friends had actually attended classes here, and there it was, occupying one whole side of the small block of buildings before me. Dozens of artsy-looking folk with eager faces crowded the narrow sidewalks, spilling into the street; some were posing for group pictures. Apparently a new session was about to begin, and they too had just that moment arrived on the scene.

The one public space at the Workshop was a photo gallery on the second floor, which I entered. Several dozen black-and-white prints of high quality were mounted on the walls of the small space. Someone had snapped a series of celebrity shots that included one of a predictably petulant Sean Penn, and another of an enigmatic Marlon Brando leaning against a split-rail fence somewhere on the great western range. Through an open door leading to a theater space, I could see a class in progress, conducted by a working screenwriter. Annie, the gallery curator, told me that emphasis at the Workshop was on the nuts and bolts of photography or writing. "It's about making a living," she said. And when I asked her what else Rockport had to offer, she told me to take the back road into Camden and check out the buffaloes being raised on a farm there, which looked like Oreo cookies. "Really," she insisted, "go look at the Belted Galloways. They're hysterical."

Before driving on, though, I wanted to see what was happening in the other buildings across the street, one of which was an informal restaurant, a kind of coffee shop you might find near any college campus. There was also the Rockport Opera House, staging in its season everything from hootenanny to *Hamlet.* The only other store with a public face was called Le Paon, owned by Leslie and Carlton Leavitt. They had just opened this store to sell the furniture that Carlton builds in his shop in Monson, Maine, hand-painted and designed in a style suggestive of that in vogue in eighteenth-century Europe. The store was already a success after only twelve weeks, despite the absence of street traffic in tiny Rockport. The building itself is so attractive and beautifully set, perched above a curving road before the water, that at night especially, when the store's decorative interior is artfully lit, the passing motorist is left with the image of a mise-en-scene.

CAMDEN

A t a fork in the road a few hundred feet beyond the Workshop, I followed the right turn, taking one of several back roads that lead into Camden. In due course, I passed a spread that gives new meaning to the term "gentleman's farm," and sure enough, there they stood: enormous black buffaloes with wide white stripes circling their midsections, the funniest-looking critters I'd seen for quite a spell. A mile or so out of Rockport, I turned right again on Bay View Road, and was treated to a breathtaking display of old-line affluence over the remainder of my ride into Camden, each home and estate more elegant than the one before. This road enters Camden at the quiet end of the harbor, where a chic inn occupies a privileged solitary spot, the other local lodgings for the most part being found along Route 1 at the opposite end of town on the way to Lincolnville Beach.

The Camden Harbor Inn, first opened in 1874, recently underwent a complete renovation. The inn now has a spacious dining room offering a full menu and many lovely guest rooms with balconies, and is on the pricey side by Maine standards, but not necessarily by Camden's. Whether for over-nighters or day-trippers, during the summer months and shoulder season alike, there is no hotter destination than Camden in the whole state, with the possible exception of Kennebunkport when the First Family is in res-idence at Walker Point. The desk clerk at the inn was a man named Bill, a grade-school teacher most of the year, and a recent transplant to the area. "After three years," he volunteered, "the tourists are starting to get to me." Then, however, as if to release himself from the power of negative thinking, he added, "but the town still isn't too commercial."

Well, if Camden isn't too commercial, I don't know what is. My visit took me there during the end of August, and the town was still virtually overrun with tourists. Furthermore, a great many of the shops and businesses exist for the sole purpose of catering to the consumer whims of visitors. And the traffic—well, I don't want to go off on that tirade again. A friend I talked with who has a shop on Main Street put it this way: "Camden is a great town for a business, but I wouldn't want to live here." Residents like Bill, the teacher, are really caught in a bind, I guess. They move to a place like Camden because of its undeniable charm and sophistication, the same qual-ities that draw tourists by the thousands, who for the most part can't or don't stay long enough to do more than have a rushed and probably medi-ocre meal, and make a few purchases. The kind of tourism you see in Camden strikes me as boring at best, and downright antisocial at worst, with most human encounters being mediated exclusively through the mar-ketplace. If I were a bureaucrat in Augusta concerned with impact of tourism on the quality of life in Maine, I would want to study one single question in particular: How do you keep a town with Camden's attractions from being overrun, and ultimately ruined, by too much popularity?

That being said, I did find a few shops—an art gallery, a sporting-goods store, and a bakery—that stimulated more interest than disdain during my romp in Camden. Harbor Square is the name of the two-story, multiroom gallery where the art—most of which didn't say much to me personally—is displayed with a touch of curatorial taste and imagination, so that the two or three pieces I did fancy were easy to spot and appreciate. Maine Sport has some of the magic of L.L. Bean, but is limited strictly to sporting goods and apparel. "Work hard," the sign said in the Camden Bakery, "so the angels will relax." I didn't get that, but the slice of carrot cake with creamy butter icing that I ate at the counter was right up there with the best I've ever sampled—and I consider myself a carrot cake connoisseur. The round loaf of rye bread I took home—made in part with mashed potatoes, if I heard correctly—was equally delicious.

Down on Sharp's Wharf, Camden's slightly honkytonk touristic core, a half-dozen booths were set up where interested parties could sign on for Windjammer cruises. I learned from the representative for the good ship *Appledore* that most of Camden's schooners are termed "windjammers," even though they possess full engine power in addition to sails. The smaller schooners are day sailers, while larger boats go out for several days on end. To visit a few of the stately B-and-Bs that line Route 1 on the northern end of town, I decided to walk rather than fight the traffic, especially since I would have to stop frequently and then struggle to get back in the flow. In contrast to the hubbub of the town center, the northern, residential neighborhood is shady and peaceful, though the drone of rubber spinning over Route 1 asphalt never ceases on summer days. Walking, I found, was an intimate way of seeing without necessarily going into the many very large homes here that have been converted to B-and-Bs. Each inn—the Mansard Manor, the Hawthorn Inn, and, of course, the little stone castle called Norumbega—seemed a paradigm of elegance and comfort. There were homes hidden from sight that also sparked my curiosity, because you know that when a driveway runs for more than 300 feet and then curves from view, there must be something pretty stunning at the other end of it. Whitehall Inn, here on High Street, as this stretch of Route 1 is known locally, is one of those larger, traditional Maine roadhouses that exercise a perennial appeal.

CAMDEN STATE PARK AND LINCOLNVILLE BEACH

As if by some mandate from on high, the crowds and traffic thin out considerably beyond Camden, and the drive to Belfast can be made most times of the year more or less at an explorer's pace. I can suggest three potential points of interest along this route, though I am sure there are many more. The first is Camden Hills State Park. The park, in the Meguntacook mountain range, is located a mile and a half north of Camden, and offers the possibilities of camping, picnicking, and some relatively nonstrenuous hiking up to such peaks as Mount Battie, which can also be reached by a service road. My son and I enjoyed a Cub Scout campover here one springtime a few years back; sites, however, are limited and in great demand, and you must get there early in the day if you expect to spend the night. Lincolnville Beach is an unexpected public strand about midway between Camden and Belfast right on Route 1. The beach is serviced by the Lobster Pound—a moderately priced, informal, and cavernous restaurant in the best tradition of Maine's shoreside seafood restaurants. Lincolnville Center can be found several miles inland along Route 173, and this entire area is a magnet for artists, many of whom are quite famous, but whose studios are seldom open to the public.

A few miles south of Belfast, I discovered that a new Mexican restaurant had sprung up on Route 1 since the last time I'd driven this way less than a month before. Frankly, I'm a sucker for Mexican food, but I'd been burned a couple of times at a few eateries in Maine that claimed to serve south-of-the-border cuisine, and where the food tasted wholesome enough, but not even close to Latino. Dos Amigos, on the other hand, seems to be headed in the right direction. I tried a combo plate, and the only real disappointment was the green chili soup, which tasted something like canned brown gravy. The rest of the platter, from the refried beans to the salsa for the taco chips, had that intangible something in consistency and flavor that rang the right set of bells in my palate. Also, I was out of there for less than ten bucks, including tip and a Dos Equis beer, and I was full.

BELFAST

I guess Belfast is about my favorite town along Penobscot Bay's western shore. For one thing, it's not a place you have to go through to get somewhere else. Yet Belfast is surprisingly large when you consider its relative distance from the region's principal coastal road. Some of the town's development stems from the success of the shipbuilding industry here during the 1800s. But Belfast also possesses the Belfast and Moosehead Lake Railroad, which has carried freight and passengers some thirty miles inland to Burnham Junction since 1870. The railroad is an anachronism along the coast, and now something of an attraction for tourists and train buffs. The line's unusual preservation resulted from Belfast's having had—with its railroad in place—the means to transport large quantities of grain to a giant poultry industry that developed in the Maine interior during the Depression, when cheap land and labor were available throughout the state.

Ultimately the chicken business failed in Maine, because even cheap labor can't compete with the mechanized innovations that have swept through the poultry industry since the 1970s. But poultry hung on in Maine, at least until quite recently, in the vicinity of Belfast, and consequently so did this unique short-line railroad. And the town, of course, grew in proportion. Belfast's long, shop-lined streets are today undergoing rapid gentrification as the local residential base has begun to shift in recent years from native townspeople employed by a traditional economy to entrepreneurs and professionals who have migrated here, discovering in Belfast one of the last frontiers along the Maine coast. New shops have names that use words like "goose," "coyote," and "Canterbury" to reflect the artsy, New Age emphasis on the commodities of personal comfort as something akin to objects of love or erudition. The reader who wishes to flip back to chapter 8, on Moosehead Lake, might be amused to compare the fliers I saw in the pizza shop in Guilford with those on a café bulletin board in Belfast advertising West African dance and drum workshops and classes in T'ai Chi Ch'uan.

On the other hand, the roughneck element has yet to totally surrender its claim to the streets of this former blue-collar seaport. Pockets here and there of restless youths hanging out and drawing attention to themselves by revving the engines of their old coupes and pickups suggest not menace but the boredom of the young trapped between their backwater roots and the inevitable shock that occurs when new wealth and new ways are introduced by outside forces into a once-homogeneous community. Shades of the old wharfside culture are retained at Jack's Place, a tavern with a sign on the door listing "9 Bar Rules":

1. One fight, permanently barred, no exceptions.
2. No foul language.
3. No horsing around.
4. No weapons of any kind.

5. No smoking or drinking on dance floor.
6. No bare feet.
7. Twice removed from bar, not allowed back.
8. ID required.
9. When shut-off, you must leave.

An almost carnival atmosphere exists on Route 1 between Belfast and Stockton Springs, especially on weekends when the weather permits. Along with the usual complement of gift and craft shops are several fields where permanent flea markets have been mounted. The Route 1 flea markets in general are the retail centers for items purchased at wholesale prices at local lawn sales and auctions. But you can still find good bargains at these markets, since markups tend to be reasonable, and the merchants as a rule are less interested in big killings from single items than they are in a quick turnover of goods, making their money on volume. I will also point out Nickerson's Tavern, just outside of Searsport, not because I have eaten there, but on the strength of a credible recommendation.

Searsport is a small village that seems to boast yet another genteel shop each time I drive through. When I stopped one Sunday in late summer to take a closer look at the town, everything was closed except for the local convenience market. Of note, I saw a bakery, a tavern, and several shops selling quality goods, and four or five very elegant-looking B-and-Bs just north of town. Stockton Springs, however, is off the main route, and is a village of the past. At its slightly widened center, a few old wooden buildings stand like architectural elders guarding memories of more active days. Near the village center, I paid a call on the Hichborn Inn, a Victorian home newly restored by Bruce Suppes and meant to appeal to an upscale B-and-B crowd. Judging from the workmanship and decor in the parlors and guest rooms, I would say Bruce is a perfectionist and a good innkeeper as well. He and his wife, Nancy, serve full gourmet breakfasts on an enclosed porch that is very bright and inviting, and frankly the $70 asking price for double accommodations with breakfast seems very reasonable on the strength of the ambience alone.

A few other attractions in the Stockton Springs' area are worthy of mention. The Book Barn on East Main Street offers an immense collection of secondhand books, and Cape Jellison, beyond the village, is the site of earthworks from old Fort Pownall, where the British for a time held their line against the French in New England. There, at Fort Point, the state maintains a park suitable for fishing and picnicking. Our itinerary turns northward here on Route 1A, and returns to the opposite side of Penobscot Bay at the island of Verona.

IIIIIIIIIIIIIIII ■ IIIIIIIIIIIIIIII

INFORMATION ■ *Rockland Area Chamber of Commerce* (596-0376), P.O. Box 508, Rockland 04841. ■ *Rockport-Camden-Lincolnville Chamber of Commerce* (236-4404), P.O. Box 919, Camden 04843. "A Studio Guide of Artists and Craftspeople" is available for the Camden area. The brochure contains twenty-eight local listings; for further information, contact Laurie Adams (236-4023). ■ *Belfast Area Chamber of Commerce* (338-2896), Belfast 04919. ■ *Searsport Chamber of Commerce* (lists no phone), Searsport 04974.

ROCKLAND

LODGINGS ■ *Strawberry Hill Motor Court* (594-5462), Glen Cove. Just north of Rockland.

FOOD ■ *A Touch of Class* (594-9410), 410 Main St. The only café in town.

SHOPS ■ *The Store* (594-9246), 435 Main St. Gourmet kitchenware. ■ *Worldly Goods* (594-2145), 373 Main St. An emporium that sells tasteful crafts and gifts.

SPECIAL ■ *Farnsworth Museum and Homestead* (596-6457), 19 Elm St. Open year-round, though closed Mondays from October 1 to May 31. ■ *Shore Village Museum* (594-4950), 104 Limerick St. A lighthouse and Civil War museum, open from June 1 to October 15 daily from 10:00 A.M. to 4:00 P.M. and by appointment throughout the rest of the year.

ROCKPORT

LODGINGS ■ *Samoset Resort* (594-2511), Waldo Ave. A big and popular resort that bills itself as "the Pebble Beach of the East." ■ *Sign of the Unicorn Guest House* (236-8789), 191 Beauchamp Ave. On a quiet lane overlooking Rockport Harbor.

CAMPING ■ *Megunticook by the Sea* (594-2428), Route 1, three miles north of Rockland. Campsites with ocean views. ■ *Robert's Roost Campground* (236-2498), in West Rockport on Route 90, the shortcut to Camden.

FOOD ■ *The Sail Loft* (236-2330), Public Landing. Many knowledgeable diners put this restaurant on their lists of favorites in Maine.

SHOPS ■ *Le Paon* (236-2328), 23 Main St. Traditional painted furnishings. ■ *The Maine Photographic Gallery* (236-4788), Main St. The second floor of the Maine Photographic Workshop, where classes are staffed "by the world's greatest photographers." ■ *The Maine Coast Artists Gallery* (236-2875), Russell Ave. A nonprofit art center exhibiting the work of artists working in Maine.

CAMDEN

LODGINGS ■ *Camden Harbor Inn* (236-4200), 83 Bayview St. Soon to be open only during the season. ■ *Whitehall Inn* (236-3391), High St. A full-service inn, open year-round.

(A brochure listing Camden's many B-and-Bs is available through the Bed and Breakfast Society of Camden, P.O. Box 1103, Camden 04843.)

FOOD ■ *Cassoulet* (236-6304), 31 Elm St. Continental country cooking, as the name implies. ■ *The Belmont* (236-8053), 6 Belmont Ave. New American food.

(Both of the above restaurants are favorites of the president of Colby College and his wife, who recommended them to me.)

CAMPING ■ *Camden Hills State Park* (236-3109), Rte. 1. Camping season extends from May 15 to October 15, and sites tend to fill up by 3:00 P.M. during July and August.

SHOPS ■ *Camden Home Bakery* (236-2661), Mechanic St. The real McCoy. ■ *Harbor Square Gallery* (236-8700), One Harbor Square. Owned and run by goldsmith Tom Donovan. ■ *Maine Sport* (236-8797), 24 Main St. Sporting goodies.

SPECIAL ▪ The *Appledore* (236-8353), Sharp's Wharf. This and other "windjammers" offer day and overnight sails from Camden Harbor.

LINCOLNVILLE

LODGINGS ▪ *The Sprouter Inn* (789-5171), Rte. 1. Across from the beach.

CAMPING ▪ *The Old Massachusetts Homestead Campground* (789-5135), two miles north of Lincolnville Beach. Wooded sites on a circa-1718 homestead.

FOOD ▪ *The Lobster Pound* (789-5550), Rte. 1. A bayside seafood restaurant.

BELFAST

LODGINGS ▪ *The Hiram Alden Inn* (338-2151), 19 Church St. Five-minute walk to downtown Belfast; open year-round. ▪ *The Horatio Johnson House* (338-5153), 36 Church St. ▪ *Fiddler Green Farm* (338-3568), Rte. 52 on the outskirts of Belfast. A working farm where organic wheat, fruit, and vegetables are grown.

RESTAURANTS ▪ *Belfast Café* (338-2949), 90 Main St. An attractive local hangout.

SHOPS ▪ *The Fertile Mind Bookshop* (338-2498), 13 Main St. Book dealers in the old tradition.

SPECIAL ▪ *Belfast and Moosehead Lake Railroad* (338-2330). Some passenger service is available to Brooks, generally on weekends.

11

ON THOREAU'S TRAIL

BANGOR TO BAXTER STATE PARK AND BACK TO
BUCKSPORT VIA SECONDARY ROUTES THAT FOLLOW
THE PENOBSCOT RIVER

On my way to Bangor about six-thirty one Saturday morning, I turned up Route 1A from Stockton Springs, trying to connect some vague and melancholy emotion in my own soul with the image of another man who had once passed this way. His admirers refer to him with familiarity and affection as Henry David, though in truth he was christened David Henry. He made the name switch himself both because it suited his stubborn fancy and because he was called Henry at home so as not to be confused with an uncle for whom he'd been named. Almost a century and a half ago, Thoreau had his own reasons for traveling up the Penobscot River, and he fashioned an itinerary suitable to his metaphysical and botanical inclinations. He traveled by several means: rail, steamer, ferry, stagecoach, bateau, canoe—and a good deal on foot. My own journey was to be considerably more constrained on this occasion, confined mostly to my trusty Jeep Cherokee, and riding the margins, not the center, of the Penobscot River.

Pretty little Frankfort was the place where I made my first pit stop. The village was the picture of a colonial river town. On one end, spanning a tributary that flows into the Penobscot, was a small suspension bridge painted green—the scale and perhaps the vintage, for all I knew, of the early steel bridges designed by Thomas Paine. On the other end, outside an old white church, a sign proclaimed a turkey dinner that evening. In between was a general store where a man near me at the counter was sorting through a mound of lottery tickets. "Ever win anything?" I asked him. "Sure," he said, "all the time." "Well, are you about even?" I persisted. "Not too far off," he replied. "I won $800 once." "How about this town?" I wanted to know. "How'd it get its name?" "I haven't got a clue," he said, and then, as an afterthought, he looked up at me and grinned. "I wasn't around then."

Winterport was the next town up river, and the homes here looked like relics of a past when the word *port* in a town's name had some teeth to it. A restaurant called the Stew Pot appeared promising, just the right image for these cooling pre-autumn days, what with the garden filled with potatoes, turnips, carrots, onions, and parsnips just waiting to be chopped up and dropped into a simmering cast-iron kettle with a good rump of beef. Well, actually, the cooling days had lapsed for the moment into the category of things once and future. Indian summer had bloomed a week after Labor Day, and now the weather had turned summer-hot again. That first "killing frost" can't be too far off, though, I thought, and the stew pot will soon be a common sight at dinnertime in our house.

Bangor's urban spread begins a few miles from the small city's downtown district. And all the familiar faces, from Big Mac to Mack Truck, are there to greet you as you drive down the strip. Downtown, on the other hand, has a storybook Victorian look about it, and if you were going to build a little river city in scale for the elaborate train set you run down in the basement, Bangor would be the perfect model. The town has a symmetry and balance that is almost fanciful in the best tradition of the elaborate sets of Hollywood and Disneyland. Bangor is also remarkably clean and uncluttered, and very quiet just before 9:00 A.M. on a Saturday—a good time to visit if you want to watch a town like this wake up on a beautiful weekend morning.

My initial impulse, however, was to skirt the downtown section, driving first to the old wharf where pleasure craft have replaced the scows and barkentines that once bobbed there when Bangor was the biggest lumber port in the world. But as Thoreau had predicted in the journals of his tramps through the Maine woods when, as early as 1846, hardly a great white pine still stood, there would be in due course little forest remaining to tempt the woodcutter's ax; by 1880 the lumber boom was over and pulp mills had replaced sawmills up and down the river. Leaving the abandoned water-front, I then drove up the hills on the south end of town and admired the remains of the big wooden mansions and the old factory-town-style wood-frame apartment buildings that marked this as Bangor's working-class neighborhood. Only then did I return to make a circuit of the downtown streets.

I followed northward the street I'd entered town on, starting near the Greyhound station, on past where it branches into a horseshoe loop of one-way traffic that doubles back on itself, encircling an island of stores and a segment of Kenduskeag Stream that runs beside a small park shaped like a midway. Then I returned and parked opposite the bus station, having liked what I'd seen, and deciding to repeat the circuit on foot. Mostly I wanted to ferret out a few interesting shops and just get a feel for the town. At the end of Broad Street I spent some time looking into the window of the Standard Boot Shop, which showcased a display of workingman's boots: steel-toed, rubber, hiking. Half a block away on something called Market Square, I spotted the Phenix (*sic*) Inn, a comfortable, downtown hotel with thirty-six rooms, which caters primarily to visiting businesspeople. Concierge Kim Shane showed me a large, nicely decorated room, termed a suite, with a four-poster bed that rents for $70 a night. Other rooms range from $53 to $63, depending on the number of persons and the size of the bed. She also volunteered the names of a few restaurants that the hotel recommends to its guests, like Sequino's, back on the strip, for Italian food, or the nearby Panda Garden, a Chinese place that had just opened.

I discovered another restaurant that appealed to my imagination, Vincetta's La Cucina, in a storefront at 199 Harlow Street, but of course the place was still closed this early in the day. As I looped the outer ring of streets, I passed a store that sold big, black cast-iron cookstoves trimmed in nickel; one brand, Wood & Bishop, is actually manufactured in Bangor. When I came to the little park beside the Kenduskeag, I walked to one end to identify the statue. It was of Hannibal Hamlin, Lincoln's politically innocuous vice-president during his first term, and a "Citizen of Bangor," as the inscription proclaimed. On Central Street, a large ground-floor space in a long building that may at one time have housed an old "five-and-dime" is now a dance club open nights from Friday through Sunday; contests for cash prizes include "dirty dancing" and "sexiest outfit." Across the street is Gourmet to Go, a fancy carry-out with a "Pick Your Picnic" menu featuring such items as poached salmon, cold lemon-fried chicken, a pâté, and a fruit and cheese plate, all priced from $5 to $7.50, plus lots of exotic edibles on the shelves.

A few homeless men and women were about the only other pedestrians I saw on the Bangor streets until around ten o'clock that Saturday morning. On the other hand, the small bus station was full, which is to be expected anyplace where the "Dog" is the only form of mass transit. Bangor did have a taxicab, though, a rare enough sight in a town this size. The remainder of the action that morning was at the Main Street Restaurant, up the street from the bus station and across from the Bangor Opera House. It was a breakfast crowd, a cross-section of folk out and about early for whatever reason. I ate there and had a pretty fair breakfast, a cheese-and-sausage omelette, for about four bucks.

The ride upstream on this same side of the Penobscot continues along Route 2, and Orono—home of the University of Maine—is only about eight miles above Bangor. The U. of M. campus is immense and, while not exactly ugly, very institutional in the Maine tradition of keeping the frills to a minimum where the public purse is concerned. In contrast, while passing through the small Orono village center, I'd seen a bit of plumage in a boutique called Material Comfort—bright, almost gaudy New Age clothes; modern hippie costumes, but very tailored and far from the hand-me-down price tags of the vaunted sixties. Old Town, above Orono, is still very much a mill town, the canoe bearing the town's name being one of its most famous products. One of our first acts as a family when we moved to Maine was to build a rack for the pickup, then drive to Old Town and buy a canoe right from the factory showroom; I'm not sure we saved any money, but the experience was fun.

Old Town is also the home of the Penobscot Nation, descendants of the tribe who called all of Maine between the Kennebec and the Penobscot their home before the Europeans came, but who have occupied Indian Island here for many generations. Over breakfast back in Bangor, I'd read an article in the local newspaper that marked the tenth anniversary of the latest "treaty" between the Indians and the federal government in Washington. The terms of the deal called for Maine's Indians to relinquish their claim to two-thirds of the state's territory in exchange for slightly more than $80 million. Now, a decade later, Native American activists were claiming they'd been swindled once again. Another article in the same paper referred to former "American Bandstand" host Dick Clark's latest venture to build a rock-and-roll theme park in Memphis at a cost of $200 million.

The juxtaposition of the two stories put the Indian claim into a sympathetic context for me, and seemed to demonstrate that when it came to dealing with the redman, the white man hadn't lost his penchant for making a sweet real-estate deal.

In the same article about the Penobscots, a tribe member was quoted, saying in effect that tourists come to Indian Island and stare at the residents as if they were "animals in a zoo." When I crossed the bridge onto the "reservation" (the Indians call it a sovereign nation), I had this injunction very much in mind. Sure, I wanted to see what the place was like both to distinguish it from and relate it to my own reality, which is the whole reason for traveling anywhere away from your own hearth. My only concrete business, however, was to look for the gravesite of Joe Polis, the man who guided Thoreau and his companion on one of the poet-naturalist's Maine adventures.

Ralph Waldo Emerson, delivering Thoreau's eulogy, faulted his friend for lacking "tenderness" (which translates as something between politeness and social sensitivity), and by extension, some critics have characterized as bigoted Thoreau's treatment of Indians in his writings. Yet Polis is one of the few Native Americans who appears in our literature as a credible human being, rather than a romantic or racist caricature. Thoreau's Polis is a consummate woodsman, a genuine Indian nationalist, and also bit of a rascal. Thoreau was no diplomat, and neither was he skilled in the genteel art of "making nice" like his remarkable mentor, the great bard of Concord. His art was candor. He took the persona that Polis presented him on face value, and did not attempt to discover the "noble savage" within. In the end, though he and his guide came from two different and perhaps incompatible worlds, after reading Thoreau's *Maine Woods*, you get the sense that the two men arrived at some kind of mutual understanding, which is more than you can say about most human encounters, whether between intimates or strangers.

I found a graveyard not far over the bridge when I crossed onto Indian Island. On one side of the narrow road was a wooden church, like the one on this island in which the marriage of the Baron de Castin to the daughter of a Penobscot sagamore took place in the seventeenth century. Castin, a landed knight from France, assimilated himself to the Indian life, and became a great warrior chieftain in his own right during the French and British wars that ravaged New England from 1689 to 1763. Opposite the church, a respectfully tended burial ground held the remains of folk more recently departed. More than half of the markers were simple wooden crosses, contoured two-by-fours painted white, the names neatly lettered in black. A few of the crosses were rotten in places, indicating perhaps that there were no longer any descendents of the deceased left to attend the family plot.

To find Polis's grave, hit or miss, in this small forest of granite and wood, would have taken some doing. But some women were walking in the cemetery and I asked one if she might know the grave's whereabouts. Sounded familiar, but she couldn't really recall the name. She was a handsome woman, white-haired and full of vitality, but not one necessarily given to keeping up on the tribal lore. But she seemed to know the man working on a building at one edge of the graveyard, and she posed the question to him. He was a big man who looked something like Anthony Quinn, and oh yes, the knew about old Joe Polis. He was down here in this corner. "Why," the man said with good humor and intended irony, while waving his hands holy-roller style above his head, "he visited me only last night." So I looked around the corner he'd indicated, but could find no physical evidence that Joe Polis's spirit resided in that vicinity. I did find the marker of Louis Sockalexis, who'd played baseball for Holy Cross and later with Cleveland in the major leagues around the turn of the century. Most of the names I read were clearly Anglicized, with a few exceptions like Chief Poolaw, the death date still blank beside his name, and his Princess Watawasco, who died in 1969.

Presumably, after rethinking his position, the large man called out to me, "Say, I think old Joe's maybe in the small cemetery up there," and he pointed to a place I'd already passed. Thanking him, I drove back the way I'd come, and sure enough, there it was, a small granite marker with a carved urn on top. Joseph Polis died a relatively young man in 1861, a year before Thoreau died of tuberculosis at age forty-four. On the little road, more than one tour bus passed me by, originating from where I do not know, but the darkened glass of the bus windows did convey the image of passengers staring out without being seen, a lack of visual accountability on the part of the looker.

I too followed in the path of the bus, in the sense that I drove around many streets to satisfy my own curiosity. Most people I saw ignored me; a few, whose eyes met mine, conveyed with their expressions a slight annoyance at being intruded upon. Mostly, people lived in homes of three or four different styles, on moderate plots of ground. Thoreau had observed with some disapproval that the homes on Indian Island in his day were all "backside and woodshed"; but there was nothing of the cottager in the Indian, and no need to mirror a formal domesticity that was foreign to him. Many of the homes here still fit Thoreau's description; some are what Mainers call FHA homes—stark, rectilinear boxes, devoid of trim and detail. Still others reflect a preference for genuine architectural self-consciousness in their design and landscaping. A large section of the island was wooded and did not seem to be inhabited. Along one back road, two young "braves," accompanied by a hound, walked along the shoulder, their .22 rifles pointed at the ground as they scouted the treeline with their eyes.

Route 2 crosses the Penobscot at Old Town and follows the opposite bank. Route 116 (reached via short segments of routes 43 and 16) stays to the left bank, and the ride toward Howland and West Endfield was long and relaxing, with nothing in particular beyond the beauties of nature and a faded blue sky to distract my eye that day. A week into September, the roadside trees were already beginning to show their colors; drying clumps of fern lit the fields with autumn bouquets of gold and brown. For the most part, the river is not in view, while the homes are plentiful and varied, but the farms are few. My immediate destination was Lincoln, where I planned to cross the river to pick up Route 2 again and make for Mattawamkeag, intending to camp there for the night. I had placed a call to Baxter State Park earlier in the week and was told that my chances of finding a campsite there were slim for Saturday night. So I had decided to take potluck at Mattawamkeag Wilderness Park, about an hour's ride south of Baxter. At Mattawamkeag I would set up my tent when I arrived in the afternoon, and then complete the drive to Baxter for a short visit before dark.

In Lincoln, at a store called Steak & Stuff, I bought a sandwich for lunch, and two thick center-cut pork chops, plus a split of dry blueberry wine for dinner. Then I drove on to the Mattawamkeag Park, run by the local county, not the state. To reach the park, you must follow the sign from the middle of Mattawamkeag village, and drive over nine miles of narrow dirt road, through lumber-company lands, accompanied a good part of the way by the Mattawamkeag River. There are forty-plus campsites at this park, and since it was virtually empty, I had my choice. The mosquitoes, unfortunately, had not gotten the word that their season was over. They swarmed around me as I set up my tent, making me regret that I had come here. But the $8.50 site fee (which can include up to six persons) was nonrefundable, and the long ride in had already eaten up some of the time I wanted to spend at Baxter, so I decided to stick it out. And even though the temperature must have been nearly ninety degrees, I gathered fallen and rotted wood and chopped it to size for the campsite fireplace. I piled my reserve wood next to the grill, and laid out other sticks and paper teepee style, so that all I needed to do was strike a match and produce a smoky fire to discourage the bugs when I returned that night.

Percival Baxter, a former Maine governor, bequeathed 200,000 acres of this region—most of it logged over since the early 1800s—to the state, and a park was created in his name. Today, with the mile-high Mount Katahdin as its glorious centerpiece, Baxter State Park is one of the nation's most splendid outdoor recreational facilities. It is also one of the most popular. Baxter is the nature lover's equivalent of Boothbay Harbor on the Fourth of July. Campsites must be reserved, in writing, months in advance of planned visits. Parking lots for the park's most popular trails and campgrounds—Roaring Brook, Abol, and Katahdin Stream—often fill up by 8:00 A.M., and remain closed until the end of the day. Other camping areas, in the park's northern sector, are in less demand, perhaps because to arrive at them adds an additional two to three hours' driving to your journey. And chances are you've come here to hike or at least be outdoors, not to spend the day touring the park in your car.

As it is, Abol is about twenty-five minutes by car from the park's southern entrance, and Katahdin Stream is another ten minutes beyond that. When I finally arrived at the park, late in the afternoon, the ranger let me drive out to Katahdin Stream, even though all three of the lower campgrounds were closed to additional traffic. It is virtually impossible, given the corduroy surface of the dirt road, to go any faster than the prescribed twenty miles an hour. When two cars confront each other going in opposite directions, one or the other scurries to the road's edge so they may both squeeze by. When I pulled into the parking space before the ranger's cabin at Katahdin Stream, I could see a dozen hikers cooling themselves in a large, clear pool of water that has been allowed to collect there for just that purpose. Like Ken Libby, with whom I talked, most of the other bathers had just descended the mountain after a full day of hiking. Ken and his party had begun at eight, climbing the Abol Trail, and by the time they reached the summit—Baxter Peak—about a hundred other people were up there, he said. They had descended to Katahdin Stream, where they would camp the night, and now Ken sat by the pool, soaking his feet after eight hours of strenuous trekking.

His account reminded me of my own experience climbing Mount Katahdin in the early seventies. My girlfriend at the time was an avid hiker, and she had turned me on to the sport over a period of time. I had climbed many trails in her company, including Mount Washington in New Hampshire's White Mountains, and so I believed I was ready to take on Baxter peak when she suggested we spend a vacation week in Maine. We stayed in a commercial campground just outside the southern gate, since we could not get a space in the park itself. But we arose early the day after our arrival, and drove off to Roaring Brook to begin our ascent. Leigh had studied the trail guides and had mapped out our course to include the Knife Edge, a rough stretch of jagged rock along a ridgeline not far below the summit. By the time we'd reached that point, I remember we were climbing hand over hand.

It wasn't until we had made the descent and driven back to our tent that I realized how exhausting the hike had been. I literally had to crawl the last ten feet from the car to my sleeping bag, where I immediately fell into a deep sleep—it being somewhere around 7:00 P.M.—and did not awake till dawn. It had taken us thirteen hours to climb Mount Katahdin, up and down, and each step was marked by beauty and excitement. From the summit, the world we viewed was a lonely, desolate place, a strong breeze blew in our faces, and all the secret powers of nature seemed to be stored in the thin, invisible air we breathed. Perhaps it is true that, among the human arts, only music can convey such power to another soul, for even today I feel the high tension of that moment, yet my mind fails to provide me with any words that could adequately express the experience.

Back at the park entrance, a gate ranger named Debbie and I tried to figure out the capacity crowd for Mount Katahdin by counting up the number of parking places available at the three major trailheads. We reckoned it at about 300 to 350 hikers a day, and for some years now Baxter has been playing to capacity crowds all summer, the season extending from Memorial Day to Columbus Day. As a resident of Maine, I entered the park gratis; out-of-state visitors pay a fee of $8, which is applied to a clean-up fund. Winter hiking and camping is allowed at Baxter under highly regulated circumstances, with permits available through application to the Park Director in Millinocket.

It was now precisely toward Millinocket that I was returning, hoping to get back to my own campsite in Mattawamkeag by sundown. Midway down the fifteen-mile-long access road that connects Baxter Park to the combined routes 157/11, I decided to stop at the trading post I'd seen on the way in. What I hadn't seen, right next door to the souvenir shop, was the Big Moose Inn, a large yellow house with a screened-in porch that I had mistaken for a private home. When I walked through the door of the inn, I couldn't believe my eyes. I could not have pictured a wilderness boarding lodge more like one of Thoreau's day than what I saw before me. I suppose if I had analyzed every detail, the picture would have been filled with a thousand anachronisms. But the overall impression—the textures, the hues, the unstudied informality and home comfort—could not have suggested greater authenticity. One end of the large downstairs room was a seating area, the rude armchairs and settees scattered like dice from a cup around a woodstove, the way people might place them in conformity with the needs of the moment. Graceful country tables and chairs occupied the remainder of the space—the dining area—and overflowed onto an enclosed veranda at the room's opposite end.

I stood at the small bar off to one side of the dining area and talked with Fredericka Boynton, who has owned the inn for ten years. She suggested that I look at the rooms upstairs, so I did, and was charmed by their tiny size. But there was nothing suffocating about them; rather, they were snug and warm, the way I pictured roadhouse rooms of stagecoach days. Fredericka told me that she leased the land the inn was on, but that the Indian Carry, a narrow strip of land we could see from a window, which separated Millinocket and Ambajejus lakes, was the only land around there—not counting the park—that did not belong to the paper companies. I told Fredericka how well her inn fitted into my Thoreau fantasy, and she remarked that she had hated reading the author as a girl. "I thought all he did was count nails and hate women. But he was just an old batch." (Maine shorthand for "bachelor.") "He was also the closest thing to a Saint Francis this country's ever produced," I added. "Or a Gandhi," said the innkeeper, having apparently, since girlhood, discovered Henry David's finer qualities.

I guess I gushed on so effusively about her inn that Fredericka invited me for dinner. If I liked the inn so well, I'd love the food, she promised. And

I could also pitch my tent, she said, in the small camping area on the grounds behind the inn. But I explained that I had already made camp elsewhere, and told her about my two pork chops and wine. So she laughed and allowed that I was well provided for. Nonetheless, I was disappointed at having to go back to buggy Mattawamkeag after discovering such an unexpected oasis of civilization only a few miles outside of Baxter.

Dusk was just transforming to darkness as I rumbled down the dirt road to where I had so prematurely erected my tent. In a minute my campfire was roaring, but the bugs had diminished to the point where they were tolerable. Still, the fire was comforting in the dark, and in minutes my baked beans and pork chops were simmering and sizzling on the burners of a camp stove. I popped the cork from the wine, and relished my simple meal. The half moon was rising in the sky just as I was about to enter my tent for the night, and the only sound was the rushing river, which was soothing and pleasing to my ears. Then I realized how much more closely my evening in the woods conformed to the experience Thoreau had written of, and how infinitely satisfied I was that the night had come to such an end.

The next morning I broke camp early and headed south, my plan being to follow the Penobscot down the east bank as far as Bucksport. In Mattawamkeag village, where the buildings give it the look of a place just come through a hurricane, I turned left onto Route 2 and drove through patchy fog till Lincoln, where I turned down Route 155. My eye had been drawn to a large pond on this road, where a teepee symbol on my map indicated the presence of a campground. As I drove, I became slightly hypnotized by the road and the passing scenery, mostly farmland, and overshot my mark, ending up on Route 188 in Burlington, a historic little corner of the countryside, judging from the many old buildings I saw. So I doubled back, and just barely spotted the honey-brown color of an adult doe a split second before the animal bolted across the front of my car. Firmly, but in control, I hit the brakes, and she lunged forward like a sprinter at the tape, just missing my front right fender by a gnat's mustache. Such accidents in Maine are not uncommon.

It was still early for Sunday morning when I found my way back to Lakeside Campground and roused Nancy Libby, one of the owners, from her apartment above the camp store. Lakeside Camping possesses a favored wedge of land on the shores of Cold Stream Pond, a stream-fed body of water with a sandy bottom. As we stood at the edge of their small but pristine beach within sight of numerous cabins that lined the shore, the hills on the opposite side giving the pond a near-alpine backdrop, Nancy told me a bit about the area. The township of Lincoln, where little Enfield is a satellite, is the biggest town in land area east of the Mississippi, she said. And Cold Stream Pond was only one of thirteen lakes in the surrounding county. But I'm sure none of the other lakes could surpass this one for pure serenity, and here I found another spot, like the Big Moose Inn, where I planned to spend a night on some future excursion.

All morning, as I drove, I had noticed that skunks in particular had had a bad night when trying to cross the road. Their dying acts were naturally to spray their assailants, albeit involuntarily under these circumstances, with that unmistakable fragrance they normally use so effectively to ward off danger. The other, more uplifting features of the drive down the Penobscot's east bank were the proximity of the river, often in view from West Enfield all the way to Brewer, and the predominance of old riverside farms, in contrast with the cottage culture that lines the opposite bank. I ate breakfast in Milford at a place called the Fantastic Restaurant—good hash but slow service—and arrived in Bucksport well before noon.

Bucksport, which overlooks Verona Island and the two channels of the Penobscot River that flow around it, certainly has the look of a town that would like to become a tourist mecca. A half-dozen stores and restaurants already reflect that hyper-colonial look that presents the form but not necessarily the substance of the past. The front drive at the genuinely old Prouty Tavern was dug up for the moment, and the inn itself was padlocked, but scheduled to reopen, I was told, in only a few weeks. Across the street, looking out on the very mouth of the Penobscot, is the Prouty Motel, a building that, were it in Brooklyn instead of Maine, would house either an Italian restaurant or an Irish funeral home. In this town, which leans a bit too heavily toward the "ye old shoppe" motif, it is the funky that seems most genuine, and the motel certainly has the best river view in town.

<hr/>

INFORMATION ■ *Bangor Chamber of Commerce* (338-2896), 519 Main St., Bangor 04401. There is also a seasonal information office at Paul Bunyon Park on Route 1A on the south edge of the city. ■ *Baxter State Park* (723-5140), c/o Reservations Clerk, 64 Balsam Dr., Millinocket 04462.

LODGINGS ▪ *The Phenix Inn* (947-3850), West Market Square, Bangor. Thirty-six rooms with private bath right in downtown Bangor, from $53 to $70, depending on number of persons and size of bed or room. ▪ *Big Moose Inn* (723-8391), P.O. Box 98, Millinocket 04462. Open May 15 to September 30 and on weekends during January and February after the lakes freeze. Eleven rooms at $38 nightly, double. A special weekend package includes two nights, two breakfasts, and two dinners for $88 per person. There are also eleven housekeeping cabins holding from four to fourteen persons. Campsites are also available, and prices for full-course dinners—everything made from scratch—range from $10 to $13. ▪ *Jed Prouty Motel* (469-3113), Main St., Bucksport.

CAMPING ▪ *Baxter State Park*. (See above.) ▪ *Mattawamkeag Wilderness Park*, (no phone), Reservations Clerk, P.O. Box 104, Mattawamkeag 04459. In addition to almost fifty campsites, the park offers ten Adirondack shelters, hiking trails, and canoeing on the Mattawamkeag River.

RESTAURANTS ▪ *The Greenhouse* (945-4040), 193 Broad St., Bangor. ▪ *Sequino's Italian Restaurant* (942-1240), 735 Maine St., Bangor. ▪ *The Bagel Shop* (947-1654), One Main St., Bangor. Kosher bakery and restaurant. ▪ *Gourmet to Go* (942-4642), 25 Central St., Bangor. ▪ *Margarita's Mexican Restaurant* (866-4863), 14 Mill Rd., Orono.

SPECIAL EVENTS ▪ *Maine Center for the Arts* (581-1755), University of Maine, Orono. Performance center building headliners in music and theater.

12

'ROUND PENOBSCOT BAY: THE EASTERN SHORE

ORLAND TO BLUE HILL

elow Bucksport, two bridges cross the Penobscot River, using Verona Island as a steppingstone to link one side of the Penobscot Bay region with the other. On the bay's western shore, I generally followed Route 1 through a string of busy harbor towns. On the eastern side, Route 1 runs well to the north of this great landmass known locally as the Blue Hill peninsula, where the roads form a mazelike network over an incomparable coastal landscape. If ever there was a locale along the coast of Maine fit for unstructured touring, this is it. The peninsula is large, and distances between villages, deceiving. The various numbered routes here crisscross each other with such remarkable illogic that only someone with a cubist's eye could see their deeper pattern. Who cares? Here, among the balmy conifers and with the omnipresent sea, you may drive for miles with no concern for time or geography, but still get your bearings without much delay when you need to.

CASTINE VIA ROUTES 175, 166, AND 166A

My mission, as always, was to wander and discover; little did I suspect during a weekend in late September that I would also be eating my way around the entire peninsula. My expectations of restaurant food in Maine are admittedly low. But I knew that there were pockets of sophistication here that would support a corresponding number of eateries where the food served would range consistently from acceptable to superior. And, of course, "acceptable" is itself far superior to "unacceptable" or "disappointing." It was in Castine, the peninsula's most cultured pearl, where I planned to spend the night, and where I first headed after turning off Route 1 onto Route 175 south.

Castine, the site of a protracted struggle between England, France, and America over which was to control northern Maine, is a town saturated with historical significance. There may be no more romantic tale associated with New England's earliest colonial days than the story of Jean Vincent de Castin, second son of a French baron, who settled here as a trader, married a sagamore's daughter, and fought for France alongside his Indian allies in the ensuing wars against Great Britain and her colonials. Castin disappeared from the annals of American history, when—no longer a young man—he returned to France to claim his baronial inheritance.

By force of habit I had followed the routes nearest the water to reach Castine, down the left bank of the Penobscot River. But since Castine is in a sense an island, the alternate routes converge just outside of town where two coves, Hatch and Wadsworth, were once linked by a canal (overgrown today) engineered by the British to ward off attack by land from the rear during their last-ditch occupation of the town at the end of the American Revolution. The imposing houses on Main Street bear testimony to Castine's long-standing cosmopolitanism. Some are manorial, others only grand; all of the timber-framed dwellings representative of the town's eighteenth- and nineteenth-century gentry. Within a few short blocks, the central street descends sharply to a small commercial district and a graceful harbor. About midway down Main Street is the Castine Inn, a small, comfortable hotel run by the cordial Margaret and Mark Hodesh. I'd noticed the inn on many prior visits to Castine, but had neither stayed nor eaten there, and I had now returned for that pleasure. There are several fine inns in Castine, but the restaurant at the Inn is commended above all others.

The day had become chilly by late afternoon, and I sat in the common room before a warming fire and chatted with Margaret and Mark. The Hodeshes became innkeepers in Castine in the mid-1980s. Mark is protective about what he calls Maine's "special quality," and he wanted the inn to retain its traditional appeal for the townspeople while at the same time remaining hospitable to discriminating guests. He accomplished this by creating an informal restaurant where the meals are consistently good and only moderately expensive. Many local residents eat here regularly, while others come only on special occasions, so, along with its complement of touring visitors, the dining room has a lively, more heterogeneous atmosphere than is often the case with seasonal restaurants.

Margaret—who is also an artist—created the terra-cotta bas-reliefs lining the inn's stairwell like stations of the cross, which memorialize local scenes. She also executed a mural of Castine on the four walls of the dining room. The mural is oriented to the compass, and various townspeople make their appearances within the respective panels according to the rounds and roles of their daily lives.

At about seven that evening, I was joined by Mark for dinner, in a dining room already filled to capacity. For an appetizer I selected smoked trout (which Mark had procured in Rockland) served with a tangy horseradish sauce. My entree was chicken pot pie. Now that may sound plebeian, but the dish was first-rate, prepared in the best tradition of good country fare. Mark ate duck—cooked to perfection—which had also tempted me but for the side dishes of turnips, red cabbage, and beets, vegetables my own garden back home was now producing in monotonous abundance. Mark then ordered a small portion of chicken and garlic stew, soaked a dinner roll in the gravy, and handed it to me. Both the bread—crusty on the outside and fluffy on the inside—and the sauce merited high praise. We took our coffee and dessert by the fireplace in the common room, and Mark pronounced the gingerbread, served with baked apple pieces and whipped cream, "a bit dry." If he is a perfectionist, it isn't a bad trait for an innkeeper/ chef to possess.

By nine I had retired to my room, a comfortable suite actually, with windows facing the moonlit harbor, and I was up the next day with the sun. A number of workingmen were already having their coffee at the corner shop down on Water Street when I walked in to get the morning paper. An early fog lay heavy over the town, curtailing visibility beyond the upright pilings of the pier and emphasizing the feeling of isolation that comes to

Maine's coastal towns with the arrival of autumn. All was quiet up and down the side streets where I strolled, admiring the village common and the old lyceum, the churches and the formal, clapboarded homes. At frequent intervals, historic signs lettered red against sober backings of gunmetal gray recalled this or that structure, citizen, or battle, these sidewalk chronicles adding detail to the story of Castine's dramatic past.

After my walk, I returned to the inn and entered the kitchen to say good-bye. Mark was slightly wounded that I wasn't staying for breakfast. He pointed to the old sign of the Fleetwood Diner, his first business back in Ann Arbor, that was hanging on the wall. It was the kind of artifact someone would pay a pretty penny for today at an auction or antique fair. In one corner of the sign, the words CORNED BEEF HASH seemed to stand at attention and salute me. I stayed my course, and decided to kill the hour before breakfast by driving around town.

A loop can be made by taking Perkins Street along the water, up to Battle Avenue, and around the cove road, returning to the town center via Spring and Water streets. Along this encirclement, the remains of barracks or houses once commandeered for officers' quarters and the ruins of many earthworks and entrenchments vividly attest to Castine's role as a fortified town, frequently under the rule of this or that military banner—French, British, or American—during the action-packed episodes of its colorful past. The last contest for control of Castine occurred during the War of 1812, when the town was again occupied by the British. The most instructive campaign, however, was a naval duel between American forces and the redcoats; the latter, despite their defeat at Yorktown, continued to hold Castine as the legitimate boundary between the original Thirteen Colonies and what had once been French but was now British Canada. The American flotilla that arrived to liberate Castine from British military occupation was led by men with illustrious names: Saltonstall, Wadsworth (grandfather of Henry Wadsworth Longfellow), and Revere among them. After a bungled siege by sea, a few failed landings, and a retreat up the Penobscot River, where the American fleet was deliberately scuttled to avoid its falling into the enemy's hands, General Saltonstall and Paul Revere were court-martialed for cowardice on their return to Boston. Saltonstall was cashiered, but Revere, who had been commander of ordnance during the expedition, was exonerated.

You will see other attractive inns as you skirt Castine's streets: the Pentagoet, across from the Castine Inn; Holiday House, by the water; and the Manor, on a wooded hill not far from the lighthouse. There is the Wilson Museum, with its collection of prehistoric artifacts and mineral specimens, and, on the same grounds, Perkins House, the town's oldest building, also open to the public. Down from these, on Perkins Street, is a narrow dirt road that leads to Fort Madison, an earthwork that I climbed to the top, from where I faced the sea patiently to scan the horizon as if with an imaginary spyglass held to my eye. Other mounds and entrenchments facing the canal off the Wadsworth Cove Road lie over lands that are so open and unobstructed that it is easy to imagine the encampments and even the skirmishes that took place there. Coming back around Water Street and in the near vicinity of its intersection with Main Street, there is a three-story brick domicile facing the harbor. The owner apparently fancies the place a noteworthy architectural creation; and so it might be in New York's SoHo or Greenwich Village. Here the plain, boxlike structure is controversial and, in my opinion, seems a willful act of obtuseness or even hostility, given the town's dominant antique appearance. As for Mark's hash, back at the inn, it was definitely a plate-cleaner—and he gave me the recipe, which wasn't a bad souvenir to be taking from a town like Castine.

THE BROOKVILLES AND CAPE ROSIER VIA ROUTES 166, 199, 175, AND 176

Leaving Castine, I followed the road up one side of the Bagaduce River and down the other, turning onto Route 176 at the sign to Brooksville, which is also the gateway to remote Cape Rosier. What you encounter here, topographically, is first one larger circle of land where the loop road, Route 176, skirts the periphery and passes through each of the four Brooksville villages in its turn. On the far side of this virtual island, between West and South Brooksville, a sign indicates the way to the Holbrook Sanctuary over a constricted, badly paved road that enters onto Cape Rosier, the second and smaller circle of land attached to the larger mass by a narrow isthmus. All that morning I had been feeling particularly good about being in this place, with not another car on the road. As I turned onto the even more primitive road that enters the Holdbrook Sanctuary, I fantasized about the maximum number of miles it might be possible to drive in Maine without passing another car, or at least avoiding anything you might be able to designate as "traffic." How much balm, I mused, can one poor soul take?

The Holbrook Sanctuary, some 1,200 acres of coastal woodlands, was donated to the state of Maine by a former resident, Anita Harris, who wished "to preserve for the future a piece of the unspoiled Maine that I used to know." The sanctuary is for people to use, however, and there are picnic areas, a boat launch, hiking trails, some beautiful prospects over the bay, and nature walks conducted by rangers like Sami Gray, who was on duty at the station that morning, scraping paint from the clapboards on the garage. She told me about Miss Harris, and said she agreed in general with her prohibitions against altering the sanctuary in any way, including selective woodcutting. Sometimes, Sami said, these strictures created a bit of inconvenience, but she too was suspicious of the commercial trend infiltrating public forest management. And she didn't understand some foresters, she said, like a man she knew at a big paper mill on upper Penobscot Bay. He told her, "Come out with us. You'll see we aren't doing bad things." "But I know they are," she said with conviction that was probably as sound as it was touching.

On I drove around wild Cape Rosier, seeing if I could remember where Scott and Helen Nearing had built their stone homestead after migrating from Vermont to Maine about thirty years ago. The Nearings, of course, are the mentors of the "good life" philosophy, authors of several books on the subject, primers in a way for practitioners of self-sufficiency who wish to lead long, healthy, productive, and useful lives. Scott, who died a few years back at the age of one hundred—an age Helen may yet herself attain—lived a full life as a college professor and socialist organizer, before packing it in, and with Helen, making a new life producing maple syrup in Vermont. Development pushed the Nearings out of Vermont, and you can almost see the highly disciplined pair studying their maps of the Maine coast, searching for a place the crowds were likely to avoid. Cape Rosier fulfilled that criterion for years, and is only now, as I gathered from certain signs, being carved up into shorefront real estate.

Scott was already around seventy-five when they settled in Maine, where blueberries instead of maple syrup were to be their cash crop. I had visited the Nearings' home, as many of their admirers had over the years, twice, the first time when Scott was still alive. I met and talked with Helen, but only saw Scott, then ninety-six, first as a distant figure down in the cove, shoveling seaweed for their garden into the back of his truck, and later in the dooryard, seated in the truck's passenger seat, a stocking cap pulled down over his ears and framing a face as deeply gnarled as a burl on an old oak tree.

The next time I visited the Nearing homestead, Scott had passed on. My wife and I and another couple—friends I would be staying with later that night in Stonington—sat with Helen in her living room as she told us the story of Scott's death. It was a moving account, for he had himself made the decision to die like an ancient Indian might have when he knew the end had come. At first, Scott cut his food consumption to only broth, and then to just water, and finally, life faded from him as if he had fallen asleep. Helen gave the account without sentiment, and we all wept, unable to contain the emotions that erupt at such moments of genuine inspiration and transcendence.

On this latest visit to Cape Rosier, I could not find the Nearing house, though I'd heard that Helen was no longer living there, and the place had been turned into a nonprofit center to continue their work. I saw only two commercial entities that invited intrusions, but chose to make a single call, at the Hiram Blake Camp, leaving the wreathmaker for another visit. A large, rustic cottage houses the camp's dining room and office, and some dozen cabins line the shore fronting the bay. Lucy Venno is, by her own admission, the camp's matriarch. She is a small but sturdy woman over eighty, whom I encountered in the lodge, where she was looking over "all the books people read here this summer," collected presumably from the cabins and now spread out on a table before her. It was Lucy's father, Hiram, who "first took in summer people," she said, though the land had originally belonged to her great-grandfather Blake. When I told her where I lived in Maine, she said she herself had lived in nearby Newcastle, in the rectory of the Episcopal church, where her husband had served as minister. I looked into only one cabin, which had a stone fireplace and was spacious, airy, comfortably furnished, and very inviting in every way. Inexplicably, according to both Lucy and her daughter-in-law, Sandy—who serves as camp manager—there are guests who cancel their reservations when they see how simple everything is here. On the other hand, reservations at the camp for the high season are booked up a year or more in advance, because many of the same families return year after year. Like Miss Harris's sanctuary, the Hiram Blake Camp also reflects an earlier vision of Maine—Lucy's Venno's Maine, I would venture to guess.

On leaving Cape Rosier, I next stopped at Bucks Harbor, adjacent to the village of South Brooksville. At a restaurant called the Landing, I talked with Peter, the owner, and Bob, who was about to install a new restaurant on the premises following Peter's loss of his French chef. Bob said he already operated a restaurant on Little Deer Isle, called the Beachcomber, but it was soon scheduled to close for the season, while he planned to keep the Landing open till New Year's Day. When Peter and I walked off to tour the inn, which he also owns, Bob—a home boy from my own New York stomping grounds—shouted after me to come eat at the Beachcomber that night. "What time?" I replied. "We open at five. Come at six." Peter originally came here from Los Angeles, demonstrating that Maine's magical appeal truly knows no bounds. I found his inn a very comfortable place, but more to my parents' taste than to mine, more to the bridge-and-golf set than to whatever I am.

DEER ISLE FLASHBACK

A long bridge built in 1938 and suspended over Eggemoggin Reach—just south of the Brookville communities—connects the mainland, via Route 15, to Little Deer Isle, and thence, over a winding causeway, to Deer Isle itself. Earlier in the summer, when I had visited my friends the Turners, near Stonington, I had been fortunate to meet Robin Stratton, who had grown up in the area and volunteered to give me a tour in her car. Bill and Julie Turner and their kids had been neighbors of mine on the mid-coast who decided to try their fortunes farther Down East, and now Robin was helping Bill's woodworking partner—also named Bill—hang some sheetrock in the old farmhouse the Turners had recently purchased. The two Bills were green with envy as I drove away with Robin while they struggled to haul a dozen heavy radiators off to a boatyard to be sandblasted clean and given a coat of primer. One of them went so far as to assume a paterfamilias posture, asking the recent college grad if she "really wanted to do that"— drive me around the island, that is. Robin, however, was not interested in the writer but in his method, and for my part, I was just old enough to be flattered by her company.

In all, Robin introduced me to a dozen scenic roads, and we also stopped at several inns and restaurants, the first being the Eggemoggin Inn, on the tip of Little Deer Isle. This inn is a real find, a former estate house looking out past the lighthouse on Pumpkin Island, and as secluded and eccentric a spot as you could wish for a true getaway. For dining on Little Deer Isle, there is Easton's Lobster Pool, overlooking Blastow's Cove, and the Beachcomber, at the foot of the bridge, which I will describe later in this section. We went to the Goose Cove Lodge, where Robin had once worked as a waitress, and which rents only by the week during July and August on the modified American plan. The attractive accommodations are mostly cabins, though suites and rooms are also available in the main lodge. The Goose Cove Lodge is a favorite for those seeking a naturalist's vacation in comfortable digs where meals are provided. Before returning to the Turners', Robin drove down an old road to an abandoned quarry. Dozens of granite quarries once dotted the Penobscot Bay region, mostly on the islands, and today only a single operation remains, on Crotch Island, opposite Stonington harbor. In the quarry we visited, great monoliths of stone lay scattered about, creating the impression of a dismantled Stonehenge. Atop the high, upright mast of an idle derrick, once used to swing the mammoth slabs onto giant wagons, an osprey sat in her nest and screeched a danger signal prompted by our unwelcome presence. She returned here each year, Robin said, as she herself planned always to return in the years ahead to her home in Sunset.

DEER ISLE

Now to return to the account of the late-September weekend that forms the core of this chapter. I departed from the Brooksville area and went off to explore Deer Isle, this time by myself. WERU, Blue Hill's community FM station—whose format is amazingly fresh—provided the entertainment. Two sisters who hailed from Michigan sang a satire on the single life with a funny refrain: " 'See you . . . in C-U-B-A. . . . ' " Near the tip of the causeway, I drove down the Ferry Road, where the Inn at Ferry Landing looks back across Eggemoggin Reach. A wonderful series of byways and back roads, beginning with the Reach Road, follows the shoreline along the quiet side of Deer Isle and ultimately leads across a series of necks and islets to Sunshine. Here, the world-famous Haystack Mountain School of Crafts offers workshops with accomplished artisans and a permanent exhibition of finished work, in a striking hall of glass and wood.

Later that afternoon, I wound my way back to Deer Isle village and stopped to call at the Pilgrim Inn, located on the north edge of the village center in a home built in 1793. Certain adjectives come to mind as I try to focus my impression of this fine inn: impeccable, authentic, tasteful, well-run . . . and perhaps a tad snooty. The Pilgrim is reputed to have the best *table d'hôte* in the state, bar none; thus, eating here can be likened to ferreting out one of those three-star Michelin restaurants sequestered somewhere in the French provinces. In a moment's conversation with innkeeper Jean Hendrick, I sensed an inherent seriousness about cooking. When she invited me to dinner, I began to have regrets about my hasty acceptance of Bob Vissicchio's offer to eat at the Beachcomber, but a deal is a deal.

When you think about it, everything about the Beachcomber is wrong: its location just off the bridge (which is not all that scenic, as is claimed), its "low-priced-spread" façade, and its connection to a motel outwardly lacking any detail of individuality. Inside, however, the Beachcomber was pleasant enough: tables covered in crisp white linen, each with a vase of fresh-cut flowers. I had hoped to an opportunity to talk with Bob in some detail, to reminisce a bit about the "old nabe," Manhattan's East Village, where we both had lived and the reason for our greeting each other earlier in the day like lodge brothers. But Bob was decked out like a New York bartender in a blue apron from midriff to ankles, waiting tables because "all the kids have gone back to school." And, of course, the place got busy, so we could only trade a word now and then as I ate my sea scallops smothered in cream sauce.

I did get to watch Bob in action, and he handled the crowd like a consummate New York charmer. Never having previously waited tables didn't mean a thing; he knew how to make people feel at home with his easygoing, almost brusque directness. The Beachcomber's menu was similarly straightforward: steaks and seafood. The diners around me seemed to be enjoying their meals, including two women from Boothbay Harbor to my immediate right who had ordered the haddock (and who confirmed for me, incidentally, that the Spruce Point Inn *was* indeed the place to eat in their village for a special occasion). Another gentleman, who had the same dish I ordered, commented on the "generous serving of scallops." And indeed it was, both generous and tasty. It is easy to overcook scallops, but these were broiled to perfection; and the sauce was competent if not terribly delicate. Fresh garden vegetables—featuring new red potatoes—made up the accompaniments; organic farmers these days are finding a ready clientele among enlightened restauranteurs like Bob or Mark Hodesh.

STONINGTON VIA ROUTE 15 ■ ISLE AU HAUT BY MAIL BOAT

After dinner I drove down the Oceanville peninsula to spend the night with my friends and former neighbors, the Turners, who had made good their escape from the forces of modernism currently sweeping the mid-coast, the region where they'd first come to homestead in Maine in search of the "good life." Homestead is really the right word; every generation has its "back-to-the-landers," and Bill and Julie Turner definitely belong to that tradition.

As Stonington was only a ten-minute drive from my friends' house, I had it in mind to breakfast there the following morning at a restaurant called the Fisherman's Friend. But being a dinner place, it was closed. Across the road, however, Connie's was doing a brisk morning trade, and I ate a good meal there. I'd visited Stonington previously a number of times, mostly en route to the Isle au Haut. A mail ferryboat makes a round-trip crossing to the island once a day, except on Sundays. And while two-thirds of the land on the Isle au Haut belongs to Acadia National Park, only a half-dozen campsites at most are provided, and the number of day-trippers allowed to visit the park on a given day is similarly limited. These stringent rules for diverting the touring crowds from this pristine spot and longtime fishing community have the full encouragement of the islanders, who for years have shown a strong inclination to avoid becoming another Monhegan. A large summer community does exist on the Isle au Haut, along with an ever-dwindling population of full-timers who relish island living as it once flourished on the Maine coast.

It was this decline in the number of full-timers on the island by the 1980s that ultimately led to a compromise in the town's policy on tourism. No inns or other transient lodgings had hitherto been condoned on the Isle au Haut, by mutual consent of the governed. Enter Jeff Bruke, with a smile that could strip a snake of its skin, and the brains to match. Now Jeff, in his own quiet, insistent way, has a tendency to move things in the direction he wants them to go. The island's Planning Board was mere glazing compound in his supple hands, and before you knew it, an inn called the Keeper's House opened at the old Robinson Head Light. No one, from what I've heard, has had cause to regret this enlightened action. Isle au Haut gained in Jeff and Judi Burke a family with a long track record for social and community activism, and in their son, Matt, another kid for the one-room schoolhouse. The Burkes were ready for a dose of island life. Judi had grown up on the Cape, where her father was a lighthouse keeper, and later she was a shop steward and union organizer in a high-tech factory out west. Years before, she and Jeff had joined the Peace Corps together, and they even lived in a Berkeley commune. By dint of good fortune, Judi also likes to cook—and she does it well enough to have opened a small restaurant at the inn where, owing to limited seating, reservations must be made at least one week in advance.

The Isle au Haut hasn't exactly been overrun by the folk lodged at the Keeper's House, which has a capacity of perhaps ten guests a night and is open only between May and October. And while my sentiment may smack of romantic elitism, I too find it a good policy to limit access to selected places in order to preserve and guarantee ways of life—not all of which favor the affluent, moreover—that may be vanishing but need not be hastened toward their extinction by some quantitative view of democracy. What the inn delivers to its ten lucky guests are handsome and comfortable accommodations with gas lighting, three full meals, and a lighthouse keeper's window on the sea. All of this—and the Isle au Haut, a nature lover's and hiker's paradise—for around $200 a couple per day. So, in addition to being unique, remote, and hospitable, the Keeper's House is something of a bargain as well—for those, at least, with the "disposable income" to enjoy such flings.

Stonington was once viewed a fitting subject by the brilliant watercolorist John Marin, whose image of the village, executed some years before his death in 1953, now hangs in the Colby College Art Museum in Waterville. The picture is remarkable both for its quintessential, ephemeral Marin quality and for its view of how little Stonington has changed in size and appearance over the past forty years or more. Much of Stonington's charm is in its harbor, a fairyland of islands that makes the forty-minute passage by mail boat to the Isle au Haut memorable, no matter how often you make the crossing. And the village itself is more a place of houses than of shops— the homes, no doubt, of people like those I saw at Connie's at breakfast time, who all seemed to know each other and were pausing for few moments of socializing before going about the business of the day. One can't really say that Stonington is a tourist town, though many visitors not bound for the Isle au Haut must come here out of sheer curiosity, just to see what the village at the tip of Deer Isle looks like. And those who want lodgings here can look to Boyce's Motel or the Captains Quarters, which face each other across the harbor street, and both of which are suitable candidates for a remote seaside overnight.

BROOKLIN AND BLUE HILL VIA ROUTES 175 AND 172

Besides Castine, the other significant pole of attraction on the peninsula east of Penobscot Bay is the village of Blue Hill, which seems veritably seized in a *Kulturkampf* of massive proportions when compared with what's happening in the rest of Maine. Blue Hill is our Tanglewood, Woodstock, and Marin County, all wrapped up in one. A strange breed of cat has migrated here, very New Age, and somewhat fragmented along class and generation lines. The first wave of cultured migrants to this area came from the top drawer of the art and music worlds. Great names in literature, world-class musicians, established artists, and, of course, "men of affairs" have summered or settled hereabouts for many years.

They've now been joined by a faction of their offspring's generation who have apparently concluded that the most humane economical model for survival our society offers, the one that allows for maximum independence and self-development, is the "mom and pop" factory. Scores of small producers—highly talented craftspeople and more than a few good artists— have flocked to this proud little corner of Down East Yankeedom, where the homes are celebrated in the National Register of Historic Places. These Blue Hill artisans work at home (filling in on the local economy as need be), making pots and pans and panchos and pictures and a thousand other commodities of distinction to be sold sometimes from private studios and shops, sometimes at local co-ops and fairs.

Thus the clock spins back to the pastoral times before industrialization, when craft skills were high and cottagers produced use objects of durability and beauty for barter and home consumption. The whole vision, as it translates to our modern world, is a bit precious, but in general the New Age life-stylers mix their emphasis on home comforts and individual growth with a fair dose of interest in what's happening in the world, or at least in the community. The ideological voice of this local movement is WERU 89.9 FM ("We are you"—get it?), probably as innovative and mind-broadening a radio station as any ever created. The talk shows are lively in the great soapbox orator tradition, and every kind of rare bird and crackpot can be heard on this station, expounding his or her recipe for good health and salvation. The musical format is eclectic and highly "listenable," heavy on folk, jazz, the Third World, and occasionally New Age cool-out music, which I suppose is meant for meditative release rather than emotional engagement, but it always sets my teeth on edge.

A nice drive for getting from Deer Isle to Blue Hill is over Route 175 by way of Brooklin. This Brooklin has about as much to do with Flatbush Avenue and Coney Island as Shangri-la has in common with the flesh pots of the Orient. Though I have never heard or read it, I am certain that E. B. White, once Brooklin's most celebrated resident, must have been amused that his refuge from the world would have been so named. And what parent, incidentally, is not a fan of E. B. White's, after witnessing how *Charlotte's Web* or *The Trumpet of the Swan* brings rapture to the eyes of his children when these stories are read to them at bedtime? On this basis alone, I formed my desire to see where the otherwise middlebrow New Yorker had made his home and penned his classic children's tales. At such shrines, writers seek spiritual refreshment, much the way hopeful pilgrims pray for miracles at Lourdes or Fatima.

There's a little village center in Brooklin where I stopped to ask directions at the general store. The teenaged girl who worked the register allowed that there were only two places in town of interest to outsiders, and she could provide directions to both. The offices of *Wooden Boat* magazine were one, and the old E. B. White homestead was the other. For White's home, she said I should continue up Route 175 and look for a "plantation-style house with cedar hedges." When I found a place that fit her description, I could see that by "plantation," she had not meant a manse with imposing columns. White's house is a nicely formed and relatively plain old structure of the "farmhouse" genre with a few outbuildings, all set on attractive, well-tended grounds. One could, however, with the mind's eye, project a tall-columned portico on the house's façade, and thereby perceive a rather close architectural relationship between this simple farmstead and the antebellum plantation houses of the old South.

What is harder to imagine when looking at the tidy outbuildings is a setting for the barnyard scenes in *Charlotte's Web*. But in White's day, family farms existed on the peninsula in sufficient numbers to provide him with an ample field for his observations. Today, just about everyone with land in this state has become a gentleman farmer by default, since it's virtually impossible anymore to make a living on a hundred rocky acres in Maine. The country fairs continue, though, and many landowners still engage in husbandry either for fun or to make a few bucks on the side. Locally, the Blue Hill Fair is a yearly extravaganza where many a critter, like Charlotte's friend Wilbur ("Some Pig!"), gets to take its bow and try for a blue ribbon. As I drove away from the White property, a perverse thought entered my mind: I visualized myself returning here someday to find that E. B. White's house had been turned into a theme park. Little people would be dressed in costumes, like Disney characters, posing for snapshots with visitors—except that instead of Mickey and Minnie, there would be Wilbur and Stuart Little, each costume a crafted original in all-natural fibers, made in Blue Hill.

The ride into Blue Hill from Brooklin is lined with long dirt drives that go down to the water and look like entrances to Southwestern haciendas. The name YGLESIAS printed on a mailbox at the mouth of one drive gave my image a weird patina of reality. The question "Could Julio actually own a spread up here?" went through my head. Later I picked up a copy of *Preview*, a free local newspaper, that featured a lead interview with novelist Helen Yglesias, resident of North Brooklin. Seek and ye shall find. And as usual, I found the drive to Blue Hill more interesting than the town itself, though I have on two separate occasions eaten well there. My health-food pizza covered with jalepeños, black olives, and fresh garlic at the Pie in the Sky Restaurant was real food and good to boot, while the spicy meat pie and

cheese-and-blueberry Danish at the Left Bank Café, outside the village on
the way north to Surry on Route 172, was equally excellent.

Before our itinerary takes us on to Mount Desert and other points Down
East, we make a final call on this peninsula at Surry. All year the Maine
newspaper I read daily gave wide coverage to the work of Walter Nowick,
artistic director of the Surry Opera Company, whose seasonal performances enliven the surrounding community. Three times during the last
several years, the company traveled to the Soviet Union to perform in the
Russian language its concert opera repertoire, including its homespun version of Mussorgsky's *Boris Godunov*. And in the summer of 1989, a slew
of Soviet opera singers were the company's guests in return, quartered in
and around Blue Hill. Yet in the corner gas stop at the crossroads in Surry,
I had to ask four local residents before I could get directions to Nowick's old
farm, where the barn houses a small theater. The farm I drove up to was
mostly in ruins, all the buildings except the barn in need of major repairs
(the house, I learned later, having burned down a few years back). There
was no vehicle around, and the place seemed deserted. Then, from the
barn, a few polished bars of piano music suddenly broke the silence, stopping just as suddenly at the ringing of a phone.

I'm afraid I startled poor Walter, who was on the phone with his back to
the door as I entered the barn. But this open-faced man of sixty quickly
recovered his composure and, with a gentle manner, drew out my story as
I drew out his. The latent biographer in me was put on alert after gathering
a few random facts about Walter's life: his formal study at the Juilliard
School; his seventeen years of Zen study in Japan and his fluency in Japa-
nese; his years of work in Surry as a dairy farmer and a sawyer with his
own mill; and his current leadership of the Surry Opera Company with its
emphasis on community involvement and cultural exchanges with the So-
viets in the interests of world peace. I asked Walter to show me a few of
the company's old concert programs, and we went into his home, actually
a shed, where the gaps created by missing wallboards were covered with
thick, clear poly sheets, and a pallet on the floor served for a bed. Also on
the floor were spread piles of photocopies of newspaper notices, and a few
filing cabinets and bookshelves filled out the remainder of the furnishings.
It was the cell of a Zen master accustomed to the ascetic life, but the old
club tie hanging on a nail by the door revealed a man who can still don a
pinstriped suit when he needs to.

■

INFORMATION ▪ *The Castine Merchants Association*, P.O. Box 618, Castine 04421. This group publishes an informative pamphlet/walking tour map. ▪ *The Castine Inn* (326-4365). Owners Mark and Margaret Hodesh update their own "fact sheets" on everything from shops to scenic diversions, an excellent source of current information on happenings in Castine and its environs. ▪ *Deer Isle–Stonington Chamber of Commerce* (348-6124), P.O. Box 268, Stonington, 04681. ▪ *Blue Hill Chamber of Commerce*, P.O. Box 520, Blue Hill 04614.

CASTINE

LODGINGS ▪ *The Castine Inn* (326-4365), Main St., P.O. Box 41, Castine 04421. Open from April 14 to October 15, $70 to $85, double, with full breakfast. ▪ *The Manor* (326-4861), Battle Ave., P.O. Box 276, Castine 04421. ▪ *The Pentagoet Inn* (326-8616), Main St., Castine 04421.

RESTAURANTS ▪ All of Castine's inns have dining rooms open to the public. More informal meals can be taken at a variety of eateries from cafés to pizza shops to seafood restaurants, located on Water Street and in the vicinity of the town dock.

CRUISES ▪ *Walter Harrington* (326-8588) can take you on full- or half-day cruises of Penobscot Bay in his thirty-foot yawl; Walter was the 1989 recipient of the coveted Keith Joyce Award for Elegance and Service.

SPECIAL ▪ *The Wilson Museum and John Perkins House*, Perkins St., Castine; open from 2:00 P.M. to 5:00 P.M. daily except Mondays, May 27 to September 30.

THE BROOKSVILLES AND CAPE ROSIER

LODGINGS ▪ *Buck's Harbor Inn* (326-8660), P.O. Box 268, South Brooksville 04617. Open from mid-May to October; $50 a night, double occupancy. ▪ *Hiram Blake Camp* (326-4951), Cape Rosier 04642. Housekeeping cabins rent by the week, starting at $330 in season to $200 off-season; modified American plan is also available.

RESTAURANTS ▪ *The Landing* (326-8660). A restaurant in a separate facility of the Buck's Harbor Inn in South Brooksville.

SPECIAL ▪ *Holbrook Island Sanctuary State Park* (326-4012), Brooksville.

DEER ISLE/ISLE AU HAUT

LODGINGS ▪ *Eggemoggin Inn* (694-6417), P.O. Box 324, Little Deer Isle 04650. Open from June 15 to September 21. ▪ *The Pilgrim Inn* (348-6615), Deer Isle 04627. Modified American plan. ▪ *Goose Cove Lodge* (348-2508), Sunset 04683. Cottages rent by the week, including breakfast and dinner. ▪ *The Captain's Quarters Inn and Motel* (367-2420), Stonington 04681. Open year-round; a variety of accommodations from single rooms to housekeeping apartments. ▪ *Boyces Motel* (367-2421), Stonington 04681. ▪ *The Keeper's House*, P.O. Box 126, Isle au Haut 04645. There is no phone at the inn; reservation messages can be left at (207) 367-2261. All meals included in daily rate.

RESTAURANTS ▪ Both the *Keeper's House* and *The Pilgrim Inn* offer excellent dining. ▪ *Connie's Restaurant* (367-2742), School St., Stonington. Open seven days a week from 7:00 A.M. to 7:30 P.M. ▪ *The Fisherman's Friend* (367-2442), School St., Stonington. Reasonably priced seafood dishes.

BLUE HILL/SURRY

LODGINGS ▪ *Blue Hill Farm* (374-5126), P.O. Box 437, Blue Hill 04614. An inn that is well spoken of, and described as "an unusually attractive old farmhouse." Open year-round. ▪ *Surry Inn* (667-5091), P.O. Box 25, Rte. 172, Surry 04684. The grand old inn of the area, with a private beach on Contention Cove.

RESTAURANTS ▪ *Pie in the Sky* (374-5570), Hill St., Blue Hill. ▪ *The Left Bank Café* (374-2201), Rte. 172, Blue Hill.

SPECIAL ▪ *Blue Hill* itself, the elevation that gives the town its name. There are some public paths that allow you to roam over the town's most prominent natural feature—for blueberry picking in season, for example. ■ *The Blue Hill Fair.* One of the great ones, every year over Labor Day weekend. ■ *Kneisel Hall Chamber Music Festival* (374-2811), P.O. Box 648, Blue Hill 04614. Sunday and Wednesday concerts in the summertime at this prestigious summer conservatory for string and ensemble music. ■ *Jonathan Fisher Memorial* (374-2459), Rte. 15, Blue Hill. Fisher built his home in 1814 after being appointed as Blue Hill's first pastor. As the exhibit reveals, the Harvard divine was a man of many parts—a gifted writer, painter, farmer, and craftsperson. ■ *The Surry Opera Company* (667-9551), the Concert Barn in Surry, Maine. A summer program of piano recitals and concert operas (the works are sung, but not staged).

13

Mount Desert Island After Labor Day

ACADIA NATIONAL PARK AND THE HARBOR
VILLAGES OF MOUNT DESERT VIA ROUTES 3, 198,
102A, 233

Forty-thousand-acre Acadia National Park covers slightly less than half of Mount Desert Island, and is currently the second-most-visited national park in the country, with an annual attendance of four million people. According to projections, that figure will reach six million by the year 2000. Naturally, not all these tourists descend on Mount Desert during the peak summer months, but most of them do. And so, a word to the wise . . .

My family and I found that Columbus Day weekend is a perfect time to visit Mount Desert, with its stunningly beautiful park and romantic harborside communities. During this holiday weekend, the island is buzzing with visitors, and most of the hospitality services and facilities remain operational.

But traffic then, while steady, does not approach the gridlock proportions that plague Mount Desert at the height of its season. The issue of traffic is critical. A comfortable, slow-paced drive around the island and on the Park Loop Road is of the essence during a visit here in order both to experience the island as an entity and to peruse the sightseeing menu for subsequent, more thorough explorations.

Mount Desert is shaped like two puffy saddlebags flung across the haunches of a thin fluvial steed known as Somes Sound, often described as the only natural fjord on the East Coast. This fjord divides the island into its western and eastern sectors, both of which contain large chunks of national park acreage. At the same time, the opposing harbors at the mouth of the sound—Southwest Harbor and Northeast Harbor—reflect not only compass opposites but the deeper social and economic differences that distinguish the eastern and western halves. Southwest Harbor is on the "quiet" side of the island, where the villages retain healthy native fishing and boatbuilding industries and have a decidedly blue-colar quality. Most of the heavy tourist action is concentrated on the Northeast Harbor side, where the elegance of seasonal residential colonies combines with the midway atmosphere of Bar Harbor and Acadia's most popular attractions—Cadillac Mountain, Sand Beach, and Thunder Hole—along the Park Loop Road. Despite the overcrowding and one or two pockets of honkytonk commercialism, Mount Desert's graceful beauty stands apart even in beauty-rich Maine, and Acadia National Park allows for the widest possible public sharing of this exceptional natural and aesthetic resource. You may want a whole week to savor fully the allurements of Mount Desert, but—as we discovered—one can also cover quite a bit of ground over a single weekend.

We had planned to leave for Mount Desert early the Saturday morning of Columbus Day weekend, just for a lark, to ward off the post–Labor Day, pre-Thanksgiving doldrums. I awoke before dawn to discover that eight inches of snow had fallen during the night. Before long, our local plow trucks had the roads cleared, and the mercury quickly climbed to a reasonable temperature. It seemed certain that the residue of this premature winter storm would soon evaporate, leaving a balmy fall day in its wake, and we all decided that the trip should not be postponed. By the time we reached Bar Harbor, at about 10:00 A.M., to rendezvous with friends who had spent the night there, the wet snow still covered the ground, but we were all in shirtsleeves. Our friends Joan and her ten-year-old son, Evan, were holed up in a modern motel room, trying to iron out how they were going to spend the day. With no consensus in sight, my son and my wife and I slipped off to find a place where we'd feel comfortable, which we—Carol and I, that is—already knew would not be in Bar Harbor.

By this time in October, the tips of the leaves had already begun to turn lemon and crimson on oaks and maples, canary and marigold on birches and ash. We struck westward on Route 233 to Route 102 and headed for Southwest Harbor, taking very suitable digs at $55 for the night for the three of us in the Drydock Inn, a former public building converted into a small hotel. Now we had the whole day in front of us to explore, and the first thing I wanted to do was just drive and look. We continued south again to get close to the water, following Route 202A, which passes the small, plain houses and prefab mobile homes I have come to associate with the kind of native day-laboring class—jacks of all trades—that have managed to survive and even to thrive on the Maine coast. Off to the left, there are views of the harbor, and near Seawall—one of two Acadia camping areas— the road runs close to the rocky shore. This day, even the scrub oak, mixed with white birch and pointed fir, added their fiery drama to the early-fall display. Beyond the turnoff to Bass Harbor, where a nature trail crosses the ledge toward a famous lighthouse that guards the channel, the habitations thin out. Tremont is a quiet coastside village, home to Duddy's Lobster Shack, where you are served a rock to crack your crustacean. As we drove along past more fisherfolk cottages and a seafarers' chapel or two, I was thinking that Mount Desert isn't really a fancy, prosperous place at all—at least not on the Blue Hill Bay side—despite the four million visitors yearly and all the money they must infuse into the local economy. This half of the island is definitely the back door of Acadia Park as well. Several roads enter the park from Route 102, leading to hiking trails and elevations such as Bernard Mountain, which was snow-topped this day. Farther up the road, we spotted an unusual picnic arrangement at Pretty Marsh. Individual picnic sites have their own parking platforms that seem to extend beyond the edge of the palisade high above the water; the shore itself is accessible by paths cut into the rocky palisade.

By midday we were ready to join the throngs of holiday visitors in the more formal areas of the park, and we drove off to the Hulls Cove entrance off Route 3, above Bar Harbor. Hulls Cove marks the beginning of the Loop Road, where a large visitors' center also provides orientation to all park facilities. The park's dramatic impact is immediate. No sooner had we begun to climb the ridge road than majestic, island-spattered Frenchman Bay came into wide-angled view, with Egg Rock and its lighthouse in bold relief on the horizon. A sign for the Wild Gardens and Indian Museum was filed away for tomorrow's program; right now we just wanted to get the lay of the land. As we approached the fee station, we saw a uniformed park employee waving people through; apparently the road to Cadillac Mountain was still inaccessible following the snowstorm, and no one was being charged the $5 fee normally collected to tour the Loop Road.

Every permutation of rock and sea and natural growth in Acadia is so perfect, so well tended, that its beauty makes you ache. An uncomplicated Sunday-in-the-park feeling swept over me; even my most unquenchable cares were momentarily suspended in the palpable presence of the all-embracing *now*. At Sand Beach we parked and descended to the strand, a carpet not of sand but of minuscule shell particles tinted reddish pink. Simon and I climbed the rocks to play hide-and-seek, while Carol hunted for rocks and driftwood on the beach where dozens of others also strolled and amused themselves in their fashion.

We decided to exit the park's Loop Road at Jordan Pond and wind our way over back roads into Northeast Harbor, a village with a social flavor light years in manner and style from its opposite number, Southwest Harbor, just a short skip across the sound. The term "old money" comes to mind, which may or may not have any practical validity in application to the contemporary residents of this privileged enclave. There can be no doubt, however, that many of the professionals and business executives who inhabit these manorial cottages today are direct descendants of old merchant families or self-made industrialists who first came to rusticate on these shores a century ago. The village center in Northeast Harbor is subdued and elegant, with a few artsy touches here and there in the form of galleries and handicrafts shops grafted onto the otherwise untouched façades of the seaside Victorian architecture. Across from the Hanson Gallery, the wild, natural landscaping of the Maison Suisse, a B-and-B, is even more eye-catching than the swank shingled cottage to which it is connected. I had a quick visit with Beth White, the innkeeper at the Maison Suisse, who, with her husband, had recently all but completed a major restoration of the old mansion, with very handsome results. She told an amusing tale about the origins of the front garden. The previous owner was a Swiss man who had trained as a landscape architect, but came to America as a hairdresser, where he eventually worked for Gloria Swanson and became her paramour. In time the hairdresser built up a classy clientele and followed them to Northeast Harbor, where he opened a beauty shop and installed this admirable garden, formal in design, but featuring only plants native to the island ecosystem.

Before leaving Northeast Harbor, we walked down to the town pier, and were surprised to see three large rubber rafts powered by outboards approach the dock, where a troop of hearty-looking passengers in colorful foul-weather gear alighted and wandered off toward the village. They were making a brief shore visit from the ship of the Society Explorer, a Seattle-based company that organizes educational expeditions for serious naturalists, both amateur and professional. We had eaten our lunches from a cooler, but with dinnertime approaching, we decided to return to Southwest Harbor for a bit of a rest, before going to a local restaurant there that had looked promising. The return route we chose was scenic Sargent Road, along the right bank of the fjord. Unfortunately, our choice of restaurant was far less satisfying than the day's visual feast. It was one of those pretentious eateries you have heard me rail about all too frequently throughout this text. The food was overpriced and had all the sophistication of some of the pioneer gourmets of the early sixties who made their sauces with canned cream-of-mushroom soup.

The next morning, with my family still snoozing at the Drydock, I roamed down to John Grindle's grocery store and joined some locals who were washing down their "sticky buns" with good, fresh coffee, warming themselves with a bit of talk and java for the day's solitary labors. John told me that despite Mount Desert's reputation for overcrowding, Southwest Harbor remained pretty quiet until the end of June, and so the pace of life was reasonable there, in the Maine sense, for most of the year. Outside, along Main Street, I took note of three better-than-average-looking B-and-Bs, and managed to visit one of them, the Penury Hall, where I sat for a bit with Toby and Gretchen Strong over another cup of coffee. When you stay at Penury Hall, you are very much within the Strongs' home, which Toby says is what real B-and-B devotees like, because "it's more personal." The Strongs limit their lodgers to six a night, and provide one of the best fact sheets on local activities I have seen in my travels. It also includes the names of their favorite restaurants, one of which, unfortunately, was the local dive we had eaten in the night before. Oh, well, tastes differ, and they are a very likable couple nevertheless.

Someone, maybe John Grindle, suggested we explore the Beech Mountain section of Acadia Park, accessible from several back roads off Route 102. We made that our first outing for the day, entering the park just north of Echo Lake and following the old road back for several miles, which was interesting in that we got a glimpse of some homesteads in what was once a back settlement on the island. We parked at Beech Cliff and then climbed to the summit, Carol and I following the path while Simon scurried up the face of the granite, with the not terribly reassuring cry, "Don't worry, Dad, I can do it," before disappearing among the trees. The view from the top was just about the same one that greeted explorer Samuel de Champlain in 1604, when he observed from here the island's seventeen sparsely vegetated hilltops from which he derived the name he gave the place, L'Isle des Monts Desert.

The Thuya Gardens kept coming up in conversations we were having with people all over the island, prompted usually by our asking about things to do, always being sure to drop necessary hints as to the range of our preferences. The Gardens' small parking lot is marked by a discreet sign about three-quarters of a mile in from the junction of routes 198 and 3. When we finally spotted the entrance, we hadn't any concrete notion of what to expect, finding ourselves across a somewhat shoulderless road from a rather steep and pretty hill and adjacent to a path that led down to a small floating dock. A good two hours passed, however, before we departed, and we by no means exhausted the psychic nourishments of the place, which took the form of a thousand delights to be discovered along a garden path. This path begins virtually at roadside, and proceeds in terraced stages up the hill to the former summer lodge of a landscape architect from Boston, Joseph Henry Curtis (1841–1928).

The engineering skill and manpower required to lay out tons of granite steps and abutments up this steep incline and still allow for a relatively gentle ascent commands as much admiration as do the many imaginatively constructed lookout stations and landings of wood and stone you will happily encounter on the way. One memorable moment involved sitting on a chair fashioned from cedar logs—seemingly built for someone troll-size—and looking down on Northeast Harbor through a keyhole opening in the trees at the masts of sailing craft bobbing like metronomes set to their slowest cadence. A strong wind stirred the fall air, slightly damp but still warm around the edges, and I mused to myself: If, having the opportunity to grasp such a moment as this, one were instead to breeze too quickly by, well, that would be unfortunate.

The lodge mentioned above now serves as a kind of museum to showcase both the life-style of its artistic creator and his rare botanical library, and it is open to the public from late June through Labor Day. Peeking through the doors and windows, set in a rude façade of logs, we saw an interior of baronial comforts, of finely crafted furniture and Oriental rugs, bathed in the maple-syrup-amber glow of polished pine floors and paneled walls. Behind the house are the gardens, a complex mosaic of flower beds and trees surrounded by a high stockade of cedar boards and posts with many gates that lead to other paths and outer gardens, and to outbuildings with no apparent function other than to display their aesthetic use of materials and design. Every detail in this construction suggests a labor of love: a grouse carved in bas-relief on a gate door, a stretch of fence paneled like a colonial ceiling, the deft placement of roots and stone to form a wall.

Reluctantly, we left the Thuya Gardens and returned once more down the Asticou Terrace, as it is called, to explore another garden, the Wild Gardens of Acadia, and to visit the Abbe Indian Museum, both of which are not far from the Hulls Cove entrance of Acadia Park. The Wild Gardens are described as "a living field guide to the plants of Acadia." Several distinct environments are displayed there, like the meadow and the mountaintop, each of which is hospitable to its own catalog of growing things, and every plant is identified by a nameplate. Thus, in a Mount Desert meadow, a botanical roll call would include rue and steeplebush, hawthorn and dogbane, large-leafed asters and rough-stemmed goldenrod, daisy fleabane and plantain-leaf pussytoes, sweet fern, fireweed, and pearly everlasting.

The Indian Museum is named for Robert Abbe, a doctor who pioneered techniques of plastic surgery and early radiation therapy. Abbe was also a devoted collector of prehistoric American Indian artifacts, and he created this tiny but very special museum so that the public, too, could "linger and dream" over his fascinating collection, which includes stone implements, projectiles, and weights and pendants used by the Red Paint People, Maine's earliest known inhabitants. There are samples of the red ocher (iron oxide) found inexplicably in their individual graves, dating back four to five thousand years. Wampum carved from clam shells reveals the fine workmanship of a later tribe, as do the bone tools such as bodkins, awls, fishhooks, and combs that fill several cabinets. The walls are hung with antique snowshoes, war clubs, lacrosse sticks, and other familiar articles of the forest peoples' everyday life.

At Simon's earnest request, we returned to Bar Harbor, where we began our weekend, our friends having since departed, but the quarry was now ice cream and a tie-dyed T-shirt. (Simon's purchase actually led to a nostalgic evening of tie-dying in our kitchen with these same friends some months later, since both our youngsters are equally into the revived fashion.) But, at one point while we walked the Bar Harbor strip, I ducked into a bookstore to examine the shelves of guidebooks devoted exclusively to Mount Desert and Acadia National Park. I browsed a motorist's guide listing the author's twenty or so "must see" locales, another book that described twelve special walks, and so on. I guess the point is that you could easily spend a week here and have a very different outdoor or touring experience every day and still leave untapped treasures by the chestful for visits in the future.

◼

INFORMATION ◼ Superintendent, *Acadia National Park,* P.O. Box 117, Bar Harbor 04609; Visitors' Center at Hulls Cove (288-3338). ◼ *Southwest Harbor Chamber of Commerce* (244-5513). A seasonal information center, located on Route 102. ◼ *Northeast Harbor Chamber of Commerce* (276-3331). This organization maintains an information booth on the town pier. ◼ *Bar Harbor Chamber of Commerce* (288-5103), Municipal Building, Bar Harbor 04609. ◼ *Thompson Island Information Center* (288-3411). Located on Route 3, on a causeway just after entering Mount Desert, the center dispenses general information on both the island and the park.

LODGINGS ◼ *Café Drydock & Inn* (244-5842), P.O. Box 1361, Main St., Southwest Harbor 04679. A former municipal building converted to a roadhouse, complete with attached café and boutique. ◼ *Penury Hall* (244-7102), P.O. Box 68, Main St., Southwest Harbor 04679. A quintessential B-and-B, and the first one on the island. ◼ *Kingsleigh Inn* (244-5302), P.O. Box 1328, Main St., Southwest Harbor 04679. Neighboring the two abovementioned establishments on Main Street, this is a lovely village house with a wraparound porch and window awnings. ◼ *Harbor View Mo-*

tel, Main St., Southwest Harbor 04679. Traditional motel rooms plus a few cabins with wooden decks and rocking chairs. ▪ *Maison Suisse Inn* (276-5223), Main St., Northeast Harbor 04662. Upscale elegance. ▪ *Bass Cottage in the Field* (288-3705), Bar Harbor 04609. Private setting, and reasonably priced. ▪ *Ledgelawn* (288-4596), 66 Mount Desert St., Bar Harbor 04609. Pricey, but well equipped for recreational and sensual pleasures. ▪ *Cove Farm Inn* (288-5355), RFD 1, P.O. Box 429, Crooked Road, Bar Harbor 04609. A nice family spot just outside town.

CAMPING ▪ *Acadia National Park* offers two campsites: *Blackwoods* (288-3274) on the island's eastern sector and open year-round; and *Seawall* (294-3600), near Southwest Harbor, open Memorial Day through September. ▪ A number of private campgrounds are also located throughout Mount Desert; consult the camping guide available through the Maine Publicity Bureau (289-2423), 97 Winthrop St., Hallowell 04347.

RESTAURANTS ▪ *The Claremont* (244-5036), Clark Point Rd., Southwest Harbor. The highly reputed dining room of this old-style resort is open to the public. ▪ *The Asticou* (276-3344), Northeast Harbor. A jacket-and-tie kind of place with a "formal dining room." ▪ *George's* (288-4505), 7 Stephen Lane, Bar Harbor. Mount Desert's nouvelle gourmet eatery. ▪ *Abel's Lobster Pound* (276-5837), Rte. 198, Northeast Harbor. Seafood on the ritz. ▪ *Decon's Seat* (244-9229), Southwest Harbor. Quality sandwiches suitable for any picnic. ▪ *Black's*, overlooking the fishing fleet in Bass Harbor, is a traditional lobster pound, as is *Beal's*, behind the Oceanarium in Southwest Harbor.

NORTHERN MAINE

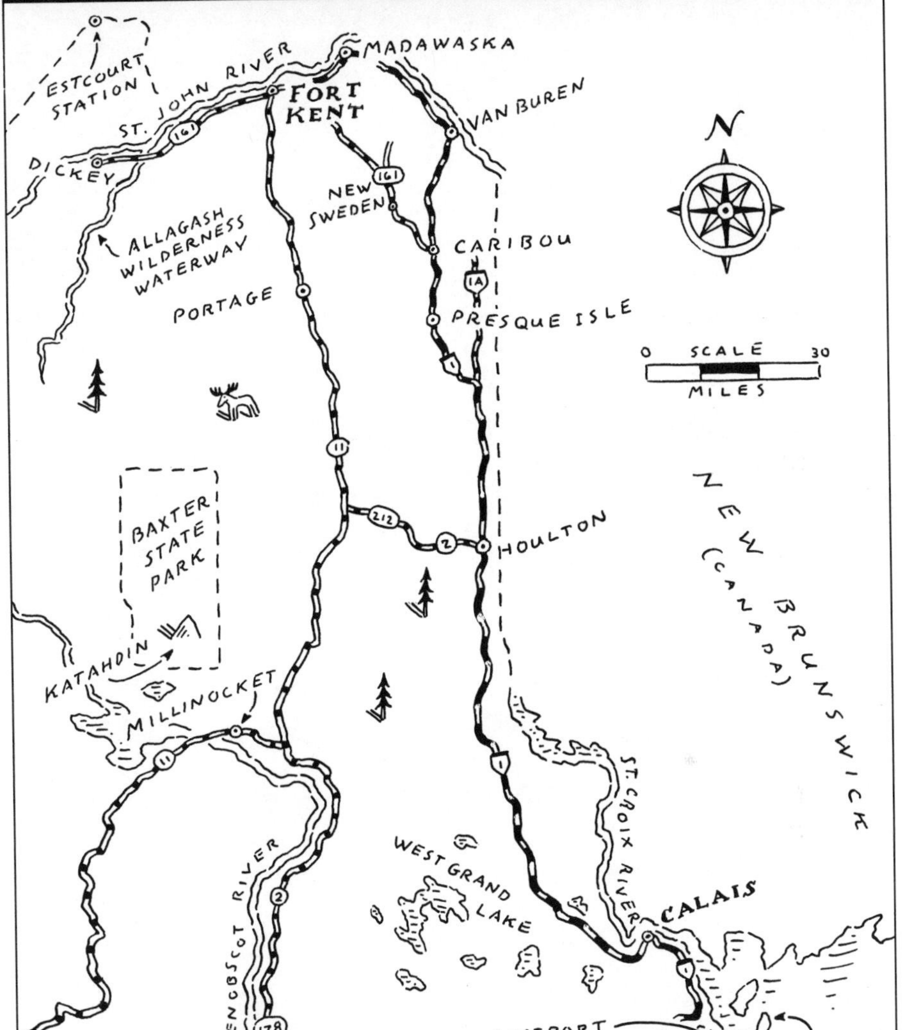

14

WAY DOWN EAST

ELLSWORTH TO EASTPORT

The term "Down East" reflects a state of mind as much as it refers to Maine's coastal geography. True, Maine's Atlantic shoreline, like that of New York's Long Island, runs more east-west than north-south. But "Down East" possesses a certain mythic property as well, signified by the following existential paradox. To a native of the Maine coast who also makes his home there, "Down East" is always somewhere farther up the coast than where he lives. But if he lives in the interior part of the state and is asked where he's from, he might easily respond "Down East," whether his place of origin is Kittery at one end of the coast or Eastport at the other. In this sense, residing on the coast of Maine means perpetually seeking a realm Down East that ever recedes before you at the same time you are actually living in the place you seek. "Way Down East," on the other hand, can refer only to those ocean fringes of Hancock and Washington counties, the latter of which borders Canada's Bay of Fundy and signals a geographic end, at least, to the Down East quest.

I was on such a quest one August not long ago, very excited at the opportunity to explore what was for me a still unknown part of Maine to the east—and ultimately areas to the north of Ellsworth as well. I'd already visited Ellsworth on numerous occasions; the town is considered the "big city" for many of my friends who live in the Penobscot/Blue Hill region.

And, in fact, this journey actually begins in the village of Penobscot (near Castine), where I spent the night with my friends Keith and Amy before beginning a trip (including the account in chapter 15), that would take me over a third of the state of Maine. I would cover some 1,500 road miles in five full days of wandering from dawn till dusk, stopping on whim and camping as I went. Total cost for gas, food, fees, and incidentals: $149.

The night before I departed, Keith and I dined splendidly on pizza topped with jalapeños, black olives, and fresh garlic at Pie in the Sky, the Blue Hill restaurant where Amy works. All the tables were full when we arrived around 9:00 P.M., so we took up ringside seats at the counter, and watched with unabashed patriarchal appreciation the admirable exertions of the seven attractive women who were preparing, cooking, and serving up the tasty vittles—capping our own feast with blueberry pie topped with whipped cream. Outside, thick blankets of fog had rolled in, cooling the modest August heat wave of the previous two weeks; and these drizzly, foggy conditions would persist with not-unpleasant consequences over the next two days of my drive Down East.

ELLSWORTH TO COLUMBIA FALLS VIA COASTAL ROADS AND ROUTE 1

Early on Sunday morning, I rallied my Penobscot friends from their warm bed to give me a quick tour of Ellsworth from their point of view, and also to gain entrance to the studio and print shop that Amy shares with several other local painters. The studio occupies the top floor of the oddly shaped Strong Building, at the corner of Hancock and Pine streets. Amy showed me around her workspace, a homy cubicle cluttered with canvases, drawings, and her latest run of proofs from the collectively managed press shop that fills the central core of the studio, known as Steammill Printmakers. Steammill welcomes the public and offers biweekly workshops.

For the next half hour we cruised the peaceful streets of Ellsworth, which were devoid of other pedestrians, as one might expect on a Sunday morning. The Grant Theater, on Main Street, is the local cultural mecca,

featuring films, live concerts, and plays; *The Pirates of Penzance* was the
production in progress at that moment. Nearby is a new Thai restaurant of
which my friends spoke well, and across the street is a branch of J. J.
Newbury, with a very fifties-looking lunch counter, the pink chairs covered
in vinyl with an abstract boomerang pattern. Amy and her friends often eat
here; "It smells like fried food," she says. I took note of some very kitschy
but not impractical "souvenirs" in the display window. Dick's Restaurant,
near where the Union River crosses Route 1, is a favorite Ellsworth lunch
and breakfast spot, accommodating everyone from local feminists to fishermen. Among the town's most interesting buildings is the Hancock Cream-
ery, a yellow, barnlike structure of unusual dimensions that is home to a
small dairy of the kind rapidly vanishing from the Maine economic scene. As
we stood in the parking lot of the Strong Building saying our good-byes,
Keith had to be restrained from abandoning his plastering job, grabbing his
fishing pole, and joining my caravan; he had made this trip many times and
was not averse to doing it again. With her man in tow, however, Amy's
parting words to me were, "Watch out for the Winebagos."

I had a bit of trouble getting my bearings on my way out of Ellsworth,
confusing routes 3 and 1, and ending up in Trenton, on the commercial strip
that leads to Mount Desert. My usual reaction, akin to that of Jesus driving
the moneychangers from the temple, was strangely muted as I passed the
swindler's row that morning, all the more unusual, given the momentary
stress I felt from being waylaid and off course. At only 10:00 A.M. on a
Sunday, the traffic was already streaming toward Bar Harbor, and I had to
retrace my route several miles back to Ellsworth. Finally squared away, I
passed through the nondescript village of Hancock on Route 1, and noticed
how radically and suddenly the landscape had transformed. The vegetation
was both thinning and turning a bit wild, and the sporadic views of Frenchman Bay were a signal that a new road adventure through lands unknown
had now begun. I'd swear today that my pulse began to quicken at that
moment, so heightened were my feelings of excitement. As I drove, I
imagined that as far as development is concerned, Route 1 along Maine's
southern coast must have looked like what I was seeing here, Down East,
perhaps as late as the 1960s, before the era of the corporate logo and the
gold-leafed colonial sign, the fast-food franchise and the instant cash machine. What I was seeing was soft and folksy, but all the "lobster pounds"
and seafood road stands also triggered a wish that the word *lobster* could be

struck from the English language. Archaeologists centuries from now, digging these lands, won't easily determine whether our dominant religious symbol was the cross or the crustacean.

At Route 186, I turned toward Winter Harbor, going right when reaching a T in that road, to visit the town itself. Winter Harbor seems a place of some size, a harbor for the opposite season to the one its name implies, however, with a number of craft shops and service businesses in wooden commercial buildings on the main street, but with no discernible center. One side street I entered brought me to a cove where a fish weir stood in low water, its construction of rough saplings following, with few technological modifications, the most ancient practices for trapping fish in tidal waters. Before leaving the village, I stopped at the Donut Hole, at the edge of a sometime mud flat, a little restaurant in a weathered old fish shanty, and an ideal screened-in spot for a coffee break or a Sunday brunch.

At the tip of this particular peninsula, on a road that comes into Route 186 just outside Winter Harbor, is Schoodic Point; call it "Acadia National Park III," the third parcel of land in Maine's disjointed federal park, and the least developed. This is the land of pointed firs and waterscapes, a place of "unparalleled views of Mount Desert and many small islands," according to my old WPA Guide to Maine, but shrouded this day by a soggy, cooling fog. Acres of rocks cover the point, and I saw dozens of people scampering over them, with one couple in beach chairs amid the outcroppings, apparently set up for the duration with the Sunday *New York Times* spread over their laps. A later drive through Prospect Harbor, while returning up the peninsula along the looping Route 186, suggests something out of Melville's scenes of early American whaling ports, while Corea—once itself a picturesque fishing village—is now a picturesque summer colony set among barrens of swaying sea grass. There is a naval security presence throughout this whole Schoodic peninsula, invisible for the most part but for the occasional road sign announcing some facility, and a few towering objects that look like giant TV antennas.

Back on Route 1, I spotted another sign almost immediately, a billboard pointing down a side road to the Bartlett Winery, a wine-producing and tasting establishment; and what could be a rarer sight on the road Down East? The winery's small parking lot, in a clearing ringed by evergreens, was almost filled with cars hailing from at least six states. A tasting was in progress as I entered a building, and no one was more surprised than I when the blueberry wine poured in my glass suggested a very potable and credible claret. From there the line went downhill; the apple and pear offerings tasted of fruit, but were more like cider than wine. The Blueberry French Oak Reserve, however, while not cheap at $11.95 a bottle, was a genuine revelation.

From just beyond the winery, Route 1 soon crosses into Washington County, proud territorial sentry that first welcomes the rising sun each day over the United States. Steuben, my first stop in the "Sunrise County," is a tree-shaded hamlet with a village circle tucked away just off the main road; even today you might expect the local Memorial Day parade here to look like a scene from *The Music Man*. Steuben is named for Baron Friedrich von Steuben, who served as inspector general of the Continental Army; whether this was done because the land was granted to him following his service to the Revolution or whether it was simply named in his honor by an admiring aide who settled here, my limited research on the point did not resolve. A few miles farther on, the town of Milbridge guards the salmon-rich waters of the Narraguagus River. On the edge of town, I decided to pay a call at Hands On Crafts and was told it is the oldest such craft co-op in the state. The work displayed there—quilts, woven goods, clothing, and so forth—was of high quality, the little girls' dresses made from Victorian patterns and trimmed with antique lace and ribbons holding a particular charm. The grand house—all garrets and cupolas—that you see when you look back down the road from the shop's front deck once belonged to a state senator, and you wonder how someone can maintain such a palace of wood today without turning it into a B-and-B.

Milbridge itself also has character, but for the rest, the town comes in a plain wrapper, not drab or dull, just without unnecessary adornment. My kind of place, if the truth be known. There's a big Christmas-wreath concern here, supplied by the local cottage industry. Milbridge has a rare bit of nightlife for this stretch, in the form of a movie theater, and there's a restaurant, the Milbridge House, that Edward Hopper would have wanted to paint, and which was written up in *The New Yorker*, no less, for its cranberry pie. Route 1 turns abruptly north in Milbridge and follows the Narraguagus upstream; at the mouth of the river, you may fish without a license for the salmon that spawn here in the early summer, if you stay beyond the brackish water on the inlet side of the bridge. On this northern end of town, a couple from Massachusetts named Janet and Ray have opened a B-and-B in their home, called the Victorian Lady Inn. The inn's three guest rooms look comfortable, and are smartly furnished in the Victorian manner. Both Ray and Janet are enamored with the rhythms of old Maine they've discovered in Milbridge; they hope to stay open year-round eventually, and offer their inn as a retreat for those with "computer burn-out," the kind of people they have long known and observed in the soft-core industrial area they come from.

Up the road, via either Route 1 or the Kansas Road on the opposite bank of the river, is tiny Cherryfield village, comprising a row of buildings as refined in their fading Victorian plumage as is the building stock in Milbridge, by contrast, a paradigm of Yankee modesty. No doubt these some-what precarious structures, owing to their inherent real-estate value, will be rescued to preserve this unique architectural composition as a set piece, if for no other reason than to memorialize some concentrated outburst of imagination by the local inhabitants of the mid-nineteenth century. Already gussied up is a home and B-and-B next to the Historical Society Museum—which itself occupies a superb old double storefront, formerly a telegraph office—called the Black Shutter Inn, which, according to a discreetly placed sign, also serves the Cherryfield community as a Quaker meeting house. Another inn to consider in Cherryfield is the Ricker House (c. 1803), decidedly out of step in its day with the local Victorian revolution, being of the sober and classical Federal style. I had met a man in Munson, Maine, in the course of my travels, who urged me to be sure to drop in on the Ricker House's innkeepers when I got to Cherryfield. Bill and Jean are their names; they are native Alabamans and, in that tradition, a hospitable pair. Their inn is attractive, but its most distinguishing mark is a scrapbook-cum-guide that orients their guests to a hundred local excursions and ac-tivities. The greatest attraction in the immediate vicinity for naturalists is a vast heath and peat bog that spreads over 200,000 acres of the surround-ing townships.

Harrington Village is the next town up the coast, and is notable for the scenic drive down to Ripley Neck and for the smelt fishery in early spring, which sees hundreds of colorful huts and shacks erected on the frozen tidal creeks that etch the village confines. The loop on the Addison Road, via Addison to Columbia Falls, follows the coastal route. Addison seemed ancient and totally seafaring as I drove among its paint-peeled clapboard houses through a thick and salty mist. Columbia Falls, on the other hand, straddles a crossroads quiet but for Ruggle's House, an eighteenth-century Adams-style home with numerous distinctive architectural features. It now serves as a museum and draws a continuous flow of travelers who pass this way. At twenty-minute intervals during working hours, visitors to Ruggle's House are treated to a guided tour of the premises. On the hilly elevations beyond Columbia Falls' principal and unassuming thoroughfare are a dozen enormous homes and buildings of great visual and historic interest, several of which date from the late 1700s. Notable are a grand hall with mustard-yellow trim and, next door to it, a glorious wreck of sadly terminal appearance that still possesses a wood-shingled roof and its original twelve-over-twelve and twelve-over-eight window sashes, or "lights," as they are commonly called.

JONESPORT TO EASTPORT VIA ROUTES 191, 189, AND 190

Route 187 traces the peninsula that separates the Route 1 river towns of Columbia Falls and Jonesboro. As I drove the initial stretch of this peninsula road, it was clear from the number of simple cottages, trailers, and rough cabins that not all of the Maine coast is owned by rich out-of-staters, which is the line adopted by many an embittered native—and not without just cause—whenever the subject of real estate comes up. Such cash-poor coastal enclaves as I was passing here are certainly more and more rare in Maine, and where they prevail, they are subject to the enormous and seemingly irreversible pressures of real-estate speculation. At land's end, I came to Jonesport, the most active of the Down East harbors, where street signs resembling lobster boats represent the quintessence of folk art in the making. You just know intuitively that someday these very signs will trade for big bucks on the antiques dealer's auction block.

A bridge links Jonesport to Beal's and Great Wass islands, popular spots for coastal hiking. After crossing the causeway between the islands, I turned right where an arrow pointed toward the "Nature Conservancy," and bumped along over a long, pitted dirt road all the way to the end, where a compound of rental cottages commanded a view of the sea above Norton Point. A half-mile back on that same road, in a yellow house, I talked with a Mrs. Beal, the innkeeper for the cottages and the wife of a man whose great-great-great-grandfather was the island's original settler. While she was clearly a Mainer, the hint of a Scots brogue in her speech is characteristic, it is said, of the population this far east along the coast. Mrs. Beal said there were some three miles of trails on the nearby conservancy lands, lovely for long walks and picnics. We also talked about the fog. "Sometimes," she said, "it stays foggy here for two weeks, maybe once a year. After a week, you want to see the sun. Yes, sir."

By the time I reached Jonesboro, back on Route 1, the day was on the wane, with perhaps two hours of sunlight remaining. I was still several towns, and a good forty-five minutes on the fly, from Cobscook Bay State Park, below Dennysville, where I planned to camp for the night. I hadn't been able to calculate in advance, of course, just how long it would take to explore the eastern coast at an unpressured pace and to my satisfaction. Now I knew that I needed a minimum of two full days to savor a taste of the region. So, feeling very pleased with what I had thus far seen, and looking forward to the next day's touring, I focused on my destination, allowing for just enough peripheral vision to skim the thinnest overall impression from the places I would pass; now I was somewhat singlemindedly bent on setting up my campsite and enjoying a tentside meal by sunset. After Machias and Machiasport, to which I would return the following day, the image of wild blueberry barrens predominated as did large signs entreating "rakers wanted" and columns of boxes, wood flats set in star-shaped stacks to hold the fruit that was now being harvested, ninety percent of the nation's wild blueberries coming from this very county.

The campsite exceeded my wildest expectations. A reliable source had mentioned that, by mid-August, Cobscook Bay State Park was rarely full. I therefore had some hope of getting a site on the spur of the moment, without the customary reservation. And I did—a private, coveside promontory encircled by trees, where a roofed structure open on all sides protected a picnic table and provided just enough space to shelter my tent as well from the almost certain storm promised by the darkness of the evening clouds. As for the other kind of shower that I was looking forward to, most of Maine's state parks don't have them; Cobscook does. The shower house is near the park entrance, and is one of those affairs where you drop quarters in a timer in exchange for luxurious hot water. I found that one quarter was sufficient, and two quarters bordered on indulgence. The sinks in the shower house deliver hot water for nothing, or at least

nothing more than your daily campsite fee, $7 per night for Maine resi-
dents, $10 for out-of-staters. Many of the campsites overlook the bay.
Well, it's a tidal flat, actually, as I discovered after falling asleep on a watery
shore and awakening at dawn to the rude shrieking of crows who were
feeding in the mud, which, I might add, did not diminish the beauty of the
spot one iota.

For dinner the night before, I had broken in my new two-burner Coleman
stove on kielbasa and baked beans, and in the morning I fried up eggs with
chopped beef. Raw carrots and cucumbers from my garden back home kept
me from totally reverting to a Cub Scout diet. But I was some tickled by
how quickly and efficiently that Coleman worked, since I didn't really have
the time to indulge a wood or charcoal fire. Hard rains had fallen during the
night, but morning brought a partial clearing. In this region, the fogs, I
gather, roll in and out continually. After breakfast, I set out to pick up the
trail I'd left off the day before, and rode over lightly inhabited Route 191
from Dennysville back to Machias, and then on to Roque Bluffs, another
state park outside of Jonesboro, featuring not camping but swimming from
both saltwater and freshwater beaches.

Fog was still thick near the ocean when I drove down to Roque Bluffs,
so I missed the panoramic sweep of the water views I had read about, but
an atmosphere of seaside remoteness created by the undisturbed woods
and barrens clung to the place and gave it dimension despite the poor
visibility. When I reached Shoppee Point, the road ended in a clearing
before the sea, opposite the summer colony on Roque Island. There was
a parking garage on the point, and a number of cars were parked outdoors
as well. A few skiffs floated at anchor offshore, and in the gray, gauzy light
they seemed fraught with allegorical powers, more like markers in an ocean
graveyard than work craft used to ferry arrivals to and from their moored
sailboats and pleasure cruisers. It's hard to say whether or not a true profile
of Roque Island's summer folk can be extrapolated from the stickers fixed
to a single, somewhat disheveled automobile, one of which read GROTON
SCHOOL and the other, JOE KENNEDY FOR CONGRESS.

Staying on the Roque Bluffs Road all the way around the peninsula, I
came back to Route 1 just before Machias. Somehow I had formed the
opinion, based on a few gossipy conversations with some neighbors, that
Machias was an ugly place. Far from it—it is quite charming and also on a
smaller scale than I had imagined. At the edge of town, where the Machias
River is split into two streams of rushing white water by a massive rocky

ledge, the community has built Bad Little Falls Park, endowed with flower beds. There are observation decks above the rapids, from which can be had a nearly unobstructed view of most of Machias and all of its waterfront. A red footbridge crosses to a picnic field, and a sign indicates a South Shore river path and a historic cemetery where many of the town's eighteenth-century settlers are buried, just a few paces up the trail. One of the buildings that is very prominent in the view from the falls is the yellow-fronted Downeast 5 & 10, well stocked with shelves of yarn, stationery, and plastic lawn ornaments. Next door is the twin-gabled 5 Water Street, a restaurant in a pretty house of periwinkle blue that serves brown rice and fresh veggies with a range of meats and seafood. On the skyline is a church steeple housing a Paul Revere bell, another subject at one time for that superb watercolorist, John Marin. Off the main square is the town's most popular attraction for visitors, the Burnham Tavern Museum, listed in the National Register of Historic Places, and the oldest building in eastern Maine. Contained therein are mementoes from the *Margaretta,* a British man-of-war captured in local waters by a small coastal sloop, the *Unity*, in what is remembered as the first naval battle of the American Revolution.

Route 92, near Bad Little Falls Park, leads down to Machiasport and several other small coastal communities. This is a true river road, and one of the most purely scenic communities that I was to drive through in all of Washington County. The river is often in view, and the old homes reflect the area's colonial roots. Machiasport itself I found unexpectedly quite small. Like most of these old shipping and boat-building ports on the Maine coast, Machiasport's economic heyday occurred over a century ago. Today there is a sardine-canning factory here, one of the few remaining in the state. And, of course, the town still possesses its proud military history; from its shores the battle between the *Unity* and the *Margaretta* could be witnessed, and later, during the War of 1812, the port was fortified to repel subsequent intrusions by the British Navy. Farther down the peninsula, east of the old air force housing units, is Jasper Beach, a favorite haunt for rock collectors, and at the tip of Route 92 is Starboard, from where, depending on the tide, visitors may cross to the Point of Main peninsula and Starboard Island, each offering its own unique and intense vistas of the open sea.

It is not necessary to return through Machias to continue Down East. An asphalt road just north of Machiasport forks to the right off Route 92 and crosses a steel bridge downriver into the historical district of East Machias, and ultimately returns you to Route 1, but only for a few seconds. The coastal route follows Route 191, and I was beginning to wonder as I drove that way if the day was going to be a complete fog-out. On the map, the proximity of the road first to Machias Bay, and next to the ocean-fronting harbor at Cutler, promised wide sea views. But the weather was against me, and my own visibility was limited for the most part to the hem between the water and the shore, where a translucent mist hung like a drawn curtain veiling the scene beyond. If the stouthearted Mrs. Beal of Great Wass Island became demoralized after two weeks of fog, well, I was beginning to unravel after only two days.

In compensation, I tried to focus more narrowly on the landscape that I *could* see, and on the salutary properties inherent in the sheer ritual of the ride. Even when the visual dimension—so central to the premise of this book—is momentarily censored, Maine roads always manage to provide some suitable distraction, some novelty if only for the mind's eye. For example, when Route 191 suddenly turned northward as it approached Cutler, I could not resist the rough side road where a small sign lettered in black paint pointed to Little Machias. Here was one of those off-road appendages that led to a backwater little visited by outsiders. The remnants of a few saltwater farms bravely fronted the ocean winds, and the way was also lined with the usual pockets of prefabricated and mobile homes that one still finds scattered along the rural seacoast. Right at the edge of the blacktop road, someone had built his kid a basketball hoop, further proof that not much traffic comes down this way.

Cutler, with its lobster hatchery, is a center of aquaculture, the new and multifaceted industry attempting to establish itself the length of the Maine coast to inject the Down East economy with a needed jolt. Cutler is also a port of call for yachtspeople, many of whom sail in from Canadian waters and then use the phone at the Little River Lodge to inform the customs officer of their arrival. The lodge is a B-and-B, open from May to October, and the owners will serve dinner by reservation in their small, cheery dining room that overlooks the harbor. Cutler also has a grocery store with a lunch counter–cum–breakfast nook, and in all the harbor hamlet is another one of those dreamy places on the Maine coast where I may want to spend a weekend someday. But the road beckoned—*toujours* the road, you might say, and not a bad fate at that. Always a new treat around the next bend. Just outside of Cutler, in fact, I suddenly became aware of a quality in the fog that was stunningly positive, something I had been experiencing right along, but had failed to recognize. The fog filters the light in a way that is especially flattering to the variety of vegetation composing the heath that surrounds you everywhere as you drive the length of Route 191. No sooner had I made this revelation than I noticed that the fog had actually lifted to an elevation that gave scope to my observations, broadening the immediate horizons over land and sea and filling me with quiet ecstasy at the detail now visible in the scenery.

It was as if I were now seeing the boglands for the first time, or at least it seemed that my appreciation was transforming from the general to the particular. I began to make distinctions in the vegetation, and was impressed by how desertlike the ecology of the heath appeared. Not Saharan, obviously, but similar in density and verdure, perhaps, to the vegetable-rich Arizona desert. With each plant growing in its distinct and separate stand, the bog is Nature's crazy quilt, with alternating grasses, flowering plants, succulents, ferns, and scrub evergreens. One space would be occupied by a patch of flat green grass, then something straw-colored, then tall stems flying fuzzy brown punks, then stunted pines and feathery ferns, and so much more, the whole crowned by the regal and complex fireweed, ablaze in pink and purple. The atmosphere of these lands was charged with a trace of midsummer madness, a giddiness in the face of the bog's powerful therapies. From this point forward, right to the tip of northern Maine, I would stop whenever a new plant or flower caught my attention. My harvest was sparse but ravishing, and the names of those specimens I both observed and picked came to be revealed in a variety of ways before my trip was over.

The defunct Fitzhenry Market with its Mobil gas pump occupies the corner of a side road just above South Trescott on Route 191. This road leads past the cove called Bailey's Mistake. Legend has it that a captain once grounded his ship here due to navigational error, and the crew, rather than continue on, off-loaded the cargo of lumber and settled the place. At the end of this road is the Quoddy Head Light and Park—the easternmost point in the United States—and en route is the Overview, a sometime B-and-B. When I passed this house, I saw the sign with its name, but no reference to lodgings, so I drove on. But my mind flashed on the discreet sign I'd just barely noticed on 191 at the turnoff back at the Fitzhenry Market. It pointed to "Overview." I decided to swing back and risk an intrusion. Indeed, the owner, Edith Heter, having recently committed matrimony, had removed the B-and-B portion of her sign, not certain whether or not she wished to continue in the hospitality business. But I fell to talking with Edith and her houseguest Ada, who was down from Toronto. "The inn is out," said Ada. "Make that with two *t*'s," added Edith. I was left with the final impression, however, that if you happen to be in the area, it wouldn't hurt to inquire about a room, which also entitles you to the use of an outdoor sauna, some tidbits from the organic garden (in season), and lots of space for ocean and woods walks, plus a glorious, isolated "overview" of the heath-bordered sea.

The great expectation for those who visit the Quoddy Light this time of year is to catch sight of some whales on migration to their summer waters in the Bay of Fundy, to feed on small fish and plankton. Several species, from the relatively small minke to the mammoth finback, appear with unpredictable regularity within view of the much-photographed, barber-pole-painted lighthouse. Once again, however, the fog had rolled in, so I could see neither whales nor the Canadian islands of Grand Manan and Campobello, which are said to be palpably visible from here on a clear day.

Lubec is the largest town in this area, and once the canning capital of Maine. Although Lubec today has many homes, most of the buildings on its main street by the wharf are boarded up and serve as warehouse space for a local fish smokehouse. One canning factory remains along this strip. At the front desk in the old-fashioned office of the R. J. Peacock Canning Company, I was told that the company had had to suspend its tours for the public several years back, owing to the hike in liability insurance rates. Furthermore, Peacock's was itself closed down at the time of my visit—whether temporarily or for good was not made clear. Apparently there had been a fire, and perhaps damage assessments were in progress. Were the factory to close, its Admiral and Bulldog brand fish steaks and sardines, whose cans were mounted on the office wall like proud sporting trophies, would go the way of other natural products of times gone by, leaving no trace save perhaps an illustration or two in some coffee-table book devoted to early designs in American packaging. My other action in Lubec, which has the overall atmosphere of an undiscovered place that might be interesting to hang out in for a while, was to peruse the listings at a local real-estate office; as elsewhere along the Maine coast, the prices have gone through the roof.

Opposite Lubec is the island of Campobello, located in the Canadian province of New Brunswick. To reach Campobello, you must cross the bridge that spans the international waters between the United States and

Canada, and pass through customs on both entry and return. Campobello, as most people know, was where Franklin Delano Roosevelt and his wife, Eleanor, had their summer cottage, a wedding present from his parents. Today, this enormous, well-administered house is the centerpiece of a park honoring the former president's memory, and it is a worthwhile stopover while on the island. The cottage certainly attests to the luxurious ease enjoyed by the upper classes during the early years of this century, a life-style out of reach for even the great sultans of industry today. But the park visitors' center yielded an even more valuable revelation, more pertinent to my own modest and immediate interests. A series of informative displays in the Flora/Fauna Room there provided names and color photographs of the environments and individual plants I had been studying en route, including a definition of *bog*: "a word of Celtic origin meaning wet, spongy ground rich in plant residue, frequently surrounding a body of open water and having a characteristic flora as of sedges, heaths, and sphagnum." Individual wildflowers of the bog, identified and shown in excellent, life-size photos, were rhodora, baked apple blossom, round-leafed sundew, bog laurel, Labrador tea, cotton grass, bluets, devil's paintbursh, yellow lichen, bunchberry, roseroot sedum, and, of course, the amazing fireweed or great willow herb, as it is also known.

A slightly more adventurous excursion on Campobello involves a stop at Head Harbor Light, located at the far end of the island. And there might be more adventure in store for you than you imagine if you fail to heed the clearly posted warning signs. Should you cross the rocks to the lighthouse itself, some distance away, a trek requiring considerable exertion up and down a series of ship-style ladders and across several stony paths and causeways, you may find yourself trapped by a tide that rises five feet every hour when the flood turns—after which the lighthouse rock becomes an island where you must cool your heels for eight hours until the ebb has once again emptied the passageway. I suppose that the danger is only great if you should choose to cross at a time when the tide waters have already begun to swell. A very adequate view of the bay and its islands can be seen from the bluffs that overlook the causeway, so that the crossing to the lighthouse—an admirable complex of buildings connected telescope fashion—is hardly necessary to enjoy the visual fruits of this attraction.

The final leg of my trip Down East was now upon me. In a half hour, after winding my way along Route 190, I would come to Eastport, and I had no idea what kind of town to expect. I had met another young traveler at the lighthouse, Tracy from Minnesota, out east on a Maine wanderlust between jobs. Tracy was also bound for Eastport, and said she had reservations at the Todd House, where I promised to look in on her when I made my rounds, visiting a few local B-and-Bs. I had forgotten, however, that before reaching Eastport I would pass Pleasant Point, where the Passamaquoddy Indians have their reservation. So, initially, I was confused by the sudden appearance at roadside of several rows of very institutional-looking, poverty-level housing units. There is considerable poverty scattered about Maine, but I had never seen such a concentration of miserable dwellings as those on what I soon realized was the home ground of the Passamaquoddies. A road to the left, before the causeway that passes on to Eastport, led to the center of the reservation, where the roads were all badly maintained, but many of the houses were of a better sort than those I had seen previously. Besides the several score residences, the only community I could see was centered around a Catholic church and an ill-stocked supermarket. It was depressing to observe how far the Indians have been forced to travel from the dignified lives their ancestors led before the Yankee invasion.

Eastport, by contrast, is a thriving town, busily refurbishing its houses and storefronts after years of an economic decline that began to bottom out throughout most of Maine during the late sixties. Only now has the boom reached this far up the coast, and Eastport is suddenly digging out from under. Five or six B-and-Bs of recent vintage line the street leading down to the town center; a dozen other neighboring houses are in the midst of major renovations. Main Street, which parallels the bayfront, is similarly under transformation. Commercial buildings whose storefronts one imagines to have been empty for years will soon house spiffy boutiques and cater to the waves of new residents and tourists who have "discovered" Eastport's undeniable charms.

Main Street yielded one immediate place of interest, Oggie's Bakery, a storefront with a half-dozen tables and a display counter filled with freshly made sweets. The pumpkin cake with sour-cream icing was all the enticement I needed. Several coffee refills and squares of cake later, I went off to rendezvous with Tracy at the Todd House. The owner of this B-and-B is Ruth, who, after having grown up in Portland, has returned to the town she was born in, and therefore—according to some of the more rigid local worthies—is considered to be "from away," an outsider to be shunned. But Ruth told me that, despite such innuendo, she fought hard to defeat the plan to build an oil refinery at Eastport, a project initially viewed by most longtime residents as having the potential for an economic boom, but later repelled as a sure environmental disaster and death to the new bloom of tourism.

As Ruth and I talked in her living room—which doubles as the B-and-B's public parlor—Tracy wandered in and told me that fellow guests from New Jersey had invited her on a bicycle trip the next morning around Deer Island in Canada, accessible only by ferry from Campobello. And Ruth had arranged for her the loan of an old bike from a neighbor. Then another new arrival came through the door, a woman from the Midwest, traveling with her five-year-old son. Finally, a third woman, who was traveling alone, joined the group. A very lively discussion then ensued when I mentioned my distress and indignation at the decrepit state of the Passamaquoddy reservation. I was amazed to hear from half of my interlocutors their opinion that the Indians had it in their power to better their condition if they wanted to, or words to that effect. The conservative values of young people, particularly females—for reasons that are patently romantic, I must admit—always shock me. Like all such encounters on the road when traveling alone, however stormy or brief, this too was a welcome release from the safe confines of my own interior monologue. I stayed with these folk until shortly after sunset, and then retreated to my private campfire—or Coleman stove gas fire, I should say—in the Cobscook State Park, happily brewing up a cup of herbal tea and reading by lantern about the places I would visit to the north during the second phase of my trip.

▪

INFORMATION ▪ *Ellsworth Chamber of Commerce* (677-5584 or 667-2617), Rte. 1A, Ellsworth 04678. ▪ *Milbridge Merchants Association*, Milbridge 04619. ▪ *The Eastport Area Chamber of Commerce*, P.O. Box 254, Eastport 04631.

ELLSWORTH TO COLUMBIA FALLS

LODGINGS ▪ The environs of Ellsworth, especially along Route 3 in the direction of Mount Desert, are well endowed with traditional motels. ▪ *The Foxfair* (667-8665), 179 State St., Ellsworth 04605. A B-and-B. ▪ *Victorian Lady Inn* (546-3352 or 508-674-5227, Main St., P.O. Box 286,

Milbridge 04658. Open year-round (by appointment only during the off-season). Three rooms and full breakfast. ▪ *Black Shutter Inn* (546-2853), Cherryfield 04622. In the midst of Cherryfield's tiny Victorian village, with three spacious bedrooms. ▪ *Ricker House* (546-2780), U.S. 1 and Maine Rte. 182, Cherryfield 04622. The innkeepers here are tireless archivists of the local scene when it comes to sights, day trips, events, and outdoor activities. Also three comfortable, country rooms at $45 double, with a full breakfast. ▪ *Harrington House* (483-2232), Rte. 1, Harrington 04643. A restored Victorian inn by the quiet village green. ▪ *The Old Hotel Tea Room* (483-6585), Main St., Columbia Falls 04623, across from Ruggles House. Room and board, open from June 15 through August.

CAMPING ▪ *Mainayr Campground* (546-2690) in Steuben, open Memorial Day through Columbus Day. ▪ *Bayview Campground* (546-2946) in Milbridge, open May 15 to November 15.

HOSTEL ▪ *American Youth Hostel* (483-9763) operates a solar- and wind-powered farmhouse on sixty-two acres with a pond in Harrington; around $5 a night, but you must be a member. For information, contact AMY, 1020 Commonwealth Ave., Boston, MA 02215.

FOOD ▪ *Milbridge House*, Milbridge. Recommended on the strength of its mention in *The New Yorker* and on a hunch after seeing the place, even though it was closed at the time. ▪ *The Red Barn* (546-7721), junction of routes 1 and 1A in Milbridge. An economical soup-and-salad bar, with children's meals available. ▪ *Sugar Scoop Bakery* (546-7048), Main St., Milbridge. A local emporium for a sticky bun with coffee or baked beans and brown bread. ▪ *Old Hotel Tea Room* (483-6585), Columbia Falls. Two dining rooms and hearty roadhouse fare.

ARTS AND CRAFTS ▪ *Hands On!* (546-2682), Rte. 1, Milbridge. Open from 9:30 A.M. to 5:00 P.M., mid-June through September.

SPECIAL ▪ *The Great Heath,* the 200,000-plus-acre peat bog surrounding Columbia Falls and Township 19MD. Over 3,000 acres are open to the public, where the Audubon Society conducts periodic tours. ▪ Apparently, fishing for salmon is very good around Milbridge or Cherryfield; don't forget the license if you're in an angling mood.

JONESPORT TO EASTPORT

LODGINGS ■ *Tootsie's Bed-n-Breakfast* (497-5414), Jonesport 04649. A B-and-B in a fisherman's neighborhood, with rooms overlooking the Mooseabec Reach at reasonable rates. ■ *Micmac Farms* (255-3008), Machiasport 04655, on Rte. 92, two miles from Machias on the river. Gourmet dining available. ■ *East River B-and-B* (255-8467), Rte. 91 (High Street), East Machias 04630. Overlooks the salmon pools on the Machias, and rooms have cable TV. ■ *Beals Housekeeping Cottages* on Great Wass Island (497-2232), P.O. Box 172, Beals 04611. Four cottages available. ■ *Little River Lodge* (259-4437), P.O. Box 237, Cutler 04626. A small inn over pretty Cutler Harbor, including full breakfast, and dinner by reservation. ■ *The Overview*, (733-2005), P.O. Box 106, Lubec 04652. Lovely site with three rooms near Bailey's Mistake, plus wood-fired sauna and tent space available. ■ *Home Port Inn* (733-2077), 45 Main St., Lubec 04652. In-town lodgings with dining room. ■ *Todd House* (853-2328), Eastport 04631. Eight rooms with Colonial decor, some with access for the disabled. ■ *The Inn at Eastport* (853-4307), 13 Washington St., Eastport 04631. Five guest rooms with antique furnishings, plus a hot tub with a water view. Breakfast included and other meals available.

CAMPING ■ *Cobscook Bay State Park* (726-4412) Rte. 1, Dennysville. Open mid-May till mid-October. 150 campsites, mostly for tents, in a 900-acre park overlooking the water. ■ *The Seaview* (853-4471) Rte. 190, Eastport. Full-service private campground. ■ *Campobello Haven* (506-752-2360), Herring Cove Rd., Campobello Island, N.B., Canada. Campground with a drive-in seafood restaurant.

FOOD ■ *Ships Wheel Restuarant* (497-2403), Jonesport. Local crossroads and family-style restaurant specializing in seafood. ■ *5 Water Street* (255-4153), Machias. Good food in the brown-rice-and-veggies tradition, with curries, chicken, meat, and seafood. ■ *Austinwoods*, Water St., Machias. Ice-cream parlor and snackery. ■ *Cannery Wharf* (853-4800), North Water St., Eastport. Seafood and steak plus service bar and takeout. ■ *Oggie's Bakery & Luncheonette* (853-2325), 50 Water St., Eastport. Brand new, but soon to be a local hangout, I predict, and a good bet for breakfast, lunch, or coffee break.

CRAFTS ▪ *Lubec Baskets,* Bailey's Mistake. Two basketmakers work in a shed behind the Overview B-and-B, and do most of their business by mail order. But you can also drop in.

HISTORICAL SITES ▪ *The Narraguagus Historical Society* (546-7979) operates a small museum in Cherryfield, open Saturdays in July and August, or by appointment. ▪ *Ruggles House* in Columbia Falls is a Federal-style home functioning as a period museum. ▪ *Burnham Tavern* in Machias is a restored inn of the Revolutionary War period. ▪ *Roosevelt Campobello International Park* contains FDR's summer cottage.

SPECIAL ▪ *West Quoddy Light State Park* near Lubec for the light-house, the seascape, whale watching, and the surrounding bog. ▪ *Head Harbor Light,* Campobello, for its dramatic setting and unique lighthouse complex.

15

CANADIAN MAINE

CALAIS TO FORT KENT VIA ROUTE 1 AND
ALTERNATES ■ RETURN ALONG ROUTE 11
TO I-95 OR ROUTE 220 IN NEWPORT

Before retiring that last night in Cobscook Park, I spent some time going over my Maine map. The area to begin exploring the next morning was vast, comprising fully a fifth, perhaps even a quarter, of the state. As with my journey Down East, I did not have the luxury of an open-ended visit, so the plan here, too, was to cover as much of this enormous territory as possible within the limits of my circumstances, without feeling rushed. I would drive as much as I needed to, and stop whenever the spirit moved me, which, as it turned out, was often enough for a deep impression to be left in my mind of a land rich in natural, agricultural, and cultural diversity. And if this chapter's title strikes a contradictory note, I suggest you take another quick look at your own map of Maine. All the way north, this itinerary parallels the border with Canada, along which, as I was to learn, the daily ties between citizens of both nations are central to the social and, to some degree, the economic fabric of this entire region.

CALAIS TO AROOSTOOK STATE PARK VIA ROUTE 1

Nonetheless, for the lion's share, this narrative concerns itself only with the Maine side of the border, because—if the reader will excuse an obvious pun—the line has to be drawn some-where. And that line begins in a town called Dennysville, just below Calais, the latter pronounced by Mainers as if referring to some hardened skin on the ball of the foot, that is to say, "callus." As for Dennysville, large homes lining a ridge above the river are relics of the town's prosperity in the days of the great lumber runs. The grandest of the old homes is an inn called Lincoln House, built originally in 1787 for the son of the Revolutionary War general Benjamin Lincoln, who, at the Battle of Yorktown, directed the laying down of British arms. Lincoln House still radiates a certain country elegance and offers the touring public an ambitious dining menu, while overnight guests may choose the modified American plan or simply bed and breakfast. The Woodshed Pub occupies an adjoining building, and is said to provide a spirited nightlife just about year-round for residents of the area.

At Pembroke, two approaches to Calais confront the motorist. The first follows Route 1 north along the St. Croix River; the second combines a stretch of Route 214 with a back road entered to the right across from a store marked "Hatton." It is the road on your map that winds close by the shores of Round Lake, and then through the countryside, before coming out on Route 1 at the north edge of the Calais commercial strip. Actually, I jumped ahead of my story by driving into Calais—known as Maine's only border *city*—via the river route the first night I stayed in Cobscook Park. Approximately three miles before Calais, a large green sign indicates a road going down to the river, from where visitors may get a view of historic St. Croix Island (known today as Dochet's Island). Here, in the summer of 1604, a French nobleman landed with his lieutenant, Samuel de Champlain, and some eighty colonists to establish a trading post and settlement. A combination of scurvy and a severely harsh winter wiped out many of the unprepared colonists, whose story is told in sympathetic detail by the American historian Francis Parkman in his study *The French in North America*.

Calais, like Presque Isle and Caribou—the other large towns I was to visit during this swing to the north—is a marketplace and shopping center for its sprawling environs. In the course of the modernization necessary to fulfill these important municipal and commercial roles, each of these three municipalities has sacrificed the quaintness and historical character still visible in other, smaller towns of the region, while failing to develop any qualities that might be considered genuinely urban. Therefore, Calais, Presque Isle, and Caribou occupy the vague suburban space between the poles of my own preference for either true city life or a more clearly defined small-town or village atmosphere. And as such, the three "moderns," as I shall call them, receive short shrift in this account, failing on the narrow grounds of visual appeal to have triggered my admittedly selective and eccentric curiosity.

It was about seven o'clock the first evening I drove through Calais. Monday night, the deadest night of the week, and Calais's principal artery—a long, curving street mostly in view of the river—reflected this moment of extreme torpor in the normal weekly cycle. Prominent on the opposite riverbank is the skyline of the Canadian town St. Stephen, a mirror image of Calais in its rough scale, and even considerably duller in appearance, as I discovered after crossing to that side. In one detail, St. Stephen was remarkably distinct from its foreign twin, at least on this particular summer night: the streets of the Canadian town were lined with cruising, promenading, and peaceable teenagers, some with the inevitable expressions of boredom and longing that come with the territory at that state of life. I am certain that many of the young faces I saw there were those of American kids, because residents of both countries treat the two towns as one, and take for granted the inconvenience of customs checks both ways when crossing the border.

There are many opportunities for crossing into Canadian towns all the way north along the Maine border. And each time you make the crossing, you explain to the Canadian guard that you are an American tourist, and he opens wide the gates, pointing toward some office where you may fill your arms with promotional brochures on local inns and sights. On return, the American border guard looks suspiciously into your car, eyes you with his most guilt-provoking gaze, and asks you where you were born. For Canadians, one imagines, the intimidation works in reverse. Their guards are looking for contraband, mostly cigarettes, booze, and jerry cans of gasoline, all of which are cheaper on the American side; our guards, one assumes, are looking for bad guys trying to smuggle drugs, perhaps for terrorists in these dark days, or for illegal immigrants looking to cash in on the American Dream. Thus the "good guys" are inconvenienced in having to submit to a few moments of humiliation imposed by our normally discreet and anonymous state; and the "bad guys" are also inconvenienced, being forced to cross either over land or at low water on some moonless night far from a border station.

Calais by day was my first stop heading north, after I visited Lincoln House in Dennysville. Having taken the faster "back route" described at the beginning of this chapter, I came in above the town and had to double back south, parking as soon I reached the edge of the downtown district. My object was to find the Calais Chamber of Commerce or some other source of tourist information about the scene from here northward, so that, informed of all the bases, I could then touch—or not—the ones that appealed. To ask directions, I walked into the first open door that presented itself, that of Big Bad Bud's Bar, which is also the Portside Inn (rooms $20 to $50 a night). At eight in the morning there were already ten gents seated at the bar and at the few tables, and whoever tried to answer my question got a good-natured ribbing from his bemused mates. A typical exchange: "You don't know where your own home is, Red." "Neither do you," shot back Red in a wounded tone. "Sure I do," replied his taunter. "Home is where my hat is. And right now my hat's on the backseat of my car."

They all laughed like hell at that, these men who struck me as players without chips sitting around waiting for some way to get back in the game. And I laughed too, grateful for that tension-breaker and even a slight warming dose of communal mirth. Finally "Sam" was located, the only one at Bad Bud's, I guess, authorized to reveal where the town keeps its promotional brochures, and I got the directions I was seeking. I walked to the efficiently run information booth located at the opposite end of town from Bad Bud's, and a very attentive lady provided a useful orientation, suggesting I might want to stop at the nearby Moosehorn Wildlife Refuge. This was tempting, but I had a craving for some active town life, so I set my course for Houlton, eighty-five miles distant, the seat of the state's gigantic Aroostook County.

Calais lingered on the landscape for several miles north, past the drive-in movie, past Route 9, the Bangor Road. On National Public Radio, my favorite DJ, Robert J. Lurtsema, was telling me that on this day, August 15, in 1870, the "golden spike" was driven into the tie that officially linked the eastern and the western railways; a nice arcane note, and in keeping with his announcement on the previous day that as it was Julia Child's birthday, he had, in her honor, selected a few compositions of culinary inspiration for the "Morning Pro Musica" menu. Up the road, the village of Princeton crossed Big Lake at a narrow gut, and the now unmistakable signs of another Indian reservation began to appear, more ticky-tacky boxes of careless construction, all rundown except for a very few. Here, at least, the tribe had not been robbed of the most desirable frontage at lakeside. Involuntarily, another meditation began in my head on the grotesque plight of the Native Americans, who by design or default had come to such an unenviable state. Just at that moment, Robert J. spun a new disk on the radio, a piano rag that sounded like Scott Joplin to my unschooled musical ear. And I left those sad reflections in a trail of gray exhaust, thinking that if I were to die that very moment, it was this song—as it turned out, from Rossini's "Pleasures and Peccadilloes"—I would want to reverberate in my head for all eternity.

I was aware of passing many worthy places and roads, potentially fruitful for my own brand of casual exploration, as I drove resolutely for Houlton, enjoying that familiar rush of freedom from being "on the road." Down Route 6 at Topsfield, though, I went searching for a place where canoe trips are outfitted, but turned back when I realized the digression would take longer than I fancied at that moment. My next stop was in Danforth on Route 1, just below where Aroostook County begins. Once a booming lumber town, Danforth today is a flag stop for the Canadian Pacific passenger train that connects Quebec with the Canadian Maritimes. Canoe excursions of some three days, as I learned during an informal chat with a pedestrian, link Danforth via the Baskahagen River with Mattawamkeag, located on the river of the same name. At the Guest House on Route 169 (but still in town), I was told that most tourists come to Danforth for the hunting and fishing. The inn is actually a B-and-D—bed-and-dinner—since most guests are gone by five or six in the morning, and the hostess makes dinner available for a minimal fee.

The road can be traveled quickly over this mid-northern stretch of Route 1, with mostly trees for companions as you speed onward. So absorbed had I become in this background of "green noise," that I had just glimpsed from the corner of my eye a very queer sort of junk display at roadside on the outskirts of Hodgdon. In fact, I drove right past Albert Kelso's exhibit of antique farm equipment, and had to swing back to make certain that I had actually seen something worth stopping for. The elderly, white-haired gent I had noticed standing shirtless at the door of the one-story building— surrounded by what looked like sculptures in the "found object" tradition— reappeared in a flowing white shirt and wide-brimmed straw hat as I entered the drive. A native of the region, Mr. Kelso's first words when he learned I was a reporter were that he and his collection had been filmed recently by a Belgian television crew shooting material from Maine to Key West. One of the crewmembers had asked him, "Where'd you study art? You're an artist, you know."

"But I never studied art. I've always had to hack it on my own," he allowed, recounting how he'd opened a road stand and general store here in the forties, where he'd sold bulk grain from his barn, and had been the "first one" to sell ice he'd cut from local waters to the traveling campers and fishermen. As for the twenty or so pieces of equipment he so studiously exhibited on his old parking lot, he explained that "people are curious, so if you can make them more curious, if you can take nothing and make something of it, you're pretty darn smart. They don't make this stuff anymore, and young people like this stuff, like those sprocket wheels," he said, indicating an old harvester. "They were on tractors when I was a boy." As a courtesy, Mr. Kelso opened his barn, itself a work of art with dozens of objects pinioned to its siding, including the tailgate of an old Studebaker pickup. Inside was another great hoard of "stuff" (none of it for sale), including an original single-horse-pulled mower with the brand name "Buckeye," fabricated in the Michigan shop where Henry Ford worked before launching the American auto industry. Mr. Kelso culls from his treasures a spare assortment of dump pickings for sale to the "curious" public (I bought an old barrel-staved planter); the artwork is only to look at.

Not far beyond Albert Kelso's, the farmlands of "the Aroostook"—as the great agricultural county is known—began to appear, being the immediate environs of the town of Houlton. There were good fields in production, and fields gone by, overgrown with acres of goldenrod. In the midst of this agrarian plain, Houlton soon appeared, with its large central square and its profile still more mill town than modern, despite the proximity of the fast lane in the form of I-95, which passes here before skipping merrily across the border and linking with its Canadian counterpart. After parking in the square, I wandered the streets, browsing in the shops, especially Shire-town Coins on the mezzanine floor of the Putnam Arcade Building. What attracted me were the baseball-card collectibles sold there, but the owner, a coin maven and a suspicious sort of fellow, delivered himself of a homily on shoplifting, something about a kid who had once stolen a prized silver dollar from his store, but he had seen justice done and the boy sent to prison. What could I say? I just kept looking at a few antique images of Joe "D" and "the Mick," then bade the man good day.

Speaking of baseball, Houlton was about the last stop going north where
I found the daily *Portland Press Herald*, a paper with an adequate national
sports section, in contrast to the *Bangor Daily News*—the paper of record
in this region—which reports primarily on local contests to the general
exclusion of major-league box scores—except the Red Sox, of course,
whom, as a lifelong Yankees fan, I despise. Reconciled to the knowledge
that certain sacrifices would be exacted when I continued this journey
northward, I went off in search of the Houlton Museum and Historical
Society, where an animated curator named Betty narrated—with the aid of
several relevant exhibits—the tale of the bloodless Aroostook War (1838–
39), a border dispute with England that was ultimately resolved by the
Webster-Ashburton Treaty in 1842. In a sense, all of these local museums
that abound in Maine are very similar, being repositories of period pieces,
tools, documents, and so forth; yet, for me, each—and the museum in
Holton was no exception—has its special charm and can be unimpeachably
justified either as a source of entertainment or as a place for scholarly
pursuits. By the time I left the museum, the sun had finally come out with
a vengeance after three foggy, overcast days, and as I headed back to my
car in the now-sweltering heat, I reckoned that Houlton had a comfortable,
timeless quality about it. And friendly too, in a dry sort of way, I thought,
after a man on the street looked me in the eye with a bit of a sparkle in his
smile and said, "Cold, ain't it?"

My goal for the day's drive was to reach Aroostook State Park before dark,
and I spent the next several hours wandering over ground you would
probably only visit if you had relatives who lived there—folk, chances are,
in the potato business. Until you reach Mars Hill, the road is so straight you
can see the cut lines through the forest, which gives the area, though long
settled, the appearance of a remote Amazonian highway scene. After that,
all around Presque Isle, Caribou, Limestone, and Fort Fairfield, farmland
reminiscent more of the plains states than of Maine is the dominant terrain
feature—flat, relatively treeless, and, for the most part, drab. Expanses of
potato vines, and sometimes oats, blanket the land. Homes tend to be
modern and utilitarian, and in general there is an air of inconspicuous
prosperity. I drove through all of the towns mentioned above before settling in for the night, and found little to distract my eye. The state park was
the one exception, with its few dozen attractive campsites spread over

tree-covered Quaggy Joe Mountain, by the side of echo Lake. The park had
no showers, so at dusk I bathed in the lake.

NEW SWEDEN TO FORT KENT . . .
AND A BIT BEYOND

B y six-thirty the following morning, I had broken camp and was
on my way to New Sweden, a community of some historic
significance that was settled by Swedish immigrants in the last
century, and mostly populated to this day by the descendants
of those original settlers. I had already driven most of the roads around
Presque Isle on the previous day, with the exception of Route 205 along the
Aroostook River, which I had reserved for my departure. This was, ironically, the narrow country road I had been looking for, a softer landscape
than I had thus far seen in this potato-farm region. Though close to Presque
Isle, the river had the squared-off look of an inland canal, in keeping with
the general orderliness of the surroundings. About midway to Caribou, I
was surprised to see the flashing red lights of a schoolbus that was taking
on some children at a farmhouse driveway. School had already started in
Aroostook, the only county remaining in the United States that still schedules a harvest recess during the last half of September and the first half of
October, when the kids are let out of classes to gather potatoes. In response to the bus, I had stopped my car opposite another barnyard, where
a man was busy at his chores. Dressed in work clothes and a brown peaked
hat, he was ruggedly handsome and middle-aged, with a lot of boy still in his
face. I asked him why I had seen so many bales in the culverts by the side
of the road. "The ditch, you mean? Placed there by the state," he said, "to
stop the wash-out." "That's not hay, is it?" I asked; it seemed so thick and
thatchlike, compared to our coastal hay. "Yes, it is," he replied with a good
deal of assertiveness and a broad, embarrassed smile, as if the silly ques-
tions asked by folk "from away" never ceased to confound him.

At the junction with Route 161, I crossed the bridge, passing through
Caribou, bound for New Sweden along this road. As you travel west and

north here, the land begins to climb again, with homes and farms widely
scattered in the folds and contours of the terrain, making for a more varied
background than that found in the flatlands below. Something very Scandinavian flavors the air, an indefinable, almost uncanny quality that is suddenly obvious in the more elaborate houses and landscaped grounds which
begin to appear on the access road to the old immigrant village. It goes
beyond the preference for greater domestic comforts and distinguishes the
Nordic folk from their Yankee neighbors. There is no town center, per se,
but a public space of sorts, a few buildings, including a Historical Society
Museum, which I soon discovered did not open till noon, some three hours
from the moment I stood on the steps looking through the windows at the
exhibit inside. A large portrait of the current king and queen of Sweden
resting on a chair, stared back, reminding me of my amusing encounter
with the royal pair in a hotel lobby in Salvador, Brazil, in 1984, when a
nervous protocol official almost knocked me down to clear a path for the
monarchs past the front desk where I was checking in.

Down the road from the museum, Bob Persson was caulking cracks in
the stone pillars that fence the old Swedish cemetery when I stopped to talk
to him. A man of about seventy, Bob was born here, but retains the distinct
lilt of an accent in his speech, suggesting that he grew up in a Swedish-
speaking home. I told him that I had met a Gorenson down in Dresden
whose family—now vegetable farmers—originated in New Sweden; these
were people Bob had grown up with and knew intimately, as it turned out.
We talked for a fair time, and he explained why the "potato houses" I had
been seeing for the past day—and had confused with regular barns—were
built into the sides of hills or embankments, with their front and rear
entrances on different levels. Spuds, of course, like to be where it's cool,
dry, and dark, and the stone walls, banked by earth, provide perfect storage conditions. The Green Mountain potatoes were the premier tubers
planted by the local farmers in the old days, Bob said, but the species fell
victim to disease. Russets are similar, but not as versatile for cooking, he
added. Other big changes had taken place around here, too. The family
farms were almost gone, he said, most of them bought up by "concerns"
that farmed potatoes on a large and highly mechanized scale.

On the map I had noticed another town, obviously founded by the Swedes,
called Stockholm. So I returned to Route 161 and continued north, inquiring
at Everett Larson's Grocery where I might get a cup of fresh coffee, one

of the few necessaries missing from his tidy, otherwise well-stocked general store. Mr. Larson directed me farther up 161 to Stan's, just before the Stockholm turnoff. HOME OF THE 10¢ CUP OF COFFEE, read the large sign, pointing down an access road to a long, tarpapered cabin right on the shores of Lake Madawaska. Speaking of necessaries, Stan supplies many necessities for the 400 "camps"—or summer homes—that ring Lake Madawaska, from kerosene to canned goods to coffee. And the coffee really is ten cents a cup (well, my cup being a double, I paid twenty cents). Stan's is also where you come to get a fishing license and to register your game, and the shop is a meeting place for the lakeside locals. It was hopping with people the morning I showed up, the backroom tables crowded to the limit. "They come here every day for their morning constitutional," said Stan.

Driving into Stockholm, which was a downscale version of New Sweden and not picturesque in any conventional sense, it struck me that the trees were back; if there was any such thing as a wilderness in northern Maine, I might now be on its fringe. I was not yet prepared to swallow the harder truth, that there really wasn't any longer an unspoiled virgin forest in Maine, nothing so majestic as Thoreau's "Maine woods" or Longfellow's "forest primeval." And yet, as a city boy, my astonishment never ceases at the sheer volume and variety of wildlife that one still sights throughout the state. The birds are legion, and that morning on Route 161, it was the ravens that seemed to overfly my car at every bend in the road. In flight, the raven is a sleek beauty, this vulture of the cornfields that also performs the macabre but socially useful task of cleaning up the remains of road-killed raccoons, porcupines, and skunks. Thus does Nature maintain her sometimes bizarre symmetry.

To return to Route 1, I took a short cut over Jemtland Road south of Stockholm, and found myself only minutes from Van Buren, a town I had a hard time leaving. This whole little corner of Maine in the St. John River valley was settled by Acadians, and retains an exotic edge, or at least it is distinctly non-Yankee. Among themselves, the Acadians speak French, though everyone I met was totally bilingual and most spoke English without an accent. It was my good fortune to fall into a lengthy conversation with Dayton Grandmaison in the restaurant he had recently opened, one of three eateries in this small but apparently cuisine-conscious town—again the French influence, I suspected. Dayton, a Franco-American nationalist through and through, as I judged from our talk, was nonetheless saddled with a Waspish, matinee idol's name by his mom, at a time when the forces

of assimilation were in ascendance. Today, intelligent, well fed, and bald-
ing, he has more the mien of a small-town mayor than of a movie star.

Dayton told me that from Hamlin—just south of Van Buren on Route
1A—on up to Fort Kent, there is a high concentration of French, virtually
100 percent in some of the smaller villages. Van Buren, for example, was
settled in 1789 by Acadians who returned from the great diaspora of 1755,
when French settlers in Canada and parts of Maine were rounded up by the
English and deported to Louisiana, a course of events immortalized by
Longfellow in his famous narrative poem *Evangeline*. The town of Van
Buren, originally called Violette Brook, was renamed for Martin Van Buren, who as president during the bloodless Aroostook War, both kept the
peace and kept the town American. Many of those original Acadian names—
Cyr, Theriault, Violette, Leblanc—still predominate in the local phone
book.

The Acadians differ, Dayton noted, from French Canadians in that they
are more in touch with their heritage, but he also pointed out that use of the
language is dying among all the local youth, whatever their origin. After a
decline that peaked in the late sixties to the early seventies, however,
French is again obligatory in Van Buren's schools. People, he said, were
also losing their Catholic religion. By local custom, the public schools there
were once staffed by priests and nuns, which kept the townspeople close
to both the Church and the old culture. Today, two nuns still teach at the
public grade school, but the crucifixes that as recently as ten years ago
hung over every doorway were removed when a secular teacher com-
plained. Narrowing his focus somewhat and speaking as a businessman,
Dayton Grandmaison chided his neighbors for being afraid of new industry
and suspicious of outsiders. This shadow of modernism quickly receded,
however, in a benign assertion of Van Buren's "secure economy," of which
he said, "We somehow survive on very little. And I myself don't usually
hire strangers, because I don't know anything about them." Oh, what a
luxury to retain such strong communal ties these days, in the land of the
free and the home of the brave!

The specialty at Dayton's—as the restaurant is called—is pressure-fried
chicken cooked in a spicy batter. The other two restaurants on Van Buren's
relatively short main street are both luncheonette-style: John's in a storefront at mid-block, and Roger's Diner on the north end, next to Martin's
Pool Room. On the opposite side of Roger's is the Van Buren Hotel, a
three-story concrete building that also houses a disco and a tavern. Van

Buren, as you can see, packs a lot of public entertainment into a small space, if you count the restaurants.

Before leaving Van Buren, I needed to replenish the ice in my camp cooler, so I went into a grocery store where the checkout person told me about a B-and-B on the edge of town, heading north. The owner, she said, was a teacher and unlikely to be home.

Indeed she was not, and as far as I could tell, the Farrell-Michaud House was entirely empty. I rang at the front door, then knocked at the side entrance and at the rear of the house where I found the door ajar. Given my mission, I felt justified in taking a peak inside. What a house! Of all the B-and-Bs I have visited in the state of Maine, this was by far, to my taste, the most exquisite. I quote from the brochure, because for once here is promotional copy that, if anything, refreshingly understates ambience and decor: "Built in the mid-1800s and currently being nominated to the National Historic Registry, this classically restored Victorian mansion houses three dining rooms, two of which are separated by hand-carved arches. The sitting room has an ornate terra-cotta fireplace and decorative tin walls and ceilings. There are six large bedrooms, some with private baths, and all with ornate woodwork throughout. The house sits atop a hill overlooking a beautiful view of the surrounding valley."

A mile north of Van Buren is the Village Acadien, an elaborate and stunning re-creation of early Acadian village life in the form of thirteen impeccably replicated or restored buildings completed in 1976 as a project to celebrate the American Bicentennial. Having recently pushed back its daily opening time from 10:00 A.M. to noon, the village was closed and empty when I arrived there a half hour too early. Undaunted, I jumped the low split-rail fence and took a private tour, visiting each of the architectural treasures in turn, peering through the many unshaded windows at the wonderful period interiors. A chorus of *ooh-la-la*s resounded in my head with each exhibit: a log cabin church, a frontier hovel, a general store, two genteel homes, a schoolhouse, and, of course, the grange—a barn, which, since it was the only building open, I duly entered. After completing the circuit of this fascinating display—no doubt even more engaging when seen from the inside as well—I drove up the road and reluctantly left Van Buren behind, thinking at least half-seriously that I was lucky not to have been arrested there for breaking and entering.

Notre Dame, Lille, Grand Isle—these were some of the Gaulish hamlets I passed en route to Madawaska—often listed as the northernmost town in the United States. At Lille I passed a huge Catholic church built of wood, a rare material for the construction of a temple for the Roman faithful, who normally prefer something more solid, like stone or brick, taking literally the Lord's injunction to his disciple, "Thou art Peter, and upon this rock I shall build my church." This church is named Mont Carmel, and contains a Musée et Centre Culturel, which was also closed. Mid-August, and already the summer season was virtually over this far north, I observed. Not only were many of the cultural attractions I came upon closed, but there was only a trickle of traffic on the road. Grand Isle offered two restaurants of a very suitable appearance, but little else in the way of public buildings. In constant view, whether near the road or at some distance across the sloping ground, the St. John River was my companion on this drive. In places the water level was so low that a stone path led from one bank to the other, allowing an informal border crossing without the aid or surveillance of a customs station.

Madawaska has a similar appearance to Van Buren, with its single line of shops along the main street near the river, and the Canadian town Edmundton, across the way, very central to the general visual scene. The Fraser Paper Mill is here, down a side street that leads over the international bridge. I walked to the factory and inquired about the possibility of a tour. The tours, I was told, would recommence at 2:00 P.M., following the lunch break, so I went off to explore the little town. Other than buying a wooden postcard at a gift shop, I didn't get much farther than the Blue Sky Hotel, where I spent a half hour sitting over a coffee in the hotel's brand-new restaurant.

Back at Fraser Paper, while waiting for my guide to appear, I chatted with Nancy, the security guard, who told me a bit about her own background growing up locally in the "back settlement," one among sixteen children. Large families among the predominantly French population were the norm when she was a child, and a family with twenty kids was not that uncommon. She expressed a certain nostalgia for the simple life she had known as a girl, the old wood-fired cookstove, the putting up of wild berry preserves from fruit that she and her siblings picked by the bucketful. Then Dennis, a student in electrical engineering at Northeastern University, introduced himself as my guide, and we went off to tour the facility.

Dennis, there on a work-study program, explained that Fraser was a binational company, the pulp plant being located across the river in Edmundton, while the paper plant was here in Madawaska. The two factories are connected by a series of pipelines attached to the bridge, through which raw pulp is pumped from one plant to the other. Since Fraser's principal market is in the United States, providing the stock for such highly visible publications as *Cosmopolitan* magazine, *Roget's Thesaurus, Who's Who,* and many more, a word about the international economics involved is in order. Actually, it's all quite simple: apparently, Canadian pulp may enter the States duty-free, but not finished paper; thus this umbilical, transnational connection.

Before entering the work area, Dennis passed me a pair of ear plugs. We then followed the trail of paper production, from the vats of soggy pulp that looked like wet toilet paper through the various stages of continuous rolling and drying, to the glossy, finished paper stock, wound on massive rolls, each weighing thousands of pounds. The plant was foul-smelling, deafening, as hot as Hades (up to 120 degrees), and as humid as the worst dog days of summer. Nonetheless, the tour was compellingly interesting as the industrial process often is, helping us to conceptualize the fabrication of a given end product in reverse to its most primitive components. At the end of the tour, Dennis presented me with a packet of souvenir pads and paper, and I felt the whole experience was an hour well spent.

After leaving Madawaska, the apex of my journey was now in reach, but I chose one final detour from Route 1 at Frenchville, the town's name a broad hint that it was not settled by Meo tribespeople from the central highlands of Southeast Asia. On Route 162, I turned off toward St. Agatha, and found a very domesticated and virtually treeless shoreside community stretching all along the banks of large, slingshot-shaped Long Lake. But I was not really in the mood for a side trip, and besides, I wanted to arrive in the Allagash region with some daylight left, so I soon returned to Route 1 and passed through Fort Kent, my eyes fixed on the northern point where Maine's paved roads end in a place called Dickey.

The Allagash and St John rivers meet about thirty miles west of Fort Kent; Dickey is roughly three miles farther on. While the area is by no means overcrowded, there are a greater number of houses on this last stretch of road than I had anticipated. Apparently, the river valley and the proximity of so many Canadian townships provide conditions for settlement that are otherwise absent within the great core of Maine's northern bulge. Some old housing stock remains, but for the most part the dwellings don't seem to predate the 1930s, and many are considerably more modern, with brand-new cars on blacktop drives and TV satellite dishes that complete the region's linkage to the global information grid. The road itself, Route 161, never runs far from the St. John River, and the general landscape is neither particularly dramatic nor wild. Yet a feeling of remoteness belies the relative population density and the somewhat tame and domestic surroundings. For me, it was as if an echo of the former wilderness still sounded in the distant hills that cupped the valley, and spoke of something transitory in the human presence there.

Dickey is little more than a trading post, beyond which the road snakes back and forth across the St. John, over a series of single-lane metal bridges. When the asphalt ended, I did not want to stop, so I drove on for several miles through closely cropped woodlands, still passing drives that led to private camps and summer retreats. And I wondered if I might not reach what I had hoped would be my ultimate destination in Maine, Estcourt Station, a diminutive village that straddles the border, more directly accessible over Canadian roads than American. The woods here, however, were so sparse and over-cut that I had no desire to pitch my tent for the night on this colorless, lumber-company land, which would have been necessary were I to commit myself to this course so late in the day. So I reflected that, after all, there had to be some point where I would say, "This far and no farther." Here, three miles beyond Dickey, the tide of my journey turned, and I started homeward, resolved to find a more pleasing campsite to the south, after dark if need be, in the vicinity of Eagle Lake.

Back at the Dickey Trading Post, I learned that many of the camps I had just passed belonged to the owner of this store and restaurant, a man named Kelly, and also that if I had driven two miles farther along that dirt road, I would have come to the gate of the Irving Paper Company land. To pass that point, a traveler must pay a fee, but the drive to Estcourt—where Irving has a large lumber mill—is not much more than an hour over adequate, if somewhat lumpy, dirt roads. A similar road below Dickey accompanies the Allagash River to another lumber-company checkpoint, where I stopped for a brief visit with the tollkeeper, Earline Ouelette. She has tended this gate for fourteen years, nine of which she has also spent working on her degree from the University of Maine at Fort Kent, finishing up this year, much to her joy and relief.

Our talk covered a variety of subjects, including writing, for we shared a mutual interest in collecting local yarns. Earline herself had published several accounts in the *Bangor Daily News* about some colorful figures whose adventures from part of the lore and legend of the Allagash. All the lumber lands, Earline explained, are managed by an entity called North Maine Woods, which supervises public access and collects all fees—$7 a night for Maine residents and $10 for out-of-staters—from those who wish to camp overnight. Most people come, she said, to canoe the Allagash, generally trips taking anywhere from six hours to five days that are guided or provisioned by local outfitters. Day-trippers who wish to explore this area, but not camp over, or who want to make the four-to-six-hour drive on these logging roads to Baxter State Park, pay a smaller fee, from $3 to $4. As we talked, a pickup truck driven by a local guide passed the gatehouse. Earline mentioned his name and said he lived nearby and was probably heading home, if I wanted to talk with someone who outfits Allagash canoe trips. I turned my car around to leave just as an elderly man and his wife drove up in a camper. "You going to drive this wild road?" I asked him. "I'm gonna give it a try. Start here and end up in Millinocket," he said, his jaw set like a figure from a Norman Rockwell illustration.

Bob O'Leary and his family live in a blue-gray shingled house overlooking the Allagash River, midway between the North Maine Woods gate house and the road's beginning at Route 161. Bob is a grade-school science teacher in Fort Kent (surprisingly, the largest grade school in the state of Maine, he said), and runs his business, Allagash Sporting Camps, year-round as well.

A typical four-day canoe trip costs $300 per person, and includes fresh food (resupplied en route), an attendant registered guide, camps and showers along the way, and all canoeing equipment. The cost also covers park and road fees, as well as supervised parking for your vehicle if you drive here directly, or transportation from Allagash or Presque Isle airports if you fly in. Bob and his crew also serve as guides for hunters and fishermen, and offer a variety of packages depending on game and season.

On the way back to Fort Kent, I noticed an odd-looking two-story building in St. Francis called Kit's Motel, which has only four rooms, but charges the reasonable prices sportsmen like to pay. Dusk had already settled by the time Fort Kent appeared, but I did stop and wander a bit, just to get a feel for the place. That "feel" was of genuine backwater, despite a main street of fair length, lined with the usual services and one not-so-usual storefront where I could see a Tae Kwon Do class in progress. The Fort Kent Hotel, a square concrete building like its counterparts in Madawaska and Van Buren, also houses a good-sized tavern and offers double rooms for $42.80 a night. It was about 7:30 P.M. when I left the town, heading south on Route 11, and the sky threatened rain. I hoped to reach the state land around Eagle Lake, where I was told there were no toilets or showers, but that camping and swimming were allowed. The problem was that by the time I reached Eagle Lake, it was so dark and overcast that I could not make out any signs to indicate where exactly I might be permitted to pitch my tent. Rather than hunt around, I decided to push on, figuring to find a suitable campsite at the end of a dirt road when I tired of driving, or, if worse came to worse, to sleep in my car.

The road sign at the edge of Fort Kent announced thirty-seven miles of scenic highway, which was indeed the case, the hills and vistas, even in silhouette, having the look of true lake country. The town of Eagle Lake itself seemed like a lively summer resort complete with a couple of restaurants, but beyond town, the open land gave way to trees that closed in tightly, making a tunnel of the road, and I assume it was there that I missed my opportunity for a campsite on public lands. Then I saw a sign indicating a rest stop, and pulled into an attractive picnic area in the midst of a glade of trees. *This will do,* I thought, just about to pull out my tent when I saw another sign, loudly proclaiming NO CAMPING.

On I drove, looking for a promising side road, exploring one or two but finding nothing that felt comfortable. I just couldn't dispel the paranoid image of some local landowner waking me up at the point of a shotgun, demanding to know how I had the temerity to trespass on private property. In all, I drove for about an hour before reaching Portage, where the light was still lit at Dean's Motor Lodge. Poking my head in the doorway of the attached restaurant, my eyes met those of a woman bent over a vacuum cleaner, straightening up after the day's business. "Anywhere to camp around here?" I asked her. Her affirmative answer was my deliverance. Right there at the corner was a road, and if I drove to the end, some four to five miles distant, I would come upon a campground on the banks of Portage Lake. No fees were required, she added.

And sure enough, there it was, a small open field near a boat-launching site, and I happily pitched my tent. The sky by now had cleared completely, and a full moon appeared with just a corner clipped off its lower left-hand side. An odd phase, I thought, and then remembered what Robert J. Lurtsema had forecast that same morning on public radio. A full eclipse of the moon would take place this night, and by 10:00 P.M. the moon would be completely obscured by the earth's shadow. Over baked beans and hot dogs, I sat for a hour in my camp chair, and witnessed an extraordinary phenomenon: the extinguishing of the moon against a shower of northern lights, to a chorus of loons who howled unceasingly, whether in sympathy or horror I could not discern.

At dawn I rose to see for the first time where I had come to rest. My map told me I had driven down West Cottage Road to Indian Point, to where the Fish River flows into Portage Lake, and where campers are welcome to stay for a maximum of fourteen days. Several hiking trails also converge here, leading to what looks on the map like interesting terrain. I hadn't found a place to bathe for two days, so I went down to the lake at the landing, but thought twice about jumping in because of the slightly filmy feel of the water, which I attributed to the overuse of outboard motors. Then I decided to call on the woman who had saved me from an uncomfortable evening and who had mentioned that she lived with her taxidermist husband—Eldron Jeandreau, according to his shingle—only four houses up the road from the campsite. Not finding them at home, I did manage to peek into the taxidermy studio, where about a dozen stiff, well-posed critters—from bears to coyotes—stood posed, looking so lifelike it was a bit eerie.

A few minutes later I stopped again at Dean's Motor Lodge to see if it was possible to take a shower without renting a room. Fortunately, it was, for $5 including towels and soap. Cleaned up and refreshed, I went down to the restaurant and fell into conversation with Jim Dumond, guide and local game warden, whose wife's family owns Dean's. Jim gave me a verbal tour of life around Portage. The big industry here was logging, Jim said, and up the road was the Pinkham sawmill, largest in the state. "But logging is about finished up here," he said. "They're laying off men all the time, and we'll have to depend on seasonal recreation like snowmobiling and hunting." Jim was quite proud of a local author he had known since boyhood, a woman named Rita Stadig, who has written several books, mostly about her own odd assortment of relatives, such as one uncle, a master forger, who had known Al Capone, and who died in Alcatraz by his own hand.

After a while we were joined by Steve Cyr, who, with his dad—whose roots run deep in the Aroostook—operates a small cedar mill in Portage and produces custom decking and siding, mostly for architectural firms in the Boston area. After saying good-bye to Jim, who presented me with a printed T-shirt with the picture of a rundown-looking cow, labeled "Portage Deer," I accompanied Steve over to the mill. There were no logs in the yard, cedar being in somewhat short supply, I was told. But a shipment was soon expected, and the unmistakable balmy smell of arborvitae permeated the atmosphere. In the meantime, the sawyer, the very image of a Maine Yankee with a first name to match—something my ear heard as Freeland— was working on replacing the engine of an old tractor. And Steve was

thinking about building a workshop to make cedar products—flower plant-
ers, picnic tables, and suchlike—for the passing tourists.

Nearby Ashland was the next town I stopped in, and on impulse I walked
into an eatery called Lil's. My curiosity was rewarded by as good a slice of
homemade blueberry pie as I'd eaten in a long time. Four or five other
home-baked products were displayed on a countertop, including bread pud-
ding and custard pie. And an item on the wall menu read, "Daily Special—
Road Kill—Always Enough, Never Tough—$3.75." I decided not to ask.
Outside of Ashland, on another impulse, I turned onto a dirt road to get a
wider view of several mountains I could just barely see in the distance. For
a mile or so I paralleled the tracks of the Bangor & Aroostook Railroad until
I came to a crossing that led over the tracks onto a farm road, which I
followed out to a field of oats. From my map, I figured I was looking at
Peaked and Round mountains, and the stunning vista and setting were
further charged by the music playing that moment on the radio, Wagner's
"Entry of the Gods into Valhalla."

Eleven miles north of Patten, I spotted a line of chalets through the trees,
and a sign that announced the North Country Lodge. What I'd stumbled on
was a very comfortable, highly professional hunting operation that special-
ized in bagging black bears (also deer, moose, and coyotes). With the
season about to begin in September, the crew at the lodge was already
setting out bait to habituate the bears to an easy feed within a large area
surrounding the lodge, where hunters wait in tree stands to get their
trophies. Of course, not everyone gets his bear, but co-owner Hank Good-
man claimed a success rate of more than forty percent. Up to thirty hunters
can stay at the lodge during a given week, paying $625 for the bear hunt,
including all meals. Hunters have the mornings free, and then go out to
their stands after lunch, staying out until dark, the majority of bears being
taken around sundown. Of the several lodges I saw on this trip, the North
Country was certainly the poshest in a rustic sort of way.

Patten is a relatively long ride from Ashland, taking you through Masar-
dis, more noticeable on the map than from the road. Some of the scenery
over this segment of Route 11, however, is very pleasing. Once in Patten,
you will definitely want to pay a visit to the Lumberman's Museum, in its
own way as impressive as the Village Acadien in Van Buren. The museum,
located on Route 159, also known as the Shin Pond Road, houses its
collection in ten separate buildings—everything pertaining to the history of

lumbering in northern Maine from rough camp houses and mess halls to sheds filled with antique heavy equipment and mills. Examples of bateaux, the river boats of which Thoreau wrote with such enthusiasm, are also on display. The Lumberman's Museum was started in the late 1970s by a local physician, Dr. Lore Rogers, at the age of eighty-five; Dr. Rogers then helped staff his creation until the age of one hundred, when he died. One old caretaker, however, had a bone to pick with the museum's venerable founder, who had insisted that all camp buildings be reproduced with complete authenticity. The problem, the caretaker said, pointing to some leaky corner posts in a log structure, was that those old camps were meant to be temporary. When a crew finished cutting an area, they abandoned the camp and simply built another in the next area to be cut. Whereas the buildings at the museum are supposed to be more or less permanent.

At Route 158, I made a brief detour into Sherman Mills, which is somewhat polished in appearance and conjured up the image of a John Philip Sousa marching band, very much in contrast to the rough, plain exteriors of the neighboring hamlets along Route 11. I also liked the look of the 4-Seasons restaurant on the main street in Sherman Mills. Somewhat below this point, at Hay Brook, I picked up the East Branch of the Penobscot River, which Route 11 accompanies for a short distance until Medway. There the river is joined by its twin, the West Branch, then flows to the sea in a wide, single tributary. Route 11 swings westward toward East Millinocket, a town with few stores, where the Great Northern Paper Company stands like a feudal castle by the river, and great mounds of pulp logs rise to the height of small ski slopes. Neighboring and slightly larger Millinocket is the gateway to Baxter State Park, covered in chapter 11.

The road from Millinocket to Brownsville was fringed by a deceptive row of trees at roadside, behind which lay the raped landscape of clear-cut operations perpetrated in the never-ending quest for more and better toilet paper. Just east of Brownville, I took what was to be the final digression of this northern journey, down seven miles of gravel road to the Katahdin Iron Works. A small parking lot sits between the ruin of an old blast furnace and a registration hut for the Maine Woods–administered logging company lands that spread out to the north and west. As late as 1880, there was an active village here with a population of 193, all of whom had something to do with the ironworks. Of the homes, boardinghouses, hotel, and company buildings, only a fragment of the furnace and a single beehive kiln—used to produce charcoal to fire the furnace—remain. The red ore deposits here are believed to be the source of the minerals found in the graves of the neolithic Red Paint People who once roamed these woods. A canyon seventy feet deep, with five sets of falls, is the great natural attraction here, some seven miles beyond the Maine Woods gatehouse. And the gatekeeper told me there are some virgin pines in there that have somehow escaped the woodsman's ax.

Brownville itself is a cul-de-sac with a market, a diner, and a rather large station house for the Canadian train that passes here daily and seems to provide the *raison d'être* for the town. Here, for all intents and purposes, our journey through Canadian Maine ends. An hour's ride on Route 11 through mostly farm country terminates at Newport, connecting with Route 220 (see chapter 8, on Moosehead Lake) or Interstate 95 leading northeastward to Bangor or southwestward to Augusta. How you continue or end your own journey in Maine is up to you. By now, there can be little doubt that when it comes to choosing a route where two or more roads diverge, I myself have always inclined toward the sentiment best expressed by Robert Frost:

> *Two roads diverged in a wood, and I—*
> *I took the one less travelled by,*
> *And that has made all the difference.*

◼

INFORMATION ◾ *Calais Area Chamber of Commerce* (454-2521), Calais 04619. ◾ *Houlton Chamber of Commerce* (532-4216), 109 Main St., Houlton 04370. ◾ *Presque Isle Area Chamber of Commerce* (764-4485), P.O. Box 831, Presque Isle 04769. ◾ *Van Buren Chamber of Commerce* (868-5059 or 868-2886), 65 Main St., Van Buren 04785. ◾ *Madawaska Chamber of Commerce* (728-7000), P.O. Drawer A, Madawaska 04756. ◾ *Fort Kent Chamber of Commerce* (834-5354), P.O. Box 430, Fort Kent 04743. ◾ *Eagle Lake Chamber of Commerce* (444-5125), P.O. Box 135, Eagle Lake 04739. ◾ *Millinocket Chamber of Commerce* (723-4443), P.O. Box 5, Millinocket 04462.

LODGINGS/RESTAURANTS (The majority of the small hotels— and one inn—I visited on this itinerary had restaurants on the premises. Otherwise, diner- and luncheonette-style eateries abounded in all the larger towns throughout Canadian Maine.) ▪ *Lincoln House* (726-3953), Dennysville. Elegant country inn, plus restaurant with gourmet menu. ▪ *The Guest House* (448-7287), Rte. 160, Danforth. "Bed and dinner"—a homestyle meal for around $5. ▪ *The Farrell-Michaud House* (868-5209), 231 Maine St., Van Buren. Gorgeous Victorian B-and-B. ▪ *Dayton's Restaurant and Ice Cream Parlor* (868-5591), 52 Main St., Van Buren. ▪ *Blue Sky Hotel* (728-7513 or 728-6567), 522 Main St., Madawaska. Twenty-two rooms plus buffet restaurant and cabaret. ▪ *Fort Kent Hotel and Tavern*, Maine St., Fort Kent. Twenty rooms. ▪ *Dean's Motor Lodge & Restaurant* (435-3701), Rte. 11, Portage Lake. Specializing in steaks and seafood.

CAMPING ▪ *Aroostook State Park* (768-8341), 87 State Park Rd., Presque Isle; attractive campsites on Quaggy Joe Mountain. ▪ *Jo-Mary Lake Campground* (723-8117), Rte. 11, 15 miles south of Millinocket; located inside the North Main Woods/Katahdin Iron Works Management Forest on the south shore of Upper Jo-Mary Lake. A full-service commercial campground, $11.65 nightly.

SPORTSMEN'S CAMPS AND GUIDES ▪ *Kelly's Sporting Camps & Facilities for Campers* (398-3461), Allagash. Housekeeping cabins, $7 per person; includes stove, shower, hot water. ▪ *Allagash Sporting Camps* (398-3555), Allagash. Bob O'Leary, outfitter and guide. ▪ *Eldron Jandreau* (435-2231), Portage Lake; taxidermist and guide. ▪ *Jim Dumond* (435-6378), Portage Lake game warden and guide. ▪ *North Country Lodge* (528-2320), Patten. First-class digs and meals; specializing in bear hunting.

SPECIAL ▪ *Houlton Museum and Historical Society*, Houlton. Period artifacts and exhibit on the Aroostook War; open year-round. ▪ *New Sweden Historical Museum*, New Sweden. Open noon to 5:00 P.M. daily during the summer. ▪ *Village Acadien*, Van Buren. Open June 15 through Labor Day, noon to 5:00 P.M. ▪ *Fraser Paper Company*, Madawaska. Tours daily year-round during weekday working hours. ▪ *Lumberman's Museum*, Patten. Open Memorial Day through September, from 9:00 A.M. to 4:00 P.M. Tuesday through Saturday, and 11:00 A.M. to 4:00 P.M. Sunday. ▪ *Katahdin Iron Works*, off Rte. 11 five miles north of Brownville Junction. A State Historic Site.

INDEX